MARATHON!

The Story of the Greatest Race on Earth

Timothy Collings and
Stuart Sykes

First published in Great Britain in 2004 by
Virgin Books
Thames Wharf Studios
Rainville Road
London
W6 9HA

A catalogue record for this book is available from the
British Library.

ISBN 1 85227 114 0

Typeset by TW Typesetting, Plymouth, Devon
Printed and bound in Great Britain by CPD Wales

CONTENTS

ACKNOWLEDGEMENTS

This book would not have been possible without the assistance, generosity and kindness of many people. All of the following, in no particular order, contributed to the research and writing of *Marathon! The Story of the Greatest Race on Earth*, some by sparing time for interviews, some by correcting facts and providing insights and some by having provided valuable information via the public domain in books, magazines, websites, newspapers and other forms of media: Katie Hodge, Ron Clarke, Robert de Castella, Ruth Beck-Perrenoud, Monique Perusset, Evelyne Moosmann and Carine Genevey-Renaud and all the staff at the library of the Musée Olympique in Lausanne, Lloyd Scott, Loch Ness Marathon website, the staff at Bedford public library, leukaemia.org, London marathon website, the BBC, Berlin Marathon website, Uta-Pippig.com, UK Athletics, Brain and Spine Foundation, Ethiopians.com, marathonguide.com, ethiopiaonline .net, ethioembassy.org.uk, Boston marathon website, Singapore marathon website, *The Times*, *EasyJet* magazine, Sir Ranulph Fiennes, Dr Mike Stroud, Gina Rawle, *Runners World*, Reuters news agency, Chicago marathon website, *The Guinness Book of World Records*, Guardian Unlimited, *The Bedford Times and Citizen*, The National Asthma Campaign, *The Boston Globe and Herald*, marathonguide.com, Erkkii Vettenniemi (*The Life and Trials of Mamo Wolde*), running-times.com, sporting-heroes.net, Kenny Moore (*The Ordeal of Mamo Wolde*), honolulumarathon.org, *The Daily Telegraph*, Jarno Trulli, nycmarathon.org, nyrrc.org, time-to-run.com, Gail Kislevitz (First Marathons), Stan Greenberg (*Olympics Fact Book*, Guinness Publishing), Jim Webster (*It's a Sporting Life*, Macmillan), *Chronicle of the Olympics* (DK Publishing), Roberto L Quercetani (*Athletics*, Oxford University Press), Charlie Lovett (*Olympic Marathon*, Praeger), David Wallechinsky (*The Complete book of the Olympics*, Penguin), David E Martin and Roger W H Gynn (*The Olympic Marathon*, Human Kinetics), David Miller (*Athens to Athens*, Mainstream publishing), Stan Greenberg (*Whitakers Olympic Almanack*, A & C Black), Alain Lunzenfichter (*Le Roman de Marathon*, Musée Olympique),

Special thanks go to Vanessa Daubney for encouraging the idea, and then the race to write it in time, to the team of research and writing staff at Collings Sport who provided stalwart assistance – Gary Emmerson, Will Gray, Henry Brown and Amar Azam – when it was most needed and our wives and families; Claire, in Mt Eliza; and Ruth, Josh and Kitty in Hitchin, for putting up with the chaos and inconvenience of being involved in such a rush into history and print. Additional thanks to Kitty for her research work. To all: thank you.

Timothy Collings and Stuart Sykes
March 2004

1. LAUSANNE – THE MAN WHO GUARDS THE GATES OF GLORY OVER THE LAKE

There is a running man, trapped in time, sculpted to perfection, in the rising land stretching above a lake in Switzerland. He has a wonderful view, this running man, high up the hillside, overlooking his lake, the Alps all around and Lausanne stretching away on all sides. France lies across the water, Mont Blanc shimmers with sunlight reflected off its snowy peak on the clearest days. Gardens fall steeply below him towards the shores of Lac Leman, their terraces offering neatly kept tennis courts, well-trimmed hedges, paved steps and an escalator to aid elderly visitors. The running man does not see them, nor does he look around much. He does not glance from side to side, but appears to have his eye fixed on a prize in the distance.

Yet he is not a man with a faraway or lost look about him. The sumptuous hotels of the shoreline, where some of the world's richest and most powerful businessmen and politicians meet for conferences that dictate future strategy and policy in arts, industry and sport, barely catch his eye. The running man wears his simple uniform with comfort and pride. He has a vest, shorts and running shoes, none of his attire is fashionable or 'named' and none of it would attract a second glance if it turned up in a church jumble sale. But it is the uniform of a man whose athletic powers made him arguably the greatest of long-distance runners in the history of the Olympic Games, a humble runner who had magnificent power, potential and determination. The statue is that of perhaps the greatest runner of all: Emile Zatopek, a man whose feats at the 1952 Olympic Games in Helsinki turned him into a legend. There in the space of eight days – starting and ending on a Sunday – he won the 5,000-metres race, the 10,000-metres race and, in his first outing at the distance, the marathon. He took three gold medals in long-distance contests on the track. He was the first man ever to do so and it was an achievement of such greatness that it explains why it is Zatopek, the modest son of a Prague carpenter, whose image graces the gardens outside the lakeside doors of the Olympic Museum.

Not more than a few strides away to the right of the doors to the museum is an eternal flame, a symbol of the games and the meaning of the Olympic spirit. Like Zatopek, this is an unquenchable source of energy, a ray of light that throws warmth into bodies and hearts, a meaningful metaphor that helps the visitors, by coach, car and train, understand the values personified by the running man, his sport and his way of life. Within the museum, in the library, work those who preserve the memories of the games and the men and women whose feats made them great and special. They look after books, films, photographs, files and records in a beautiful environment surrounded by natural scenery, and in another room above them are the smaller and simpler items that hint at how painful it was in 1952, compared to the luxuries of the twenty-first century. The shoes in which Zatopek ran to glory are there – bent, tight and ugly, worn and worked in, uncomfortable to look at, with no cushions, no luxuries and no extras. They have no resemblance to the sumptuous trainers worn by multitudes of sportsmen and sportswomen, not to mention the general public, in modern times. But they too look like the footwear that belonged to special feet, moulded into shapes that made them part of one of the most extraordinary runners of all time; an extension of his courage.

It is no wonder that Zatopek is photographed and remembered more than anyone else. His statue stands there, where the Japanese tourists arrive with their cameras, where the schoolchildren mill around and eat their snacks, where the sporting executives stop to take in the view and the air. It is a picture of peace that hides the pain he must have felt as he ran through his most famous afternoon and made history in the summer of 1952.

His life was never the same again. Nor was the history of the marathon. If it was seen as a challenge, perhaps the greatest in track and field sport, before those games, it was elevated afterwards to something else. For runners, for long-distance runners, it was the Holy Grail, a competition between the runner, his legs, his heart, his body, his mind and the landscape and a clock that was to defy age, common sense, physical complaints and sound advice from then on. Others ran magnificently, if not like Zatopek. Ordinary people aped his efforts, in a tribute. People tried to do it, to run the 26 miles and 385 yards that made up a marathon race, and to join an elite club of runners that grew as quickly as the number of races that were created around the world. It was an international sensation. As the years went by, everyone, everywhere, wanted to run marathons. Every city wanted to host one. The great cities launched great marathon events. They mixed the historic and traditional with new and adventurous concepts to produce famous sporting weekends. London and New York joined Boston and Tokyo and Paris and Fukuoka and Rome and Berlin and Chicago and the rest. Running was not only respected by the sporting fraternity, but adopted and made fashionable by a broader public; people jogged for fun, travelled to far-flung cities to watch or participate in marathons involving the masses, where thousands of runners flooded through a city in a human tidal wave like a festival of joy, release and sport. These events generated great interest, television audiences and prize money that attracted not only fast enthusiasts, but hardened professionals. Sponsorship came to add commercial values and an attractive reward for the hardened professionals while, in a different way and at a different level, supporting the modest efforts of the amateurs who ran for charity.

The great marathon runners were always great public heroes and they knew their value. Even in the earliest years of the Olympic Games before the outbreak of the First World War, the marathon men were seduced by running for prizes. A century later, the great British female runner Paula Radcliffe was running for huge sums of money offered to her if she could succeed and win and break world records. Her painful training regimens, supervised by her husband, were no doubt endured with some help from the lure of luxuries that might be afforded by the prizes on offer. By the end of 2003, the money was being allied to rankings systems, too, as marathon organisers, led by those in New York, sought to take control of the myth of the marathon and turn it into a commercial venture with comparisons made to the rankings systems that operate in other highly developed global sports such as golf and tennis, where the agents have taken control. In early November, it was announced by a company involved in the sponsorship of the New York marathon that a top prize of one million American dollars would be paid to the top-ranking runner after a two-year period of assessment involving sixteen of the world's leading and established marathon events. In the proposal made at this time, the best three results of each runner would be considered over 24 months leading up to the 2005 New York City marathon. It was an idea that was not warmly received.

The organisers of the famous events in London, Chicago and Berlin had not been consulted, but their names were included. Great runners like Grete Waitz, who won in New York nine times and became the greatest woman long-distance runner of her era, establishing women's marathon running fundamentally and profoundly with her selfless and superb performances, and Alberto Salazar, who won three times in New York, were reported to be involved in the initiative. It was a project that remained unconfirmed as this one went to the start line and began its run towards the printers' deadlines. As always, the marathon was the talk of world sport.

And all of this, of course, including the great rise in competitiveness of runners, men and women alike, the unwanted introduction of drugs in sport, the platform that attracted politics and protests and demonstrations of violence and horror, came as the feats of determination, defiance and endurance embodied by the victorious and great marathon runners were spread by word around the world, later by radio and television and the Internet. This running of marathons was a job that we could all understand, all of us at any age. We had all run to catch a bus, chased a dog down the road and sprinted across fields for fun, in younger days, and we knew what long distance meant when a physical education teacher instructed us to set off on a school cross-country epic, or a race against the clock around the athletics track. Yet a marathon was something else, something apart, that became a part of the public psyche as the tales of the heroes unfolded in time. The growth of interest in running that followed, and the proliferation of marathon races of all names, derivations and purposes, all over the world, proved this as well as celebrating the euphoria shared by many in relishing the exercise.

This was a spectacular endorsement for Zatopek's gut feeling that he could run a decent marathon, shrug off fatigue and find the pace to deliver a worthy result back in 1952. It confirmed that in most human beings there is a competitive spirit that drives them to seek challenges, and succeed. It helps explain why men like Carlos Lopes could run so far so fast; why men like Sir Ranulph Fiennes and his friend Dr Michael Stroud chose running marathons as a test of their endurance instead of tackling Mount Everest, the North Pole or the South Pole again; why a racing driver, fine-tuned to the rigours of Formula One motor racing, like Jarno Trulli, would want to fly

LAUSANNE – THE MAN WHO GUARDS THE GATES OF GLORY OVER THE LAKE

halfway round the world after competing in the Japanese Grand Prix and take part in the New York marathon; or why a former boxer like Michael Watson, having suffered terrible physical damage in the ring, should want to labour for days to say that he had completed his marathon in London. It helps us all understand what makes Paula Radcliffe run and run in pursuit of fastest times and marathon records when her rocking head and spindly frame look close to collapse. The oxygen that comes with the physical exhilaration of the exercise is accompanied by an oxygen that makes meeting the challenge feel just as intoxicating. In these days of computers, televisions, cars and couch potatoes, everyone needs to run, to feel the heart pounding, the wind in the hair, the eyes stinging with cold, the sweat on the ribcage and the skyline moving nearer and nearer.

Around the world, they all run now: the beautiful, the blind, the old and infirm, the crazy and the lonely. Some work in offices, some are messengers, some are fighting weight problems and some are in need of strong legs and lungs. But all love the festival of marathons and marathon running, the simple and ancient challenge that characterised the Olympic Games from Athens in 1896 to the same Greek capital again in August 2004. In every great city, there has been a great winner of a great race: in Paris, St Louis, London, Stockholm, Antwerp, Amsterdam, Los Angeles, Berlin, Helsinki, Melbourne, Rome, Tokyo, Mexico, Munich, Montreal and Moscow . . . and in Seoul, Barcelona, Atlanta and Sydney. These runners and their races have all thrown up great stories, great personalities and great drama on and off the track as the Olympic Games were used as a platform for political and sometimes terrorist actions by extremists. Yet, nearly always, the sport rose beyond it all and the marathon, the greatest of all races, rose beyond everything else. It is the simplest examination of athletic prowess, fitness and endurance, the most original.

To run like Zatopek, with that sense of industry and pursuit of freedom, offers something that anyone can try and everyone can enjoy. Alone, or accompanied, in a city, or across the fields, in a bracing rainstorm, or bathed in warm sunshine, the same challenge stimulates the body and the mind as it did the little Czech runner in Finland in 1952. That is why the thousands stop and peer at his face, his legs and his muscles in Lausanne where he stands on guard outside the gates of glory. He has been there and done it. Others dream. He has been an Olympic champion and a master of the roads and the track. His triumph, on his marathon debut, reflected also the history of the event, the boldness and courage and defiance that saw a Greek courier, Pheidippides, according to legend, drop dead after running a great distance, from Marathon to Athens, to bring news of his countrymen's triumph in a battle with the invading Persian army. That, it was said, was in 490 BC and here we are, more than two thousand years later, still revelling in the feat and, in 2004, enjoying the prospect of a return to Greece where, at the 2004 Olympic Games, the marathon will be run again from Marathon to Athens.

According to most sources, there is little evidence to confirm that Pheidippides ran this classic distance and died, but the story has survived time and can be accepted as part of the mythology surrounding the marathon race. It was certainly in the minds of the men who resurrected the Olympic Games in Athens in 1896 and it has certainly lived on in the imagination among the runners who have taken part ever since. The fact that the first winner of the modern Olympic marathon race was a Greek, Spiridon Louis, can only have given the tale greater lustre. In the *Encyclopedia Britannica* (as good a source as any), it is stated that the modern marathon race, run as part of the Olympic Games, 'commemorates the legendary feat of a Greek soldier who, in 400 BC, is supposed to have run from Marathon to Athens, a distance of 22 miles and 1,470 yards, to bring news of his countrymen's victory over the Persians'. It adds no further detail, but the majesty of this idea has survived thanks to the running of the great marathon men and the feats of the greatest of all, Emil Zatopek of Czechoslovakia, known as 'the best of Prague' or 'the Czech Express' or 'the Human Locomotive', as much for his style of running, arms akimbo, face screwed up in agony, as for his speed and invincibility. A soldier, who joined the army following the Russian invasion of Czechoslovakia, an athlete who helped the development of his sport by relying on a new training system known as 'interval training', Zatopek is an ideal sentinel for the Olympic ideals and a great symbol of the glory of marathon running. His statue in the garden makes him an ideal running man, a perfect marathon figure, an exemplary long-striding competitor at the gates of glory and running into history.

2. HISTORY 1 – ORIGINS OF AN ANCIENT RACE

Long before Zatopek, or the great Abebe Bikila of Ethiopia, who was the first man to win the Olympic marathon twice in succession, or Carlos Lopes of Portugal, the fastest of the fastest at Los Angeles in 1984, there was a wonderful myth about marathon running of the past and centuries of confusion. Indeed the history of the race is rooted in confusion and legend. It is intertwined with Greek traditions, encouraged by hot sunshine and strong coffee, robustly stimulated by a shot of ouzo and imitated everywhere. The Greeks love talking and they love talking history. The rest of us, too often, say we cannot understand and leave it at that. So, understandably, the origins of this great and noble race are all Greek to anyone who does not understand them!

Many have tried. There are tomes of research on the origins of the Olympic Games and the origins of the marathon race. There are nearly as many words written, at a guess, on how it all began as there are on the often-amazing lives, deeds and legends of the runners themselves. Some of this is tiresome stuff, requiring great patience to digest and evaluate. But much of it is also useful, valuable and welcome.

It is difficult, as every researcher has always found, to travel back in time and find the absolute truth. In their book *The Olympic Marathon, The History and Drama of Sport's Most Challenging Event*, David E. Martin and Roger W. H. Gynn took a very methodical approach to their task. It produced plenty of statistics, some very interesting revelations, much accurate research and a reliable template of historical record. They discovered, for example, that between 1896 and 1996, only 73.5 per cent of the men who started the Olympic marathon races actually finished them. One of them, tragically, died in the effort to do so. Others collapsed in dramatic circumstances, sometimes controversially, once in such fashion, in front of the British royal family, that the man involved was awarded a special medal for his extraordinary, if vain, efforts to stagger to victory. By contrast, 84.1 per cent of the women who started their marathons (in the four Olympic Games in which their participation was accepted and studied by the authors) managed to complete the task. Martin and Gynn also pointed out that it was erroneous to talk about medallists in relation to all the Olympic marathons because in the early years only the top two finishers were given medals and in 1900 the first runners to finish were given pottery prizes instead. Indeed, to further confuse the issue, and spoil the neat idea that gold has always gone to the winner, the first Greek to win the Olympic marathon race, in 1896, was awarded a silver medal. Given all of this, it is important not to attempt to find a unique truth about the origins of the marathon more than 2,000 years after it began.

The origins of the race are not to be found, furthermore, among the sporting events of the ancient games, but, as we learned in the opening chapter, in the legend of Pheidippides and the name of the village from where he began his fabled run to Athens. The town, still standing, of course, is a good place to begin the search for an understanding of how this long and arduous event emerged from centuries of Greek history and established itself, even burned itself, into the sporting calendar. It is worth remembering, too, at this point, that Greece is no ordinary place. It is the cradle of ancient civilisation and philosophy, a place where history and mythology are so interwoven that even such a guide as the Lonely Planet's book on Athens has to admit that it is 'impossible to disentangle fact from fiction'. Thankfully, this book is not about Greek history or philosophy, so we can leave Socrates ('know thyself'), Plato ('until philosophers are kings . . . cities will never cease from ill, nor the human race') and Aristotle ('he who exercises his reason and cultivates it seems to be in the best state of mind and most dear to the gods') aside as we hunt for clues about how, or why, or if, a man did actually run a very long way to deliver a message about a battle won and then die.

However many books are read, or scanned hurriedly, in search of this truth, it is difficult to find many that differ significantly from the generally accepted notion that the original games date back to Mycenaean times. Most sources refer to a great goddess, identified as Rea, who was worshipped in Greece during the first millennium BC, as the instigator. By the time of the 'classical era', however, Rea had been surpassed by her son Zeus, who is widely and popularly believed to be the founder of the Games. Indeed, it is often said that they were created in his honour. The first record of an official quadrennial Olympic Games is said to have been made in 776 BC. The Games were said to be open to all male Greeks and took place at the time of the first full moon in August. (Wild rumours that link their behaviour then with later outbursts of frivolity and levity in the Greek islands at the same time of the year are also to be dismissed.) The athletic festival, as it was, lasted for five days and included wrestling, chariot and horse racing and the pentathlon (wrestling, long jump, running, discus and javelin).

It is reported that, in later years, Romans were allowed to enter these original games of Olympia, which ballooned in status (as they have in modern times) to become festivals of other activities including the arts and politics. Writers, poets and historians became involved, reading aloud to vast audiences, and tradesmen completed deals. According to one theory, the Games continued until AD 394 when they were banned by Emperor Theodosius I as part of a purge of all pagan festivals. Some 32 years later, Emperor Theodosius II ordered that the temples of Olympia should be destroyed. The Games – in which the athletes were made to compete naked from 720 BC – were ended, but they were not forgotten. But it is a surprise to learn that the reinstitution of the Games was due to the activity and imagination of a Frenchman rather than a Greek: Pierre de Coubertin, a man who was disillusioned by the aftermath of the Franco-Prussian war in the nineteenth century, found hope for the future in his belief that sport, particularly the kind of team sports played in England and the United States, had the potential to revive spiritual faith, belief in life and a sense of purpose and hope for the future. He also believed that sport could encourage peace and that a revival of the Olympic Games would do much to achieve this. He first talked of his beliefs at an international conference on physical education in Paris in 1892. He gained little or no support. But two years later, in June 1894, he tried again at another congress to study athletics, held at the Sorbonne, where he reportedly introduced an unscheduled eighth item to an agenda of seven items – this was 'regarding the possibility of the revival of the Olympic Games'. The conference was said to have lasted nine days and his infectious enthusiasm this time carried the day and, on 23 June 1894, the revival of the Games was supported unanimously and, at the same time, the International Olympic Committee (IOC) was founded. The first Olympic Games of modern times took place two years later, in 1896, in Athens, 14 nations sending 311 athletes to participate in 42 events in 10 sports. Greece entered 230 athletes and all the contestants were men. De Coubertin was happy, even if the French were not running; his dream was realised. He became president of the IOC in 1896 and stayed in the job for 29 years.

All of this, of course, merely supplies the historical backdrop to the restoration of the Olympic Games that were organised, in Athens, by de Coubertin's friend Demetrius Vikelas, who served as the IOC's first president from 1894 to 1896. But it does not explain the creation of the marathon, an event that was dreamed up by a friend of Baron de Coubertin, Michel Breal. He was born in 1832, in Bavaria, and his parents were Jews of French descent (Martin and Gynn). When he was five, following the death of his father, the family moved to the French Alsace where Breal learned French and other languages and developed a great interest in philology and mythology. This carried him into the realm of Greek culture and history. He became deeply interested in the ancient Olympic Games and, in supporting his friend's proposals for a renaissance of the games in Greece, in Athens, he suggested that the introduction of a new event that had relevance to Greek history would add to the hosts' enthusiasm. So, in this moment of intellectual and sporting creativity, was born the modern marathon race. To support his idea, Breal wrote de Coubertin a convincing four-page letter in French that resulted in him also awarding a silver cup to the first winner. In his letter, Breal hoped to push for a 'race from Marathon to the Pnyx', a steep hill in Athens. He also asked, in vain, to establish the time that was taken by the legendary Pheidippides in his run from Marathon to Athens in order to establish an early record to be beaten.

Like most scholars, Breal was aware how difficult this task would be and he was also aware of the conflicting tales surrounding the story of Pheidippides' great run, or runs. In summary, it is generally accepted that, in 490 BC, King Darius of Persia landed a force of 20,000 men on the shore at Marathon from where they were expected to march on and conquer Greece. The Greeks sent an army to defend their country, but they were outnumbered heavily and sought assistance from the nearby Spartans. To carry the message of their plight and their request for help, the Athenians, according to a Roman historian known as Cornelius Nepos, sent 'a runner of that class known as *hemerodromoi*, to report how urgent was the need for aid'. Despite their painful name, these runners were trained to run very long distances. According to some estimates, the distance that this poor man was asked to cover was in the region of 145 miles. It is also said that he covered it in less than two days, though there is not much documentary evidence around to prove this claim. And then, as if this was not enough, the same poor man, presumably exhausted, turned round and ran back to Athens to report the latest news – that by the time the Spartans reached the battlefield at Marathon, General Miltiades and his Greek army had performed their own miracle in defeating the Persian army in a famous battle that saw the Greeks allegedly lose only 192 men and the Persians 6,400. A massive tomb, built, it is said, to accommodate the bodies of the Greek casualties, was built on the battlefield and remains visible to the eyes of the discerning tourist and passing runner. On his return to Athens, the exhausted Pheidippides reached the king and gasped a single word: '*Nenikhamen*' (rejoice, we conquer). After this, he collapsed and died.

Many questions remain unanswered about the two runs and the man. No one has satisfactorily proved that the two long runs were performed by the same man or, indeed, that either story is absolutely accurate. Nevertheless, the tale of the run from Marathon to Athens has become part of Greek and Olympic folklore while the run from Athens to Sparta is commemorated regularly in modern times with an exceptionally long race over the same distance. This is known as an 'ultra-distance' competition and is called the Spartathlon, held annually in September. The overall distance is 246 kilometres and the run is completed frequently by the fastest man in 24 hours, or less. The record in recent years has been reported to have gone to a Greek, Yannis Kourous, who ran from Athens to Sparta in 20 hours and 25 minutes.

Strictly speaking, of course, the Spartathlon is not a marathon, but it certainly played a prominent part – at least the original run did – in the creation of the marathon as it is now known. The Spartathlon was created in 1983 by a British RAF Wing Commander called John Foden who was consumed by a desire to see if it was possible, as narrated in Greek history by Herodotus, the fifth-century BC historian, to run this kind of long distance in 36 hours. He attempted to do so himself in October 1982, and succeeded. The following year the rest of the world joined in. As a result, the International Spartathlon Association was created to organise the race every September in memory of the efforts of Pheidippides and the success of the Greek army in the battle of Marathon of 490 BC. According to the Spartathlon website's history section, published in early 2004, the battle of Marathon was notable not only for its dramatic victory by the Greek army, but also because it

> constituted a landmark and a starting point in the history of civilisation . . . The genius of (General) Miltiades and the self-denial of his soldiers made the hordes of Persians flee and rescued Athens and Hellenism from the utmost danger of subjugation to the barbarian invaders. The effects of victory at Marathon continue to influence the present. It was the first victory against the planned domination of "Asianisation" over Europe and an event with momentous significance. Because of this victory, Athens was able to achieve a great deal and bequeath the benefits of its knowledge, arts and virtue to mankind.

In all of this drama and mythology, it is worth noting that Herodotus, an historian who, according David Wallechinsky in *The Complete Book of the Olympics*, 'thrived on such juicy tidbits' did not even mention Pheidippides' run back to Athens from Marathon, or his legendary announcement and death. Indeed, Wallechinsky said that this wonderful story did not appear in print for the first time until the second century AD, more than 600 years after it was reported to have happened. So, despite such a rich tapestry of colour and intrigue and importance, the truth about the origins of the marathon remains mysterious. Nevertheless, it was run as part of the modern Athens Games held in 1896, and it did start from the place called Marathon, where it will again start in 2004 when the Games return to Greece. About 26 miles northeast of Athens, and lying in the plain of Marathon that runs down to the sea and the Bay of Marathon, the small town of Marathon has a population of about 10,000 people. It is, in all fairness, an unremarkable place to look at, but a place with a remarkable history and a significance that far outweighs its looks and its reputation among tourists.

The plain, of course, was the battlefield for the famous Battle of Marathon across which so many runners have hauled their limbs in the searing heat and dust of the Greek peninsula, their minds untroubled by nostalgia, history or mythology. If they follow the classic route, as the runners in the 2004 Olympic Games are expected do, they will start from the town of Marathon, follow the coastal route south to Mati and Rafina before turning inland and west to traverse an incline that will take them via Pallini and Stavros to the finish at the famous Panathinaikon Stadium, following in the footsteps of Spiridon Louis. It will be a marathon that reflects history, a race more significant than any other in its completion of the full cycle of time since the 1896 race.

It will, of course, be impossible for spectators gasping in the hot conditions not to sympathise with the runners at the second Athens Olympic Games when they run their marathon in conditions that are far from perfectly suited to their task. According to the world's leading environmental watchdog, Greenpeace, the high levels of pollution in the Greek capital city, coupled with the heat and the dust, may endanger the health of the runners. This thick smog that hangs over Athens in the summer is known as 'nefos' (the cloud) and has been conceded by organisers of the event as presenting a potential threat to easy breathing for the athletes. In the final months of the build-up, there were stories in the sports pages of most European newspapers suggesting that many runners may use specially developed 'masks' that fit inside their mouths to assist their breathing in the difficult conditions.

Marathon historians, reminded by these concerns, will recall the agonies of many runners at St Louis in 1904 when an American, William Garcia, from California, almost died due to the choking dust on the chosen route. He was forced to retire with stomach haemorrhaging after inhaling huge quantities of dust that had coated his oesophagus and moved into his stomach. That Tom Hicks, another American entrant (although he was born in Birmingham, in England), won mostly due to his steady intake of brandy and some stronger stimulants is another story for elsewhere in this study and celebration of a great event with such great, confused and ever-fascinating origins.

If the origins matter, of course, it is because they add a deeper understanding to the event, even if Zeus is hardly likely to call in and remind the hordes that descend on Athens to witness the 2004 marathon that he was the man whose efforts began it all. According to some, it was Zeus's defeat of Kronos in a wrestling match of the gods that stimulated the first ancient Games as a commemoration of his feats. These Games were held at Olympia, where there was a vast 60,000-seat stadium, a hippodrome and a gymnasium, but no marathon. That only came, as we know, with the merging of mythology, or history, and the vision of de Coubertin, whose ideals for sport were to be enshrined in the Olympic movement, in 1896, and through the efforts of Breal. His marathon was the start, the stunning beginning of a modern series for the ancient race. Those who chased Louis home in 1896 were amazed by the event and the atmosphere and its history, especially the Americans. A year later, the Boston Marathon was born, to be run each year in April. This race, in turn, spawned a host of imitators as the greatest long-distance event on earth took hold. From Athens to Athens, from its dusty origins to Olympic glory, the marathon has grown to become sport's most spectacular and regulated test of human endurance.

3. SINGAPORE – BLOOD AND GUTS, DEFIANCE AND ENDURANCE

On a hot day, it is difficult not to perspire heavily in the heat of the shimmering tropical island of Singapore. Dark stains spread across shirts from wet armpits, sunglasses have scant effect against the glare and even the slightest sign of a breeze in the palm trees is welcomed with a shaking and loosening of clothes. The sun rises remorselessly in a heavy, blue and humid sky. Tourists, in shirts of exotic colours, walking through the colourful shrubs and flowerbeds on the pavements, hide under wide-brimmed hats and seek the dark side of the road. Spicy food aromas waft through the high-rise modernity of hotels and office blocks, hiding the traditional whiffs of Singapore's great historic past as one of the world's finest, most natural and most important harbours, a trading and business centre for Malaysia and Southeast Asia, a world centre for the rubber and tin markets, oil refining and shipbuilding, imported food and high technology products.

Most visitors come for the history as much as the vivid scenery and the climate, a significant past that explains why Singapore has an atmosphere of old Britain entwined so deeply into the fusion of modern Asia that permeates the waterways, streets and shopping centres. Few, apart from the usual 'mad dogs and Englishmen', would consider flying into Singapore to go running, let alone attempt a marathon that leaves its participants drained, physically, emotion-ally and mentally, and, in certain cases, so exhausted that they are passing blood and gasping for breath. If ever there was a single marathon race that was designed to examine the limits of human suffering, it would be run on the streets of this city-state at the southern tip of the Malay Peninsula.

The small nation-state of Singapore, with a population of 3.5 million people, stands at the confluence of the Strait of Malacca, the Java Sea and the South China Sea. It is separated from Malaysia by the Johore Strait, but linked by a causeway that ensures water and supplies are consistently available. Lying on a trading route of great and historical importance for strategic and economic reasons, between Malaysia and Indonesia, Singapore is also at the crossroads of several contrasting civilisations. The island, with its deep and natural south-facing harbour, has been influenced by many different foreign and domestic rulers throughout its history – from the impact of its nineteenth-century trading links with the Dutch, to its colonisation by the British later in the same century, its occupation by the Japanese in the Second World War and now, in modern times, by its self-governing republicanism. Singapore is a mix of religions (Buddhism, Islam, Taoism and Hinduism lead the way), colours, creeds and nations; a place where an adventurous diner can choose a dish from virtually anywhere in the world at any time of night, knowing that it is still warm enough to eat in shirtsleeves and sit outdoors. But each and every year in recent times, on the first Sunday of December, the perspiring city, glowing in its diverse entirety, comes to a standstill to watch some 7,000 human beings contest in the Singapore International Marathon, an annual ritual of suffering and pain, satisfaction and glory, that has delivered many great moments and hours in the annals of long-distance running.

Singapore, of course, is not one of the most famous of the world's city marathons. Nor is it one of the oldest. It is, however, one of the most challenging road-race marathons of all. Despite climatic conditions that make any short run an uncomfortable experience and viewing the marathon a minor examination of patience and persever-ance, millions of people flock to witness the event for themselves. They hang from trees, balance on bollards and endure crowding and scorching sunshine to claim a clear view. For the casual visitor, the high level of local interest in the event and its host of competitors from all over the world is as remarkable as the idea that anyone should wish to run in Singapore at all. The city is, quite literally, steaming with heat, day and night, plagued by a strength-sapping average temperature of 30 degrees Celsius and a humidity level of around 90 per cent. These conditions are accompanied by around 250 centimetres of rain each year and monsoon seasons that last from June to September and from November to March. It is nothing remarkable to stroll down the immaculate streets of a city where chewing gum is discouraged and the cleaners, weaving among a tide of humanity, have uniforms to rival the police, and feel sodden wet with sweat, or rain, or both. Yet, every year, thousands of foolhardy and determined souls take to the streets of this remarkable equatorial metropolis and run 26 miles and 385 yards, not minding the weather or the sweat that rolls from their brows. Around 105,000 bottles of water, and 50,000 isotonic energy drinks, are consumed during each race. Sweat bands? Better to use a bucket.

The competitors come from all over the world, giving the race a multicultural flavour that reflects that of the smiling crowds, a mix of every conceivable background from a history that has turned Singapore into one of the most recognisable and colourful conurbations in the Far East. The marathon begins in the Singapore National Stadium, built in 1973, already showing its age, and continues on a course that takes its participants within a stone's throw of the world-renowned Raffles Hotel, a throwback to Singapore's links with the old British Empire. Winding through low-rise and high-rise buildings, the runners travel past international banks, restaurants specialising in local cuisine, stock markets and mosques, hotels and run-down seedy motels. History, economics, architecture and the social sciences all feature on the wide-ranging curriculum offered to observers and thinkers by the unique Singapore Marathon.

None of these edifying reasons, however, could explain the presence of two ageing, slightly pale, lightly dressed, but heavily sweating middle-aged Englishmen on the streets of Singapore on 7 December 2003. Clad in their loose-fitting running gear that had seen better days, these two agonised figures shambled their way in a throng of competitors. They were barely noticed by the masses, but it was they who had embarked on the biggest adventure and greatest challenge of all. Both breathed heavily, the second man barely moving faster than walking pace as he shuffled along, stubbornly placing one foot in front of the other, despite obvious pain. However it seemed, given their outfits and their outward appearances, these were not two 'ordinary' Englishmen attempting to live up to the proud British tradition of brashly refusing to be perturbed by adverse weather or long distance. Indeed, these two men were not taking on the Singapore Marathon as an act of bravado, a last hurrah for their lost youth in their final mid-life years. Nor were they, in the best traditions of British expansionism of the past, seeking to assert any kind of colonial superiority in one of the old empire's most treasured historical outposts. They were, in fact, two of the world's greatest living adventurers and they were halfway through a challenge that was, ultimately, to see them set a record as the first human beings to run seven marathons, on seven continents, in the space of seven days. Even Pheidippides would have blanched at this one.

A closer examination of this intrepid duo is essential even if they passed anonymously in front of the vast numbers of Southeast Asians on the streets of Singapore that day. They were certainly not passing anonymously through the consciousness of the western world's media even if they looked dressed to be forgotten. Shorts and vests, drenched in sweat, their faces contorted with a mixed look of agony and bloody-minded determination that only a marathon seems capable of evoking, they were grinding out the distance to complete their goal. The first figure on the road was Sir Ranulph Fiennes, described by the *Guinness Book of Records* as 'the world's greatest living explorer'. Take a history of expeditions to the North and South Poles, throw in his time in the British Army's Special Air Service (SAS, arguably the toughest specialist military force in the world) and the occasional discovery of a lost city in the Middle East and this man, Fiennes, emerges as a dashing figure and a very English adventurer. Some commentators have described him as an English public school's Indiana Jones, others as an eccentric version of 007, James Bond. He is rather more modest in describing himself. 'The problem is knowing what people mean by the word "explore",' he says. 'I've done thirty-two years of expeditions, only one of which was as a true explorer, as opposed to what I call myself – an expedition leader.' Fiennes, almost casually, in his own quintessentially British way, is taking on the seven-marathon challenge as a 'break' from his normal fare of Arctic or Antarctic expeditions. Despite his modesty, Fiennes has been responsible, almost single-handedly, for keeping the British end up in the adventure-rivalry between British and Norwegian explorers, which can trace its roots all the way back to the famous rivalry between Captain Robert Falcon Scott and the Norwegian Roald Amundsen in 1911 when the two nations, and personalities, battled to be the first to reach the South Pole. In his spare time, he writes books – sixteen so far, with more in the pipeline. For a man who has done many things that others can barely contemplate, the marathon – albeit a modified 'super multi-marathon' – is still challenge enough to whet the appetite. And, as if it was just to make things interesting, he took on this extraordinary challenge just six months after suffering a life-threatening heart attack.

'I finished researching my book, a biography of Scott of Antarctica, in 2003, and at that point I wanted to get back to some kind of physical challenge,' explains Fiennes. 'So, I rang up a friend of mine, Mike Stroud. We thought, as we weren't doing a polar expedition, we could do something shorter, like climb Mount Everest. All our neighbours had climbed it and, if the weather's good, it is dead easy, but Mike could not get the time away from home!' So Stroud told Fiennes about a plan he had concocted, with a group of American friends, to run seven marathons on seven consecutive days on seven different continents. The Americans had dismissed it as logistically impossible, but Fiennes was immediately intrigued. 'Mike and I thought it could be worth trying ourselves,' he said, his understatement so flat and dry that it could have been added to tonic water and ice and served instead of a famous gin sling in the Writers' Bar at Raffles Hotel. 'I found flights that would work, but we were told that we would have to finish each marathon in less than six hours as none of the flights would wait for us.'

The plan was researched, dates set and sponsors found. Then Fiennes experienced what he modestly described as 'a slight setback'. He suffered a heart attack on 7 June 2003 while sitting in an aeroplane waiting for take-off. The event almost cost him his life. When his heart stopped, it took paramedics thirteen attempts to get it going again. 'I was on a plane, strapped in,' he explains, 'and as it was revving to take off, I collapsed.' His deadpan delivery suggests he had been only slightly inconvenienced by a minor case of heartburn. 'I can't remember anything, but I know there was a kind nurse a couple of seats away who put me in the aisle and did all of the initial stuff. The captain immediately called the airport fire engine and lowered the steps. The fire engine people rushed on board with a defibrillator and that saved my life. I was so lucky that the plane hadn't taken off and that I was at Bristol Airport. Not at home – or on the motorway. I could not possibly have been in a better place.'

Fiennes was in a coma for three days after going under the knife at Bristol Royal Infirmary. He was later told by his surgeon, who ironically held the Italian record for the 800 metres, not to drive, or do any physical activity, for eight weeks. This was to protect the fourteen-inch gash through his ribcage, stitched up with wires that will be with him for life. The doctor might just as well have gone outdoors and turned cartwheels to entertain the great explorer as give him sensible advice. For, if it did anything, the heart attack, coming when it did, just as Fiennes was beginning his training regimen in the build-up to the first marathon of the series, in Antarctica, actually increased his resolve to return to his usual active, or, as some might say, eccentric lifestyle. This, after all, is a man who routinely jogs across the hills that surround his home in Somerset weighed down by motorcycle tyres and backpacks to emulate the strain of lugging supplies across the desolate wastelands of the poles.

'It was too late to postpone or cancel the event,' he recalls, somehow conveying a notion that he could not possibly put other people out just because he had experienced the inconvenience of a heart attack. 'It was not practical to postpone or cancel it. The marathon started on October twenty-sixth and it was written in concrete.' This bald statement was a clear signal of proof of the obvious: Fiennes is a special kind of man, who ran a very special type of marathon sequence. Remarkably, too, as if it was just to prove his confidence in himself and his repaired heart, he had only taken out ordinary holiday insurance for the challenge that lay ahead on those seven continents and their races, including his agonising jog through the heat in Singapore.

There, on the punishing and unforgiving course on asphalt and concrete, in the sweltering city, a drama occurred that was shared and only truly experienced by the two men involved. About halfway through the marathon, the second bedraggled and pain-wracked figure, Fiennes's friend and running partner, the aforementioned Dr Mike Stroud, was lagging behind. Stroud is a senior lecturer in Medicine and Nutrition at the University of Southampton and a consultant physician at the Southampton University Hospital Trust. He is, in short, as near to an expert in pushing the human body to extremes as can be found anywhere in the Anglophonic world. This expertise, it seems, has developed mainly because he has used his own body as a test bed on which he has carried out experiments in order to know how to base his judgements. Stroud is a regular accomplice of Fiennes in his many and various adventures and challenges. His name was written into the history books that record such achievements when he was declared the first man to have walked unaided across the Antarctic. He also holds a record for the longest unsupported Antarctic walk in history and he has a history of marathon running that dates back to 1984. Like Fiennes, he has always been a man apart from what passes as normal. Where most seek pleasure from life, he has always, it seems, sought pain. This explains why, too, in 1994, when he was apparently bored by the prospect of another routine 26.2-mile marathon challenge (he ran his first marathon race with barely 12 hours' notice, buying a pair of trainers on the way to the start line), he chose instead to try taking on the 135-mile Sahara Marathon, known as the 'Marathon of the Sands'. For him, he said, beating the marathon was always about the head and the heart, rather than the strength of his sinews. It was a piece of personalised jargon that may have returned to haunt him when he began experiencing difficulties beyond even his rare thresholds while running in Singapore.

'In my opinion, I am more surprised that not more people want to do marathons and physical challenges rather than vice versa,' he reflected later. 'I don't think it is in my physiology. I am not, by any stretch of the imagination, a gifted athlete. People who run marathons at great speed and in very fast times are. I think, what it is, is that I discovered by chance that you can do a great deal more than you think you can and, having discovered that, I am not daunted by things that others see as huge obstacles. Because they do not daunt me they become more attractive. It is the case that the mental side of running a marathon is important – for me, more important than the physical side of things. I think it is different when you are attempting to run a marathon where you want to "win". I don't know what that feels like. I've never ever attempted to win a marathon or, if it comes to that, to do a marathon in the best time possible. I'm more than happy to compete against myself, but also find it easier to compete against distance rather than the clock.'

It was as well that Stroud had this kind of philosophy to drive him on in Singapore. At the halfway point, it appeared that only sheer determination kept him on his feet. He was in serious trouble, his body rebelling with pain, blood passing in his urine, muscles abandoning their work and his feet staggering from one step to the next. Just moving forwards was a major challenge. But he was one of the two adventurers who had chosen this madness and he refused to buckle. The duo, who had a world of options open to them when they were choosing their next escapade, selected to run the modern marathon of 26.2 miles seven times. It was a challenge which both men, by the end, insisted was the hardest thing they had ever done.

Their presence on the streets of Singapore helped to stress the global appeal of the Singapore Marathon and of marathons in general. It confirmed the marathon as a mass medium for self-expression by ordinary athletes and as an extraordinary test of anyone's commitment. The adventurous pair had already run marathons at Punto Arenas, in southern Chile (instead of King George Island, in Antarctica, where bad weather prevented them from landing on schedule and so forced a late change of plans), at Stanley, in the Falkland Islands, and in Sydney, Australia. After Singapore, the most gruelling of all, they went to London, Cairo and New York, where their self-inflicted ordeal came to an end. The pictures, sounds and stories of their record-breaking runs were broadcast to millions around the world via television, radio, the written media and the Internet. Aghast at the challenge, the viewers, listeners and readers were fascinated by the efforts of these two men, at least twenty years beyond what should have been their physical peaks. They learned, too, that Fiennes and Stroud demonstrated without doubt that the marathon is as much about the pain of competing as the pleasure of reaching the finishing line. The lure of the challenge enticed them to fly 38,000 miles in 7 days and run a total of 183 miles on their increasingly bruised, blistered and tattered feet in the same period. A study of Fiennes and Stroud is a lesson about the mentality of the 'non-athlete' marathon runner for whom the mental battle of completing such an arduous physical challenge is far more important than how fast he can run. In this test of endurance, everyone could share and anyone could empathise.

The Singapore shock may have been the worst on the road for both men, but the entire sequence was a test of their resolve and physical strength. It was also a test of their logistical powers as Fiennes reflected frequently in his own account of events in that amazing week. Even before he had started running, he knew how profound was the test that lay ahead. 'In essence,' he said. 'This is a seven-day race, sub-divided into fourteen stages, seven of which are physical – the marathons – and the other seven logistical. The physical challenge is largely unknown. Although I've spent a lifetime pushing myself physically and my partner Mike Stroud is an expert on the effects of stress, the truth is that I've never even run two marathons on consecutive days. We believe it's possible – and in seven days we will know . . . That is, of course, if we can get off the ground!'

Twice, while waiting in the south of Chile to fly to their first marathon venue on King George Island, they were thwarted in their attempts to get away. In their first, the left engine in their two-engine plane failed. In their second, poor weather made them turn back when they were in the air. In the end, they abandoned that idea and ran instead on the mainland of Latin America, in the southern tip of Chile. 'It was a pragmatic decision,' says Fiennes. 'Without a change of plan, the challenge would quite simply have ended before it began.' Instead, they ran a makeshift course in good conditions, but ran faster than planned. Fiennes blamed Stroud's timekeeping. Energy expended on pace on the first of seven successive marathon running days was energy wasted. After the maiden event, they transferred to Santiago and flew by private jet to Stanley, luxuriating and resting in the leather-clad interior of a Gulfstream. The second run, in a desolate landscape redolent of the Falklands War, was completed relatively comfortably, five hours having been made available for the jog back to Stanley Cathedral. Only the last ten miles were painful, Fiennes admitted, adding that he then became bothered by worries about food intake and proper rest schedules during the days ahead. 'The normal recovery time for a marathon is measured in weeks, whereas we have hours, and not many of those. So it was rice, fish, potato and power bars at three in the morning.' Thankfully for both men, the Gulfstream was refuelled and ready to return to Santiago where they caught their flight to Sydney and began to face the really difficult tests their extraordinary challenge was throwing up.

'The long trip to Sydney allowed us a precious opportunity to sleep,' says Fiennes, with the nonchalance of a man who, in 2000, had cut off his own fingers at the knuckle, on his left hand, after contracting frostbite on an expedition to the South Pole. 'And we needed it because the ground schedule there was particularly tight. From landing to taking off again, for Singapore, we were set to be on the ground for barely seven hours including five allowed for the marathon. So, of course, it was hand luggage only . . .' Listening to Fiennes, or hearing of his feats, it is little surprise to learn that he took his dog, a Jack Russell called Bothie, on his expeditions to the North and South Poles. Or that his full name is Sir Ranulph Twistleton-Wykeham-Fiennes. Or that, as we know, he underwent a double bypass operation on his heart several months before he began his seven marathons in seven days challenge. He is, after all, no ordinary man; indeed, he is no ordinary marathon man. 'The first signs of physical deterioration showed before Sydney,' he said. 'My fatigue was manageable, but I had already abandoned my shoes, thanks to a blister where a toe used to be! That sounds like a joke, but after suffering severe frostbite in Antarctica several years ago, I'm short of a few toes and the site of the subsequent skin graft has always been prone to blistering . . .'

Next to this colossus of adventure, who has cut such a glamorous figure, Stroud was not eclipsed, but he was certainly less likely to steal any metaphorical limelight that strayed across their paths during their painful odyssey around the world. But Stroud's marathon of marathons was an expedition of equal, if not greater, courage and strength, particularly by the time they had left Australia and gone to Singapore where, as we know, he suffered very considerable pain. A veteran of marathons for twenty years, Stroud had already had to call for medical back-up after seven miles of the race, fearing that his symptoms of heat exhaustion, in addition to the inconvenience caused by fatigue and the passing of blood in his urine, might result in a need for serious and immediate assistance. He was followed by an ambulance from Singapore's Alexandra Hospital. As a doctor, one might have thought Stroud would know better, but his case demonstrates just what a human body can be put through and his motivation to continue against all sensible advice was a testament to the sense of achievement, and kudos, that can be gained by completing a marathon. It is a drug that causes sensible, normal, intelligent people – perhaps like Fiennes and Stroud, in fact – to put themselves through hell.

Stroud, it should be noted, ran without the tensor fasciata in his right leg, a strip of muscle that connects the hip to the knee. Sports medicine experts assured him that to do so would cause him terrible physical problems and agonising pain, but he insisted that he could not understand how he could further damage a muscle that had already been torn off. So, he plodded on, and on. And on. Of more concern to him was the fact that he suffered from blisters and cramp, his blackened toenails began to fall off and he developed symptoms of influenza. The blood in his urine was put down to repeated running on hard asphalt surfaces, causing the crushing of capillaries in his feet and the transfer of haemoglobin into his water.

Fiennes, despite his heart attack and subsequent operation only four months earlier, coped somewhat better despite being aware, at all times, that another heart attack was a real possibility should his rate of heartbeats per minute exceed 130. The fear of another attack prompted Stroud to pack a defibrillator in his pack of running essentials, despite being confident that his friend had been 'success-fully replumbed' after his heart attack. 'Just in case Ran needs to be restarted again . . .' he quipped. Fiennes, as ever, refused to let such a minor consideration enter his mind and had conveniently 'forgot-ten' the heart-rate monitor given to him by his doctors.

As the two plodded onwards, perspiration-covered camera crews and photographers intermittently getting in their way, or in the way of other participants in the event, they were cheered on by crowds who probably had no idea what they were attempting to achieve or knew anything about their history or homes in the west of England. In truth, the crowds would cheer anything stumbling past, be it male, female, young, old, black, white or clad in any of the weird and wonderful costumes that shielded the identity of the runners from the onlookers. Two runners, however, did recognise the pair and were inspired to push themselves past their intended mark of a half-marathon and on to the finishing line of the event. ('If he could do seven in seven days after a heart attack, I figured I ought to be able to manage one without one,' Nina Passi, who runs a fitness club in Singapore, told reporters after the race.)

Their physical courage was impressive and inspirational for the people of Singapore. There, some 6,700 miles from London and the next marathon on their schedule, the pair ran past Mountbatten Road, near Raffles Hotel, the world-famous Singapore landmark that harks back to an age of British imperialism, which was based on a belief in hard work and Victorian neo-puritan Christianity. Such a code for life may now be long gone, but it is not forgotten. Raffles Hotel, in all its splendour, was named after Sir Stamford Raffles who, in 1819, persuaded the British East India Company to lease the island from the Sultan Johore. This move established Singapore as the greatest trading post in the eastern oceans as Britain expanded its influence from India. Seven years later, the Straits Settlements, including Singapore, Malacca and Penang, were established and in 1867 they became a British Crown Colony. This British control was to remain in effect – apart from the Japanese invasion and occupation during World War Two – until 1959, when self-government began. Fiennes and Stroud, the two running Britons, running through the historic buildings of Singapore, were symbols of this history and the great friendship that existed between the British and the island's occupants.

Furthermore, for all the differences that exist between the two nations in more modern times, with the British Empire replaced by its Commonwealth, it is interesting to note the many similarities that still tie them together. Indeed, as a primary example, there is the symbolic importance of the lion to both Britain and Singapore, which gives a sense of unity between two islands on opposite sides of the globe, even though the animal is not indigenous to either country. For Britain, and the British Empire, the lion was the physical incarnation of pride and dominion. The king of the animals, the lion is still used as a symbol of the combined British Rugby Union team for its tours abroad. The lion also plays an important role in Malay legend, which claims that a Sumatran prince encountered a lion on the island of Temasek, prompting him to found Singapura, or Lion City. As Sir Ranulph and Dr Stroud stumbled past Raffles, it was perhaps only their indomitable leonine spirit that prevented them from succumbing to temptation to bring an abrupt end to their marathon challenge by entering the air-conditioned portals for a refreshing tonic at the bar.

Instead, perhaps inspired by their historical surroundings, the pair finally stumbled across the line, Stroud finishing thirty minutes behind Fiennes. Both were clearly shattered. Stroud's problems were not helped by the fact that he had only managed to consume drinks, a banana and a muesli bar since completing the last race in Sydney. The pair were reunited on the finishing line, where Fiennes nearly collapsed. Then they were driven in an air-conditioned ambulance to the Padang Parade Ground, where Lord Mountbatten received the Japanese surrender at the end of the Second World War 58 years earlier, to recuperate. Both applied a variety of ointments and potions to the most painful parts of their bodies and limbs, hoping for a swift recovery. A 6,739-mile flight to London beckoned and, with it, another 26.2 miles of punishing marathon fun.

As they sat bandaging their feet and massaging their aching muscles, surrounded by the opulent splendour of the Parade Ground's exquisite architecture, the contrast between their apparent pursuit of pain and their ancestors' pursuit of money, pleasure and glory, was thrown into stark relief. 'Why?' is an oft-asked question for any marathon runner. The case of Fiennes and Stroud goes some way towards answering part of this complex question. While the main goal of others in life is to attain some experience of maximum enjoyment or pleasure, Fiennes and Stroud set their target as a pursuit of discovery, especially a discovery of how far their bodies can be pushed. A marathon is an ideal stage for this very personal voyage of discovery. The price to be paid is pain, but the reward is in achieving something difficult that many others may not, and may never, achieve. These men truly tested every mental and physical reserve in Singapore, the halfway point in their race around the earth.

In essence, their exertions allowed them to truly know what it is to feel human, to know the outermost boundaries of a human body and mind. While others merely experience humanity, Fiennes and Stroud have used the marathon to find the inside track on life itself. And for every one of the competitors on the streets of Singapore, and around the world in a variety of marathons, the resolve, determination, pain, agony and mental trauma experienced as the body and soul are stretched towards breaking point are made worthwhile by accomplishing a goal – whether it be beating a personal best, overcoming illness or simply proving something that was previously unproven. The marathon turns 'nine-to-five man' into an adventurer, putting him, or her, shoulder to shoulder with Fiennes and Stroud, the professional adventurers, for a day at least.

Looking back on Singapore, and the marathon as a whole, Fiennes was somewhat reticent to talk of his feelings about the event, and the challenge as a whole, other than to admit that 'it was great fun'. Yet, in his reticence, there is a sense that by forcing himself to complete the seven marathons he ran, so soon after his heart attack and surgery, he had responded to the threat on his own life that was represented by the heart attack itself. He believed that he was fortunate to have been on a plane in Bristol Airport when he suffered his heart attack and he seemed to believe that the seven-by-seven-by-seven was scheduled for him to prove he and life could go on. 'I've always thought luck can come, or it might not come,' he says, somewhat mysteriously. 'Sometimes, there's good luck, sometimes there's bad luck. You just have to say God was good to you on that particular day.' And Singapore? 'I hit the pavement and nearly fainted at the end. I felt completely knackered and not able to do another one. I decided it would be stupid for my condition to continue.

Things didn't look good at all. But after about an hour I felt better, so I thought, "I might as well continue . . ." '

Stroud underwent a series of medical examinations after struggling over the finish line in Singapore. His blood enzyme levels were found to be dangerously low, so much so that, as he puts it, 'My muscles were, basically, just disintegrating and falling off my bones.' But he still boarded the next plane with Fiennes and continued, running in London on the original and historic 1908 Windsor to White City course, and then in Cairo, from a floodlit start under the pyramids at Giza back to the airport, eventually crossing the finish line in the New York Marathon, after a feed and a sleep on the British Airways flight to the Big Apple and a brief sojourn to change and prepare in a hotel room in Manhattan. Arm in arm with his friend (despite a chronic dose of diarrhoea that forced him to walk much of the final leg), Stroud crossed the line. They both went the distance, mentally, physically and emotionally.

'I like the opportunity to travel to these wonderful places and get a lot of satisfaction from trying these challenges that I do,' said Stroud, with the benefit of two months' rest and recovery at home in England. 'But they are really physical rather than athletic challenges. The quality you really need with all these tests is a bad memory so you can remember the good parts and forget the bad. They are incredibly demanding, but I think that what you draw on when you do these things, including any type of marathon, are survival reserves.

'Humankind, from our evolutionary background, has a reserve capability that is designed to be used in life or death situations. In those situations, people who have very poor fitness have done remarkable things. People who are prepared to take on prolonged endurance events – marathons, certainly ultra-marathons – are drawing on that survival reserve that our physiology has given us voluntarily. They have found it's there. A lot of people don't even realise, when they are a bit tired after running a few miles, that there is this reserve facility that will allow them to go ten times further if they want to. People who run five marathons and say "I could never run another marathon" are kidding themselves. They just need to discover those reserves. They will surprise themselves and be amazed for the experience . . .'

4. HISTORY 2 – BIRTH OF THE MODERN MARATHON BY THE AEGEAN SEA

The first recognised 'modern' marathon of the Olympic Games took place on Friday 10 April 1896 in front of vast roadside crowds on a mild and relatively dust-free afternoon in Greece. That is accurate, strictly speaking, according to the Gregorian calendar; but if the traditional Julian calendar, in use in Greece at the time, is consulted, it was held on 29 March, a date that, for the purposes of this book, we will ignore (although it is the date given in the official report for the 1896 Olympic Games). Henceforth, as is normal in our modern world, we will refer to dates as in the Gregorian calendar.

This race was contested by seventeen runners over a distance of approximately 40 kilometres, or 25 miles and 28 yards, and it was run over a course that started in the village, now a small town, of Marathon and finished in the city of Athens. It began on a bridge and finished in a stadium. The runners ran, in the simplest terms, down the coast and then uphill and downhill, to the capital. It was no surprise, looking back more than a hundred years later, that the first winner was a Greek, Spiridon Louis, nor that Greek contestants filled seven of the top eight places. The Greeks, after all, were keen to supply a strong team and they had also laid on two preliminary races to act as practice sessions for the runners involved. In short, the Greeks were ready; albeit that their training programme had, according to some reports, resulted in a Greek tragedy with the death of up to three runners whose fitness levels were insufficient to guarantee survival on such a course. Ultimately, however, it was a Greek race, devised by French intellectuals, to be won by a local hero, a modest water carrier whose occupation had given him the stamina and strength to cope with the distance; and that, of course, was exactly how it turned out.

The first of the trial marathon races, in preparation for the first Olympic event, was held on 10 March 1896. It was, in effect, the first true marathon, though it was not run as an official competitive event. The race was run over the course chosen for the Olympics, from a bridge in Marathon village to the Panathenaikon Stadium, reconstructed for the Games. Two of the runners, however, were said to have gained a small advantage by privately trying to run the course by themselves during February. One of them completed the distance, reportedly G. Grigorou, but it was of scant use to him. In the trial race, twelve runners from Greek sports clubs took part, the winner, Charilaos Vasilakos clocking a time of 3 hours and 18 minutes. The second trial was held shortly before the Olympic Games and was won by a man known simply as Lavrentis with a time of 3 hours, 11 minutes and 27 seconds. A team to represent Greece was selected from the first event, but it was changed after the second with the addition of a little-known runner called Spiridon Louis, who had finished fifth in the second trial. This man, a shepherd or a farmer or a messenger (depending on your source of information) from a simple rural village, was not to remain unknown much longer. His running and his marathon triumph left an indelible mark on the culture and the language of his country.

The race began with seventeen men assembled on the bridge in Marathon. There had been eighteen entrants, according to some sources, but one – an unidentified German athlete – was left behind. The field of entrants was mostly made up of Greeks, but it included a few international runners: the Australian Edwin 'Teddy' Flack, Gyula Kellner of Hungary, Arthur Blake of the United States and Albin Lermusiaux of France. Flack, an Australian accountant who lived in London and who held the Australian record for the mile, had proved his form by winning both the 800- and 1,500-metre races, the former earlier on Thursday before he travelled to Marathon. Blake had finished second, behind him, in the 1,500 metres and Lermusiaux third. If the Hungarian had not shown speed on the track over any distance, he had the advantage of having run a long race close to the length of a marathon before. None of the other non-Greek runners had.

Some controversy was added to this international assembly to give the maiden Olympic marathon and Games a taste of what lay in store for the future. The experienced Italian long-distance runner, Carlo Airoldi, who had travelled to Greece on foot to take part, was barred from participating because he was regarded as a professional and, therefore, contravened the strict code laid down by Pierre de Coubertin's initial idealism. It mattered not that the poor man was exhausted anyway after a journey of nearly a thousand miles. He was ruled out.

Most of the competitors allowed to run had travelled to Marathon the previous night in various horse-drawn carts and coaches. This allowed them plenty of rest and preparation before the race began at 2 p.m., their starting positions having been allotted by the drawing of lots. By the time the official starter, Major Papadimantopoulos, completed his brief introductory speech and fired his pistol into the air, there was small crowd in attendance to witness what seemed to be a novel event. Nobody knew it was the start of an era. As the runners moved off, they were followed by officials on bicycles and medical doctors in horse-drawn wagons.

The race, regarded by the swelling groups of spectators that gathered to watch the runners as the highlight of the Olympic Games, began at high speed, by any standards. The Frenchman, Lermusiaux, reached the village of Pikermi in about 55 minutes and held a lead of almost 2 miles. Flack was second, Blake third. The Greek crowd was disappointed, but did not give up. Americans had enjoyed great success in most of the Olympics until then. The Greeks, however, still believed they could achieve a triumph in the event they revered because of its strong cultural associations with their country and its history and mythology. These were, after all, only early days in a very long struggle. This was the view also of Louis when he reached Pikermi, as one of the runners in the anonymous pack behind the leaders. It is said he took a glass of wine in the village and made it clear he believed he would go on and win the race.

The Greek runners' slow start, compared to the foreigners, was, of course, eminently sensible. Knowing that the first half of the course would take them down the coast on level ground before the climb up through the hills towards Athens, they had conserved their energy. After Pikermi, the leaders were therefore left to regret their early haste as their Greek rivals, in almost leisurely style, passed them. Blake dropped out, then Kellner was passed, but Lermusiaux battled on and, at the village of Karavati, he stayed at the front of the field. The villagers, filled with enthusiasm for the marathon, smothered him with a floral wreath as if he was the victor. It was a premature gesture. Soon afterwards, he retired in extraordinary circumstances when a compatriot, probably his helper who was believed to be the gymnast and athlete Alphonse Grisel, riding a bicycle, first gave him an alcohol rubdown to revive him (each runner was permitted to have one assistant with him for the race), but then – depending on the accuracy of sources – collided with him as he staggered along. He was in agonised exhaustion. Courageously, he regained his feet, but he could barely walk, let alone run and, after reaching the twenty-miles mark, he collapsed again. This time, he was carried away to recover.

This left Flack in the lead and, in an act of foolhardy confidence, he sent a message ahead to the stadium by bicycle, a message that was intended to pronounce his impending victory. The news, once it spread around the huge crowd, silenced the spectators. But not for long. Behind Flack, Louis had gathered pace and strength on the climb, passing several runners to arrive in second place. He was closing on the leader and, as Flack slowed with fatigue over the closing miles, he ran past him and, after struggling with his attempt to stay with him, opened up a commanding advantage. Flack, his competitive energy spent, his hopes of victory burst asunder, crashed to the ground and abandoned his race not long after his helper, an Englishman, was said to have accidentally conspired to upset him. This helper, sensing that his man would need a blanket, asked a nearby Greek spectator to help him stay standing, but Flack misinterpreted what was happening. Instead of thinking the Greek was helping him, he thought he was attacking him and so he punched him to the ground. Flack fell and, like Lermusiaux, was carried away. According to Wallechinsky, he was then transported to the stadium where he was revived with a drink of eggs and brandy served by Prince Nicholas! (According to Martin and Gynn, the helper was a British butler W. Delves-Broughton, a staff member from the British embassy who had gone to school in Australia where his father worked as master of the Melbourne mint.) In another useful source, H. Gordon (*Australia and the Olympic Games*, 1994), as quoted by Martin and Gynn, offers a vivid description of the start of the race and Flack's mood.

As the runners cantered away backed by an odd caravan of attendants, there he was, a tall and angular figure among so many smaller, swarthier ones, with his chest cased in his old school vest (dark blue with a white mitre on the chest) and his head protected by a small tasselled cap, attended by the faithful Delves-Broughton, pedalling a pushbike and looking thoroughly incongruous in a bowler hat.

All of this dramatic competition, with retirements, endorsed Greek confidence in their distance runners and Louis's mid-race prediction that he had the potential to win. Another messenger went ahead to the stadium and this time, when the crowd was told that the Greeks were running in first, second and third positions in the marathon, they went wild with excitement. The official starter, on his horse, rode in to inform the King of the joyful news. The news spread 'with the rapidity of lightning', according to Wallechinsky, quoting the official report. The crowd, by now 100,000 strong, shrieked, '*Ellen! Ellen!*' (A Greek, A Greek). Unlike Pheidippides, he survived the experience. The royal family was delighted. Prince George and Crown Prince Nicholas, or it may have been Crown Prince Constantine (again, the sources differ on this fact) danced with pleasure and, when Louis entered the stadium, ran with him to the finish line. Then, according to one report, he went to rest and drank two cups of Greek coffee and met Queen Olga, who congratulated him and embraced him. When she discovered how calloused his hands seemed to be, it is said that she asked about his occupation. Learning that he was a common labourer, she took off her rings and gave them to him, saying, 'The honour that you have given to Greece is worth more than these simple rings.' It is impossible to know if this story is true, but in Athens, as he approached the finish, the triumphant runner had been almost overwhelmed by his welcome as thousands of Greeks packed the streets to cheer him. There was barely room for him to run.

Louis, confident, unflustered and strong, still had time to take some orange slices from his girlfriend Eleni – whom he was to marry on 19 April the following year – near to the finish, where she was in the crowd and waiting for him, before he ran on and completed the race in a winning time of 2 hours, 58 minutes and 50 seconds. Charilaos Vasilakos, winner of the original trial race, was second, more than seven minutes later and another Greek, Spiridon Belokas, was third. Kellner, the plucky Hungarian, finished fourth, but promptly complained that Belokas had not run the entire distance and had, instead, cheated by travelling for some of the time in a carriage. Challenged on this, the Greek runner agreed it was true and he was disqualified. Kellner was promoted to third. He was happier, but not as happy as the Greeks who, forgetting all else that had gone before, ensured that this first marathon, run at the first of the modern

Olympic Games, signalled the arrival of an event that has ever since been synonymous with heroic long-distance running.

Two days later when the King held a celebratory feast for his athletes, three days before the prize-giving ceremony, Louis, who was reported to be 23 or 24 years old, arrived wearing the national uniform of Greece and was given an exceptionally warm welcome. Most surviving photographs of him show him in his Greek costume for this special occasion, in a black waistcoat, white frill-cuffed shirt and knee-high boots. When he travelled home afterwards, through the streets of Athens, he was greeted like a hero. His father, who was with him, basked in the glory he shared with the marathon's first winner. For his victory, the following Wednesday, at a downcast and wet ceremony, he received a silver medal and an olive branch as well as the silver cup presented by Michel Breal. He also received a vase donated by Ionnis Lambros that showed a runner of the ancient Olympic Games in action. This vase was later donated to a museum by Louis whose legendary feats attracted much attention in Greece and established him as an almost mythological figure in the modern age. He was fêted and lavished with gifts including money, all kinds of material wealth, jewellery, wine, free haircuts, watches, clothes, food, coffee, shotguns, even a Singer sewing machine, so it is said, and an offer of marriage. Steadfastly, he turned them all down and chose instead to return modestly to his home in his village of Amaroussion, often shortened to Maroussi in later times. According to many of the stories that emerged from the aftermath of his great triumph, he asked for only one gift in recognition of his success and this was a horse and cart so he could carry water for the villagers. This may be a significant, if small, tale to remember for those Olympic followers who travel to Greece for the 2004 Games, for it is in this famous old village that the new magnificent marble Olympic stadium complex is to be built. It is also the village where Louis is buried in the local cemetery, his grave a simple surviving symbol of the life and feats of the first marathon winner.

His normality, such as it was after 1896, was to be interrupted again, however, by the Olympic Games, later in his life. This time, it was not to run a marathon. Instead, in 1936, he was rediscovered by the German Olympic Games organising committee and invited to Berlin. There, in a ceremony that stretches credulity, he presented a laurel wreath from the sacred grove at Olympia to Adolf Hitler. He also, thankfully for us, gave an interview in which he talked candidly of his run in the 1896 marathon. His comments, as reproduced by David Miller in his extraordinarily detailed book, *Athens to Athens*, in 2003, gave an insight that provides a startling contrast to the cosseted life of modern athletes preparing for such an event.

The day before the race, a decrepit old horse and cart pulled some of us from Maroussi, my home village, to Marathon,' he said. 'It was raining and the journey took almost five hours. It had rained and even hailed in the night and, as a result, we were shaking with cold. The people of Marathon kindly lent us their jackets. That evening, the mayor plied us liberally to get us warm again, to keep our strength up for the race. "Is there anything else you want?" he asked. "Yes!" we cried in unison. "Bring us some more wine, please!" That rainy Thursday, we celebrated in a way that probably no other athletes have ever done before a competition. What did we know about abstaining during training?

'The next morning, when the foreign runners were being massaged by their helpers, I said to my companions, "Let's do a couple of laps around the village square to stretch our legs a bit." In that way, we wore in the new shoes which the people of Maroussi had bought for us. They were good and cost about twenty-five drachmas a pair, at the time an enormous sum for shoes. At eleven, there was milk and two eggs for each man. At two, we were in the street and ready to start. After some way, my future father-in-law, standing by the roadside, offered me a beaker of white wine and an Easter egg. I slurped down the wine, felt much stronger and quickly caught up with my colleague Christovoulos. The crowds were shouting, "Go, Louis, go," and that spurred me on. A policeman who shouted "the only ones in front of you are foreigners" had to ride a brisk trot on his horse to keep up with me. A few hundred metres in front of me was the American. I thought, "I'll show him what's what," and I stepped up the pace. It was enough. Vasilakos overtook him, too, and I said, "Let's run together," but he was exhausted and he couldn't keep up. I left him and came up behind the Frenchman. He did his best, but suddenly he collapsed. He was all in. Once I was past him, I realised that the front-runner, the

Australian, was there. Everyone was bellowing, "Catch him, Louis. You've got to beat him. *Hellas, Hellas!*" Ambition took hold of me. I lengthened my stride and it did the trick. He was a tough lad, but I closed on him. When I caught up with him after 34 kilometres, an officer shot his pistol in the air and everyone cheered. For 500 metres, we ran side by side. I kept watching him from the corner of my eye. I didn't let him gain a foot of ground. At last, he got short of breath and fell further and further back.

Four years later (1940), when the movement to which he had contributed much was held in suspension, unable to hold its Games, he died. Born, according to best reports, on 12 January 1873, he died on 26 March 1940, following a heart attack, aged 67. He was the fifth and final child of Athanasios and Kalomira Louis, and he grew up helping his father with water transport and distribution, after serving in the army. He and Eleni had three children, all boys, but he never ran another marathon and did not enjoy a life of wealth or subsequent fame or happiness. He fell on hard times and, in 1925, according to Martin and Gynn, was arrested and jailed for forgery. He was found innocent and released in March 1926, but lost his wife a year later when she died from diabetes. His contribution – a superb run, a modest public appearance, a shy man's inspirational effort – had fired the marathon and the Olympic Games into being. He had helped to establish the event and to give flesh and reality to the theory, realising a dream for those brought up on the mythology of Pheidippides' fabled run from the battlefield of Marathon.

5. BOSTON – HOME OF THE 'STAR-SPANGLED' MARATHON

Some cities fizz with the vibe of living in the here-and-now while others slumber in the past. Some offer beautiful scenery, sumptuous tourist luxuries and streets crowded with exclusive hotels, department stores and up-market shops. Others are commercial, high-rise, stiff collared, unforgiving and competitive. Some are dull, poor and unattractive. Others are chic, romantic and atmospheric, alive with music, sizzling food and laughter rising from river boats. Some are industrial, working places, dark with toil, lit up by humour and wit. Others are academic and tweedy, or agricultural and flat capped and pungent with rural odours. Boston, the ancient bosom of American dreams, is all, and yet not entirely any, of these. Sitting with aplomb on Massachusetts' eastern coastline, facing Europe and its forebears, it takes everything in its Ivy League embrace, boasts Harvard – arguably America's finest university, with its Cambridge addresses and manifold academic departments – has a fine harbour, enjoys being a financial, commercial and cultural centre and has a range of restaurants as good as anywhere in the United States. Yet Boston is really a city made famous by invisible threads carried forwards from the past, not gimmicks or casinos or vulnerable reputations. In short, Boston is where they have always made history; and memorable history at that. Few visitors, after all, will not have heard of the city's most significant act of ancient unrest. It led to some important repercussions and it was known as the 'Boston Tea Party', though there was not much bone china in use.

To some, Boston is a poor relation in the vast, gleaming, but chintzy family of American cities. It lacks the sombre pomp of Washington DC, the high-rise grandeur and night-time thrills of New York or the bright lights and razzmatazz of Las Vegas. Nor does it have the silicon-enhanced charm of Los Angeles, the sheer industrial drive of Denver or Chicago, or the laid-back allure of dreamy New Orleans. But Boston still holds a remarkable place in American history. For it is the spiritual birthplace of the United States itself and, for our purposes, the founding city of the first regular non-Olympic marathon. There is no trusted academic proof to hand, but the pioneering spirit that created both great institutions is likely to have come from the same line of bloodstock and to have been drawn from the same well of human endeavour.

It was on 17 December 1773 that the feisty inhabitants of Boston landed the first blows in a dispute with Great Britain that would ultimately spark the Revolutionary Wars and see the United States of America emerge as a country in its own right. Increasingly outraged by tax hikes imposed from Britain by the ill-advised actions of George III (despite the American colonies having no representation in the British parliament) around 200 colonists, disguised as Indians, descended on three ships of the East Indian Trading Company docked in Boston's harbour and dumped their cargo of tea into the sea. The remarkable act was the first move in a series of disputes between Britain and the colonies that would lead to war and, after a bitter struggle, to the independence of the United States.

By 19 April 1897, 113 years and 4 months later, America was established as a major world power. It had experienced its own brutal and bloody civil war and had emerged with a stronger Union. America's industrial and military might was being taken seriously around the world and a distinctly American 'culture' was developing that would one day come to dominate the globe. And on this date in Boston, Patriot's Day, a year after the first running of the 'modern' marathon at the Olympic Games in Athens, and in the spirit of American innovation (copy it, improve it, promote it and make some money), fifteen runners embarked on the inaugural Boston Marathon. It was an event that provided the basis for imitations all over America – and all over the world.

This first event was the brainchild of one John Graham, manager of America's 1896 Olympic team and member of the Boston Athletic Association. Despite the fact that the American entry in the marathon at the Athens Olympics, Arthur Blake, collapsed well before the finishing line, Graham was inspired to imitate the event on the streets of Boston and set out a 24.7-mile marathon course running close to the railway line from Ashland to Boston, finishing with 5 miles of uphill climbing and then a 6-mile descent into the city. The ascent, similar to that which greeted the runners on their way to Athens from Marathon, was dubbed Heartbreak Hill. The event drew a small crowd and 'sponsorship' from Boston businessman Herbert H.

Holton and, of the fifteen runners who started, eight finished – sowing the seeds for what promoters now bill as the 'grand-daddy of all marathons'. Although Boston's development of historical roots tying it to the foundation of the marathon owed much to good fortune (a 25-mile footrace from Connecticut to the Bronx had been held a year previously, but failed to catch on) and old-fashioned Corinthian sprit, rather than a continuation of revolutionary, or inventive zeal, the development of the event and the countless imitations it subsequently inspired has provided a reflection of the progress of the 'land of the free', and of the development of the massively popular 'people's' marathon ever since.

As the nation expanded, and trends changed, so did the marathon, reflecting changes in domestic and global attitudes. Who would have guessed that 107 years on from that first field of fifteen brave souls, participant numbers would peak at 38,706. The initial sponsorship of a local patron turned into a prize fund of hundreds of thousands of dollars. Participants changed from gentleman athletes (although their influence in the marathon was not as pronounced and enduring as in many track and field sports) to a mix of amateur enthusiasts and professionals and, eventually, women and the disabled. The Boston Marathon was joined and aped by marathons in every one of America's 52 states. From Arizona to Alaska, Boston to San Francisco and New York to Honolulu races have been founded to cater for the growing popularity of the event. Succeeding generations of Americans have been bitten by the same bug that inspired John Graham to found the Boston Marathon in the first place, or at least a younger version of it.

It should be recognised, however, that the wide-eyed innocence of the first Boston Marathon was soon forgotten as the race came to the attention of professional sportsmen and gamblers. As early as 1901, the marathon fell victim to a notorious betting scandal. Organised gambling on the result of the race was rife, with Jack Caffrey odds-on favourite to triumph. His only apparent rival was one Ronald McDonald (no, not that one, this was long before his emergence as a public figure!). Caffrey triumphed with ease, but not before McDonald had collapsed and died after being handed a sponge, by an onlooker, that was allegedly laced with chloroform. Another version of events claimed that McDonald's trainer, in a bid to see his charge defy the bookmakers, had effectively caused McDonald to overdose on performance-enhancing drugs.

It is remarkable to consider that doping, and allegations of cheating, have been a cause for controversy for so long. While the outcry surrounding the race did little to cement its integrity, it did help to increase its notoriety and, remarkably, its popularity. It seems there is indeed no such thing as bad publicity. The increasing level of interest in the event would soon become apparent when thirty Americans, twice the number who competed in the first Boston Marathon, entered the first Olympic marathon to be held on American soil in St Louis in 1904. Admittedly, the only qualification needed to compete was to be at the start of the race on the right day, but American competitors still claimed most of the leading places in the event.

Even America's involvement in the Great War of 1914–18 could not stop the twenty-first running of the Boston race. The organisers simply roped in a selection of solders and sailors from the various different units of the US Armed Forces to race against each other in a relay form of the event in 1918. As the 20 April 1918 edition of the *Boston Globe* put it in a review of the race, 'Those sun and wind-bronzed young soldiers, those deep-chested patriot-athletes had each run two and a half miles at their top-most speed over some part of the historic marathon course from Ashland to Boston, and they did not even breathe deeply.' In fact, the sight of the competition between the armed forces saw the first calls for an end to the increasing professionalism of the event, perhaps sowing the first seeds of the combined professional and amateur event of the modern-day city marathon. 'Every mother's sons wore the uniform of his service. How different from other years when the specially trained runners appeared in scanty running suits and light running shoes,' the *Boston Globe* continued. 'Yesterday, the 140 fighters for democracy were clothed as they will be today. There was no difference in apparel, no unusual equipment for the race.'

The Boston Marathon course was extended from 25 to 26.2 miles in 1924 to conform with the new Olympic standard adopted after the 1908 games in London, although the course was once again extended in 1927 after it was, rather embarrassingly, revealed that the modified course was still 110 metres short. Increasing interest in the event from the medical point of view saw the first research into the physiology of marathon runners undertaken by Dr D. B. Bill at Harvard's Fatigue Laboratory in the 1920s – research that built the foundations for modern sport's scientists, long-distance training specialists and conditioning experts. But the Boston event itself continued with little incident, bar increases in competitor numbers, faster times, the occasional accusation of cheating and the odd unfortunate on-course death, for another fifty years, encompassing the disruption of the Second World War.

That lengthy and appalling conflict overcome, it was surprising that the 1960s and early 1970s saw the face of the Boston Marathon change dramatically as it was popularised and promoted more than ever by television and business interests. This was the age of the dawning of all sorts of change, reaction to Vietnam, Woodstock, women's rights and sexual freedom. As the 'hippy' revolution moved into full swing, America's conservative society was forced to react and relent. It was predictable that demands would come flooding in for women to be allowed to compete in the Boston Marathon and, so, eventually, they did. Despite the ban on female competitors, Roberta Gibb wrote her name into the history books when, in 1966, she became the first woman to run the Boston Marathon by the somewhat unusual, though low-tech, method of hiding behind a bush at the start line before joining in with other competitors. She also raced in 1967 and 1968, but was never officially recognised by race organisers. In 1967 Katherine Switzer was given a bib number after failing to identify herself as female and finished the race despite numerous attempts to remove her. By the time of the 1972 Boston event, American athletics authorities had bowed to massive pressure to allow women to compete in marathons and Nina Kuscik, from a field of eight women competitors, became the first ever official women's champion of the Boston Marathon. It had taken 75 years for women to be allowed to take part in the event. (Remarkably enough, just three years later, the Boston Marathon became the first major marathon to recognise disabled participants when Bob Hall became the first winner of the wheelchair event.)

As the make-up of the fields in the Boston marathon became increasingly diverse, so, too, the marathon in general began to expand and the 1970s saw the marathon flourish in America and throughout the world. Increased interest in physical activity in general, and among the working class in particular (as they had an increasing amount of leisure time in the increasingly technological post-industrial society), combined with the inherent American ability to identify a captive audience, and alternative events sprang up all over the place, notably in New York (1970), Chicago (1976) and San Francisco (1977). New York was soon to establish itself as perhaps the best-known City Marathon venue of all, and Chicago as the marathon city that can attract fields of up to 40,000 with ease. San Francisco was one of a number of marathons that would flourish throughout the USA on a slightly smaller, if rather more exotic, scale.

By the end of the twentieth century, marathons were being held across the United States at all sorts of weird, wonderful and often unusual venues. States, counties, towns and even geographical features (e.g. the Pikes Peak marathon in Colorado that climbs 7,700 feet to the summit of the 14,110-foot tall Pikes Peak) joined the growing list of varied events in the colourful marathon catalogue. The consequent blanket coverage of many of these events was broadcast on regional and national television. Chicago, bulging with enthusiasts wishing to compete, was forced to impose a limit of 40,000 on the number of competitors and even Honolulu emerged as an alternative and very popular venue. Honolulu proved capable of attracting a field of near to 26,000. Such is the lure of the marathon.

As events spread far and wide, and interest in the marathon continued to escalate, so, too, did the monetary rewards on offer from an increasingly affluent American society and its business community. As well as appealing to the club runner and the charity collector, huge prize funds soon developed, backed by massive corporations; to encourage the best of the world's talent to take part in marathons throughout the United States. By 2003, the prize fund for the Chicago Marathon had enlarged to 550,000 dollars with 100,000 dollars on offer to the winner of both the men's and women's events. Boston, in an effort to maintain an image as a 'special' race has, to some extent, snubbed the modern marathon's tendency to encourage the mixture of the professional and amateur seen in most of the world's leading marathons. Having seen a world record 38,706 runners complete the Boston course in the hundredth staging of the event on 16 April 1996, Boston has now, to some degree, gone back to basics, limiting participant numbers to 20,000 and setting strict qualification tests for those hoping to make it into the race. If you are in the 18–34 age group, male, and do not have an officially sanctioned sub-3 hours 10 minutes personal best, then there is no place available.

With more than eight million dollars in prize money being handed out to participants at the Boston Marathon since 1986, the race is arguably the most 'professional' marathon in the United States. However, with an increase in money came an increase in the number of overseas winners in American marathons. In races where victory had previously been the preserve of home-grown talent and locals, the best athletes from Europe, Asia and Africa now started to come to prominence. This was welcomed by some, but not by Kevin Dupont, of the *Boston Globe* newspaper, who was brought up on American marathon heroes. The fact that an American man had not won the Boston Marathon since 1973 was not a cause for celebration for him at all. 'The Boston Marathon is open to the world, and right now, Kenya, essentially, has annexed the 26.2-mile asphalt swath that once belonged to the Commonwealth of Massachusetts,' wrote Dupont, after seeing Kenyan athletes take all the top five places in the 2003 race. 'One day a year, we line up by the thousands to wax nostalgic over the land that once was ours and hope to catch a glimpse of the comet-like pack of equatorial runners as they renew their eminent domain claim on Boylston Street.'

Like many of the world's best-known sports events, the popularity and importance of the Boston Marathon lies with its place in the history of the sport. It is a showcase for this kind of athletics, an event that embraces the history and spirit of the original race from Marathon to Athens, albeit with a twist that could be managed in the land of the star-spangled banner. Boston, at least, has some identity that is separate from the modern infatuation with world records, for time, and national boasting rights for participant numbers. Like the English Football Association (FA) Cup, which is venerated through-out the world and holds a special place in the hearts of millions of soccer supporters, the Boston Marathon is the first of the annual city marathon races. As such, it is the paternal lord of them all. Other venues, like some American cities, may be more exotic, enjoy a more spectacular setting or may boast bigger fields of entries and, of course, larger reserves of prize money. But Boston is where it all started.

6. HISTORY 3 – EARLY PACE-SETTERS FEEL THE HEAT

Long-distance running may have been established in form and style by the marathon at the Athens Olympic Games in 1896, but the idea of endurance running of this type was not new and had been practised in many places before. It had been particularly popular, prior to the birth of the marathon, as a 'modern' classical race, in America, Britain and various parts of Scandinavia. It is no surprise, therefore, that these places were to produce many great marathon runners and host many great races in the years that followed. But, in the immediate aftermath of the first Olympic Games, with their great maiden marathon race in Greece, it was difficult for the event to settle down and secure its future. High temperatures, unproven courses, unreliable organisation and various problems experienced in coping with the logistical challenge of putting on such a great event tested the next Olympic host cities to their limits. It was a credit to the pulling power and sheer fascination of the event itself – the marathon race – that it survived this period in the light of some of the dramatic stories that emerged.

Heat and dust best sums up the experiences of the poor runners in this period. In Paris in 1900 the marathon was run in virtually intolerable weather conditions. The temperature was 39 degrees Celsius in the shade. The course was also problematic, designed around a confused itinerary that involved too many of the French capital's various streets and lanes. In St Louis in 1904 the weather was again unpleasant: very hot, very dry and the race was run in extremely dusty and polluted conditions. One runner almost died and needed to spend several days in hospital to recover from a choking experience while the marathon winner, it was revealed, had enjoyed being revived and encouraged during his race by various administrations of strychnine served with egg white and copious slugs of brandy. The Games, and the marathon men, were glad to return 'home' when the Greeks organised the 'interim' games of 1906, an event that was left in an unrecognised or unofficial category by the IOC. This mattered little to the athletes. The habit of holding great games had continued and, after the previous two events, it was good to return to a place where the hosts were well organised and the welcome was warm.

A taste of the feeling towards Paris – an inevitable destination for the Olympic Games at the turn of the century given the work of the Baron Pierre de Coubertin in establishing the Games and the IOC – was given in the words of Ion Pool, a British marathon runner who took part. He revealed in an interview that appeared in the *South London Harriers* magazine, as reproduced in David Miller's official history of the Olympic Games, *Athens to Athens*, that the entire organisation for the race was farcical and that the French public's behaviour, in his opinion, was appalling. This, and the fact that the event was won by a French gardener, or carpenter (again, depending on the source), Michel Theato, a former citizen of Luxembourg, sweltering in the sun with a white handkerchief on his head to protect him, did not warm the marathon and 'foreign' racing much to the British long-distance men at this time.

'The marathon turned out to be a dismal fiasco,' said Pool.

> The whole conduct of the race on the part of the responsible organisers, beginning with the tardy date of the announcement sent abroad, down to the smallest details of providing, or rather failing to provide, for the conveniences of contestants on the appointed day, and the entire absence of precautions to ensure fair play, can only be characterised by a single word: Preposterous, with a capital P. Add to this the non-sporting demeanour of the French populace and it will not be necessary to cite fully the extent of the troubles that variously beset the foreign runners. At best, it proved a steeplechase, with bicycles and cars for obstacles. Twenty-five miles is really too far for a steeplechase, but that was a mere incidental. Suffice to say that when the first three finishers in last year's London to Brighton race found it necessary to retire within four miles and Arthur Newton, that well-known long-distance record-breaker in the United States, who was unwise enough to finish, took almost longer than walking time to complete the distance, it shows that everything was very, very wrong.

There is no doubt that Pool made his point! The Paris marathon of 1900 was not for him and not for the British or any of the foreign visitors to enjoy. French runners took most pleasure from it with Theato completing the distance of 40,260 metres (25 miles and some 30 yards) in a winning time of 2 hours, 59 minutes and 45 seconds. Photographs of the event, with Theato in them, show a pained man in a typically Gallic striped shirt and dark shorts being hosed down by water sprayed at him from spectators. He was followed home in second place by fellow Frenchman (so to speak) Emile Champion. Theato's nationality, like the entire organisation and record-keeping surrounding this particular Games, was for years afterwards a source of argument and conjecture, though it later emerged that he was born in Luxembourg, but had taken up French citizenship. Either way, he looked French and he spoke French!

Newton, the American mentioned earlier by Pool, was the clear pre-race favourite, but suffered ignominy. Lost in a mazy circuit of twisting streets, he finished eventually and believed, partly no doubt due to the heat and the sheer nature of the challenge, that he must have won. He could hardly believe it, therefore, when he was told that three Frenchmen and a Swede had done the job and finished well ahead of him. Newton, according to Miller, claimed he had taken the lead midway through the race and had not been passed thereafter by any other runner. He claimed, also, that he had passed Theato on his way, an allegation that could not be proven in the confusion that followed. Scheduling errors, chaos, poor planning and bad organisation, including no proper marshalling and various obstructions to the course that had not been anticipated, meant that no one was certain who, if anyone, had completed the correct Paris marathon course for this event. Theato, who was said to have worked as a baker's delivery boy, as well as working as a gardener, was accused of using his local knowledge to take short cuts through the backstreets. Few could understand how he had finished more than an hour ahead of the favoured Newton if it was not for this reason. Theato, it was said, remained unaware that he was acclaimed as an Olympic champion for several years afterwards. In one version of affairs, Theato did not understand that the marathon he ran through Paris in 1900 had anything to do with the Olympic Games at all until he received a medal through the post twelve years later.

Nobody was impressed. Dick Grant, an American, who finished sixth, attempted to sue the IOC because he had been knocked down by a cyclist just as he was about to overtake Theato. The crowds, as they had been in Greece in 1896, were very enthusiastic and may, in this case, have crossed the line from respectable behaviour to something less attractive or fair. In retrospect, it is relatively easy to see how the 1900 marathon suffered in this way, given the appalling organisation of the Games and the race. Paris was, at this time, also the host city for the 1900 Exposition Universelle Internationale, a vast trade show that married the delights of a country fair with the commercial grit of a trade show and, as de Coubertin found himself locked into an increasingly bitter dispute with the local French athletics associations over who should control the event, he proposed merging the Olympic Games with the Expo'. The outcome was that the French athletics administrators lost control of the event and so did the IOC. So, too, did everyone else involved. In the end, according to Charlie Lovett, in his book *Olympic Marathon*, of 1997, the organisers of the Exposition appointed Daniel Merillon to take charge of what were to be called the 'international championships' run over a five-month period of confusion.

It was a classic case of something of value being dropped between two stools in a struggle. Indeed, the word Olympics did not appear in the official literature of the Expo' surrounding the games at the time – the event was called the 'Concours Internationaux d'Exercises Physiques et des Sports' – and the marathon was not included, to start with at least, at all. When the IOC did produce its own programme of events and sports, again the marathon was forgotten, left out of the list of contests that were to run from 14 May to 28 October that year.

Yet, of course, it took place; otherwise it could hardly have been recorded as the hottest Olympic marathon of all and dubbed, by the French, the '*marathon de fortifs*'. This was a reference to the course that took the poor runners around the inside of a wall, once known as the 'farmer's general wall' to protect about half a million people in the eighteenth century, a barrier that was punctuated by 57 '*portes*', or gateways, and dozens of other obstacles, following four laps of a track at the Racing Club de France and a run through the Bois de Boulogne. It was, without doubt, a challenge. Motorists who are frequent visitors to Paris will recognise it as something close to a run around the inner '*peripherique*', with such temptations as the Porte de Chatillon, Porte de Vincennes, Porte de la Villette and Porte Maillot on the route. It was hardly an alluring and beautiful natural course and it was made no more attractive by the steaming conditions as Paris, in 1900, sweltered in a hotter-than-usual summer. The temperature when the marathon began soon after half past two in the afternoon was reported to be close to 39 degrees Celsius. The heat, the bad organisation, the obstructions created by the crowd and the general public caused trouble for most runners. In one report it was said that George Touquet-Denis, who led for the opening four miles, decided to stop at a café near the Porte d'Ornano after realising he had gone the wrong way and run an extra 480 yards for no good reason. He was thirsty, but found the bar had only beer, drank two and decided to retire from the race. Close to the Porte Villette, the site of the main Paris abattoir, the road was blocked by sheep and cattle.

Through all of this, with good fortune, Michel Johann Theato ran on and on. His win, ahead of only six other finishers from a starting field of sixteen, made marathon history due to the heat, the curiosity of the conditions, the occasion and the myths that built up around him and his performance. The suggestion that he was a baker and that he had delivered bread and croissants all over Paris, so learning the streets intimately, remained no more than that. It ignored the more commonly accepted fact that, in Paris, most people go to the baker to collect their bread and croissants each day and deliveries are not common. Also, it ignored the fact that the course looped around the edge of the central city and did not go through it. It is more likely, according to most sources, that he was a gardener, or possibly a woodworker. In either case, whatever his job, it is probably more significant that he was born in Luxembourg, according to research by Alain Bouille (1990), and that, in common with two other 'Frenchmen' who have won the marathon at the Olympic Games, he was celebrated as a French winner, though it was not his country of origin. The other two to have won for France, so to speak, were Boughera El Quafi, in 1928, in Amsterdam, and Alain Mimoun, in 1956, in Melbourne. Neither was born in France, but in Algeria, which remained a French colony until 1962.

As in Paris, the 1904 Olympic Games in St Louis were held in conjunction with an international trade show. Again, it was a near-disaster for both the event as a whole and for the marathon. By 1904, in the United States, marathon running was beginning to become popular. There had been a marathon in New York in September 1896 and the first Boston Marathon was run in April

1897. Long-distance running was understood and enjoyed else-where, particularly in Canada. Yet the IOC and the Olympic Games still did not have sufficient confidence or reputation to establish the Games as a freestanding event without any association with, or support from, another event like the World Exposition in St Louis. Again, too, the Games ran the risk of being eclipsed by other activities; in Paris, poetry reading, among other things, had attracted more immediate attention than athletics.

In 1904, St Louis emerged as the host city after beating off a challenge from Chicago, the originally favoured host city in America. This was achieved by luring the games away from them through prudent politicking with the IOC in general, and de Coubertin in particular. It was his final decision that took the Games away from Chicago and put them further south in mid-America. He clearly believed that it was better to join forces with the city that was hosting the World Exposition (an event that celebrated also the Louisiana Purchase), as well as the United States national track and field championships (which were carefully scheduled to clash with the proposed Chicago Olympics, thus ensuring no American participation) than to set up a rival attraction, without any local participants, less than 300 miles away. It may, or may not, be difficult to believe, but it did seem that there was a little political interference in the decision-making process even in such distant days when the foundations of the Olympic movement were only just being laid.

De Coubertin's decision, however, certainly ensured that the marathon had an interesting field, including 18 Americans among the 32 starters and 2 Tswana tribesmen who, along with a man called Robert Harris, were the first Africans to show their continent's potential. Some of the Americans had proud reputations to protect, but there were also nine Greeks, men that could cruelly be described as immigrant waiters by some, and a Cuban who was only 5 feet tall (152 centimetres). This last was Felix Carvajal de Soto, who was born at San Antonio de los Banos, near Havana, and he was running, according to Martin and Gynn, in his first marathon at the age of 29. In Cuba, he was a postman and was used to running long distances with heavy bags of mail to deliver. Contemporary photographs show that the two Tswana tribesmen were Jan Mashiani and Len Tau, the first in shoes, the second barefoot. Both were described as Zulu tribesmen who were in the United States because they were veterans of the Anglo–Boer War of 1899–1902 that was 'on show' as an exhibit at the fairgrounds at the time. Later research, reported by Martin and Gynn, suggested they were not Zulus at all, but Tswanas and that they had probably never run a marathon before. Carvajal, however, had reportedly paid for his boat trip to New Orleans by demonstrating his running ability in Cuba and then reached St Louis by hitchhiking, learning a new foreign language as he went, having lost much of his money in the gambling houses of New Orleans. Lovett said he lost in a crap game. Photographs show him wearing heavy street shoes, heavy outdoor trousers cut off at the knee and a long-sleeved shirt. His trousers were reduced in length, it was said, when the American discus thrower Martin Sheridan produced a pair of scissors and performed the necessary task before the start.

By contrast to the muddled and chaotic marathon in Paris, the race in St Louis was well ordered. Information about the course and the event remains relatively scarce and sketchy, some of it allegedly quite inaccurate as it is derived from one principal source, Charles P. Lucas, who wrote a book about the Games, including a chapter on the marathon. His impartiality was questionable, given that he was, after all, the personal assistant and manager of the eventual winner! Nevertheless, by piecing together supporting information from local newspaper reports and comparing stories from all sources, a decent picture has emerged; and the most startling tale of all is that the winner, Tom Hicks, was given drugs and alcohol in a bizarre battle for survival that resulted in him sitting, seemingly numbed and dazed, in a car after winning the race. The look on his ashen face, described charitably as that of a 'blank stare' by some, said it all; this was a man who knew little of where he was or how he had arrived.

Another important story to emerge from this marathon race was that the man who ran into the stadium first, seemingly at the head of the field after a torrid square loop of the city on difficult roads in terrible conditions, proved not be the winner, but a cheat. He had not run the full distance – a trick performed twice more in the history of the Olympic marathon, usually by a man who thought his prank would be amusing, but who found out pretty soon afterwards that marathon runners and spectators take their sport seriously. Such jokes are not appreciated. Hicks, the true winner, had to start and finish in Francis Stadium, the track and field headquarters of Washington University, St Louis. Over the course of the race he had to endure dust, heat, dehydration, the strain and pain of the distance of 24 miles and 1,500 yards (just short of 40 kilometres), the stimulus of a variety of performance-enhancing substances including strychnine, brandy and eggs, not to mention being sponged down by Lucas from time to time. Quite what Paula Radcliffe, or her meticulous and competitive husband Gary Lough, might have made of this if they had been involved in this contest is not difficult to imagine!

The marathon of St Louis began at three minutes past three in the afternoon of 30 August with a large part of the 9,000-seat capacity of the Francis Stadium occupied by spectators. It was hot, the temperature around 29 degrees Celsius. After a mile, Hicks, of Cambridge, Massachusetts, but born in England, took the lead, then lost it and fell back into the pack as various men toiled to run at the front. The first water stop, for fluids to replenish their bodies, was not for six miles and came in the form of a roadside water tower; the second, after twelve miles, was a roadside well. How the poor runners, choking with dust and heat, drank any water at these places is unknown. As dehydration set in, even the best runners suffered from cramp and began to retire, usually collapsing into a nearby car that was driving along with them at the time. These cars, basic and rudimentary vehicles of the very early age of automobiles, may have offered somewhere comfortable to collapse, but they also delivered clouds of polluted air, stirred up dust and other objects, caused stress and worry for everyone, and in Lucas's opinion added the best part of half an hour to the run time. For William Garcia, from California, it was almost fatal: he was choking badly with the dust, retired from the race and, after being found collapsed and lying in the road, was taken to hospital with a stomach and cerebral haemorrhage caused by the inhalation of so much dirt that his throat was lined and his stomach filled. Thankfully, this is not a common problem in modern times, though there are some who have raised concerns about the air quality expected at Athens in 2004. There, however, unlike in St Louis, they are unlikely to be chased into the surrounding fields by stray dogs.

The preferential treatment given to Hicks by Lucas and Hugh McGrath, of Charlesbank Gymnasium, Boston, would not have been allowed in later years. Hicks was physically in poor shape during the race, but was given aid and stimulated. Carvajal, who finished in fourth place, was in decent shape and at one stage stopped at Lucas's car. Lucas reported that 'a party were eating peaches and he begged for some. Being refused, he playfully snatched two and then ran along the road eating them as he ran.' Later, said Lovett, he picked some green apples in an orchard, suffered stomach cramps when he ate them, but continued. Hicks was given water, that was stored in a bag by the engine of Lucas's car, grains of sulphate of strychnine, with raw egg whites and French brandy to keep him going, the popular belief of his team being that these depressants were stimulants and would aid him. The combination of these substances is understood to have provided a brief kick to the athlete's central nervous system before leaving him more drained than he was before.

After twenty miles, Lucas said he looked at Hicks and, seeing that he was 'ashen pale', decided that more of the same cocktail was required as well as a warm-water rubdown. 'He appeared to revive and jogged along once more.' The same routine followed for the last two final hills before Hicks entered the stadium to finish in 3 hours, 28 minutes and 53 seconds, in what he thought was second place. The false 'winner' was Fred Lorz, who had finished sixteen minutes earlier after dropping out after nine miles, completing ten by car, and then running the final section to the stadium. He passed Hicks on the road after nineteen miles.

Hicks's team and the officials who were with him hurriedly told the stadium officials that Lorz, who was about to be given the gold medal by Alice Roosevelt, the famous daughter of the American president Theodore Roosevelt, was an impostor. When Lorz was confronted with this, he admitted immediately that he had not run the full distance and said that it was only a prank. The Americans were livid. Lorz was later banned from sport for life, but this ban was rescinded. In 1905, he won the Boston Marathon in a time that proved he was a great runner and that such practical jokes, as in St Louis, were not necessary for him.

Albert Corey of France, who had been working as a strikebreaker in Chicago, it was reported, looked relatively fresh, finished second and so made up for a disappointing experience in the Paris Marathon. American Arthur Newton came third and become the first man to finish two Olympic marathon races. Of the 32 starters, 15 finished. Of the non-finishers, one was in hospital and many others were vomiting and severely ill, or badly dehydrated. Hicks, looking the worse for wear, was left to recover from a bizarre hangover. It was no wonder he felt so bad. At 29, he was the perfect age to have run well. A study carried out afterwards by the Department of Physical Culture at the Exposition showed he had lost 10 pounds in weight (4.5 kilos) during the race, equivalent to 7.5 per cent of his body weight, according to Martin and Gynn. There were post-event protests at the help and support given to Hicks, but these were rejected later by the Olympic Games director James Sullivan.

More worrying for the organisers, for the Olympic Games in general, and for the marathon in particular, was the manner in which it was used to allow a joker to demonstrate how easy it is to cheat and to win. It was the first of three events in which an impostor took a false victory: the others followed in 1908, in London, where Italian Dorando Pietri was helped to his feet several times after collapsing, and in 1972, in Munich, where Frank Shorter entered the stadium at the head of the field only to discover that another man had begun false celebrations in front of him by joining in at the very end to run home first.

St Louis, however, was the first Olympic marathon venue to give the triumphant three leading athletes medals to mark their successes. Hicks, thus, became the first Olympic 'gold' medallist, for winning a marathon, although as certain sources have revealed, his medal was actually made of silver and merely gold plated. Hicks, blank and dizzy, barely cared. This, too, was not unexpected. He was born in Birmingham, in England, he ran for the United States and his victory was his first in any marathon at the fifth attempt. He had run in four Boston Marathons before St Louis and, afterwards, he ran in three more as well as four in Chicago, winning just once more, at Chicago, in 1906. But his career will not be remembered for any of this – he will always be recalled as the man who swilled brandy, swallowed strichnine and took eggs on his way to finishing first after a dust- and heat-smothered battle of endurance.

By 1906, the Olympic Games, and the marathon in particular, needed a return to Greece as much as the great Mediterranean nation wanted the sporting spectacle back on its original soil. The interim games, as they were, came about after King George of Greece had suggested that his country be the permanent host, a proposal that was not supported by de Coubertin. Instead, he responded by suggesting that Athens host an interim Games two years after each Olympiad. As it turned out, the first and only interim Games in 1906 were important in re-establishing the ideals of the original and in resurrecting standards of organisation and reputation. Furthermore, many of the teams were recognised and supported by their national associations for the first time in moves that added credibility. Hence, there were 20 nations and 884 athletes reported as attending in Athens where, of these, 53 runners from 15 nations took part in the fourth Olympic marathon. Just as before, it was the marathon that inspired excitement in the Greeks. It was their greatest event and a part of the tapestry of their history.

According to reports, the Greek people were offering substantial inducements to their own athletes to succeed. They were offered free shaves for life, a year's supply of Sunday lunches, a statue of Hermes and three cups of coffee and a loaf of bread daily for the following year. Greek anticipation was at fever pitch in the build-up to the race on 1 May, over the same route and in similar conditions to that run by Spiridon Louis a decade earlier. But they were to be disappointed; all of their natural confidence was to be dashed by the élan of a bold Canadian called Billy Sherring, who had only made the journey across the Atlantic thanks to the assistance of a barman who won the necessary money for the passage with a winning bet on a horse. Sherring had, literally, invested all he had on this and he was not going to give up. The Greeks, though disappointed for themselves, recognised his courage and warmly applauded his efforts.

Sherring had saved up all he could and had also been given a financial contribution by the local athletic club in his home town of Hamilton in Ontario, but it was not enough for the ocean crossing. He had, according to Lovell, accumulated 75 dollars, which he gave to a bartender who bet it on a racehorse called Cicely. Cicely won at odds of 6–1, and Sherring was assured of his trip to Europe and his place in the Athens marathon. After that, his victory was almost easy. He reached Greece in late February, giving himself March and April for training. He worked as a railway porter to pay his living expenses and trained every other day. When the Greeks held a trial on 17 March, they hailed the winner who finished in three hours and four minutes, little knowing that Sherring had run the same course about twenty minutes quicker not long before. Acclimatised, confident and fit, he was in perfect fettle for the race when it came.

After the chaos in Paris and St Louis, the Athens organisers took special care when preparing for their event. This marathon was the first at which proper plans and rules were made and obeyed. Each runner was allowed one assistant, on a bicycle, there were regular checkpoints with refreshments and doctors and there was an air of understanding and care. The course was longer, by about one mile, than that run in 1896 and therefore the longest to be used for a marathon, but Sherring made light of it. Running in a white vest with a large trefoil on his chest to show he was Canadian, and wearing a light hat, Sherring was content to run with the American William Frank and early leader George Blake of Australia before pulling clear after eighteen miles. Then, it is said, he simply turned to Frank, with whom he had run for three miles, and said, 'Well, goodbye, Billy.' He finished faster by seven minutes than Louis had ten years before, but received nothing like the same rapturous welcome. Even so, there was genuine warmth in the reception of him in the stadium where he was met by Prince George who ran with him around the track to the finish. Queen Olga sent a bouquet to him on the track, from where he bowed to the king. Not being Greek, he was not thereafter shaved free of charge for a year, but instead he did receive a lamb and a statue of Athena. On his return to Canada, he was rewarded with several thousand dollars while back in Europe, on his return to Italy, a little-known and disappointed runner called Dorando Pietri was recovering from a personal blow in retiring after thirteen miles. Pietri determined to try again and his effort to succeed inspired American music and global sympathy four years later.

7. ATLANTIS – A WATERY AND MYTHOLOGICAL AFFAIR

Trying to run the legendary Atlantis Marathon is certain to be a wet and uncomfortable experience, completed by few. It may also be purely mythological. Nobody knows exactly where to find Atlantis, after all. Somewhere, it is said, at the bottom of the Atlantic Ocean. So, just finding the place, let alone finding the marathon course, is a job of major proportions. But as with most challenges associated with the history and development of this long-distance race from ancient Greece, it is evocative and extraordinary. Anyone, therefore, who makes an effort to run 26 miles and 385 yards underwater not only needs to have their head tested, they also deserve recognition; and if they choose to run such a distance, the marathon distance, in Scotland's most famous lake, Loch Ness, wearing only an ancient deep-sea diving suit and for charity, then they deserve to be treated with caution. Atlantis, however, was far from his dreams when Lloyd Scott, an Englishman with what can only be described as a chequered career behind him, chose to do just that in 2003 and, in the process, set off endless debates about the myths surrounding Atlantis, ancient gods and underwater athletics.

Atlantis, according to *The Oxford Dictionary of Classical Myth and Religion*, is a word that means, quite simply, the island of Atlas. It also signifies the island lying in the Atlantic and is known as the 'oldest surviving wonderland in Greek philosophy'. The dictionary gives further details. It explains that Plato is the earliest and the chief source of the famous story, said to have been told to Solon by Egyptian priests, of a huge and wealthy island of this name outside the Pillars of Heracles, which once ruled 'Libya . . . as far as Egypt' and 'Europe as far as Tyrrhenia' (Etruria), until, in an expedition to conquer the rest, its rulers were defeated by the Athenians, the island shortly after sinking overnight beneath the Atlantic after 'violent earthquakes and floods'. The unfinished work of *Critias*, the dictionary reports, describes the island's constitution (similar to the ideal city of Plato's *Republic*) and layout of its chief city (a series of concentric circles of alternating land and water). Crantor, the first commentator on Plato, is said to have accepted the truth of the tale, suggesting that controversy about Atlantis was raging as long ago as 300 BC. In other more modern theories, it is suggested that the massive volcanic eruption at Santorini in the late bronze age resulted in a loss of most the island's land mass and that this sparked the legend.

Mention of Atlas, and Atlantis, clearly helps link the ancient Greek myths and legends to the modern challenges that are relished by certain athletes, particularly marathon runners. For them, it is as much about endurance as performance, as was shown by Sir Ranulph Fiennes and Dr Mike Stroud in their seven-by-seven challenge. Through experiencing primal pain and making self-discovery a part of their living experience in this way, they could identify with the runners who performed extraordinary feats in the past. For Lloyd Scott, the motivation was different, but the experience was similar when he established himself as the first man to complete an underwater marathon in Loch Ness, an achievement that deserved to be recognised as finishing the Atlantis Marathon.

For him, in the beginning, the scheme was nothing more than an ambitious idea to raise some money for good causes and charities through sponsorship. He felt that a two-week walk, submerged in the depths of Loch Ness, the stretch of water in Scotland famed for stories of sightings of its monster, would be challenging, interesting and rewarding. His idea turned into something else. Wearing a deep-sea diving suit and enduring the time he spent underwater finally earned him a place in the record books. Cold, dark, lonely and tiring, the conditions and physical demands were not things that he had considered when he suggested to a charity, aiming to raise funds to benefit children with illnesses, that he should go to Scotland and try. He had done many unusual things before. So, in truth, for him, this was just another challenge to add to his collection, after taking on and succeeding with some of the most daunting marathons in the world.

Scott first came to public notice in England when he walked the London Marathon while wearing a heavy and authentic antique deep-sea diving suit in April 2002. It may have taken him 5 days, 8 hours, 29 minutes and 46 seconds to complete the marathon, but the money he raised for leukaemia charities more than made up for the pain and suffering he experienced in carrying the suit around the

London course. It was so heavy and awkward, he was only able to walk 400 metres at a time before he needed a brief rest to prevent dehydration. If that was not bad enough, he decided afterwards to do more and so he walked in the same suit in the Edinburgh and New York Marathons. In New York, he raised funds for the families of the firemen who had lost their lives when they were on duty during the terrorist attacks on 11 September 2001.

The marathon, the causes and the whole challenge of these experiences helped complete a special circle in Scott's life. He is a former professional sportsman. He was a soccer player in England, playing as a goalkeeper for Leyton Orient, Watford and Blackpool in a relatively unspectacular five-year career between the ages of 18 and 23. When he gave up goalkeeping, he chose to become a firefighter instead. He had needed a new challenge. But, while working as a fireman, he was diagnosed as suffering from leukaemia, after inhaling toxic smoke when he was saving the lives of two young boys. It was the start of another time and another level of experience for him in his life.

In 1989, he ran the London Marathon three weeks before undergoing a life-saving bone marrow transplant. Nine months later, as if to prove to other people who are in a similar situation that life really does go on, he did it again. And, for this intrepid marathon man who believed in running for a good reason and for other people, this was only just the beginning. He went on and further trials followed with the completion of a marathon at Snowdonia, in Wales; completion of the Mount Everest Marathon, on which his bone marrow donor Andrew Burgess accompanied him; completion of the Marathon des Sables, a 145-mile run through sand dunes in the Sahara desert; and completion of the 135-mile Death Valley Ultra-Marathon, as well as treks up Kilimanjaro, dressed as Indiana Jones, the North and South Poles, and the Argentinean Andes mountains. All this with an artificial hip fitted after four operations.

'I suppose I'm a person who likes a challenge,' explained Scott, with some understatement after his successful completion of the Atlantis Marathon in Loch Ness. 'This is going back to before I had my illness. I'm probably like millions and millions of other people and just want to see how I get on and how far I can rise to the challenge.' Life could have turned out differently for Scott, however.

After being diagnosed with chronic myeloid leukaemia, he was not expected to survive the bone marrow transplant that followed. He was given only a 10 per cent chance of success, but he survived; more than surviving, he flourished to achieve more than most active people dream of doing. Now, he treats his extraordinary exploits as a message to other people – to show them what can be achieved. 'It was a huge battle for me,' he says of his struggle to overcome his illness. 'I think I was diagnosed with less than 10 per cent chance of coming through. We had to find an unrelated donor to have a bone marrow transplant, which was my only chance of long-term survival. Even then, the survival rate back then, in 1989, was fairly slim. I ran the marathon three weeks before I went into hospital for my bone marrow transplant just to show people that, despite having such a life-threatening illness, one can make the most of any situation.

'I wanted to do something positive for other people. Then I did the marathon again, after my bone marrow transplant, this time to show that there is life after leukaemia. At least you give people some hope, encouragement and inspiration to fight their own personal battles because that is what I needed when I was diagnosed. I needed to know that there was a chance and that it wasn't the end. Somebody each day is going to be told they have leukaemia and if they can see the guy that did that London Marathon in the diving suit, or in Loch Ness . . . That is a very personal message that I feel I can give to other people to show that the game is not up.'

That is why Scott, whose wife Carole and children Aimee, Luke and Elliott have all supported his extraordinary challenges, did not shirk at the prospect of the underwater marathon quest. It took place on 28 September 2003, the day after the Loch Ness Marathon was run on the roads surrounding the loch. Scott had come up with the idea of walking a marathon in the suit because, as he said, it was so unsuited to movement on land. The only time he had been in the water in the diving suit was for a publicity photo-shoot before his London Marathon walk, but he couldn't resist the temptation of using the suit for the purpose it was intended.

'I took a "punt" on that,' he laughed, recalling the moment he was talked into the underwater marathon. 'I was approached by a charity, Children's Leukaemia, and they wanted to launch something called the Children's Marathon Challenge. It was a fundraising initiative and I was fairly synonymous with the marathon. They said, "Can you do something in the diving suit because everyone knows you as the diver?" They wanted it to be UK-based. I thought hard about things and I had actually done one dive, in the diver's suit, prior to the London Marathon, for a promotional event at the London Aquarium. I couldn't move in it. When they asked me to think about it and come up with something, I just decided to take a risk so I suggested the underwater marathon. They thought about it and said yes.'

Equipped with a suit weighing 200 pounds, including lead boots that were 80 pounds heavier than the ones he wore when he walked the marathons, Scott spent six weeks training to become a qualified deep-sea diver. He was told of the dangers of decompression and so he had to be fully compliant with health and safety regulations. But the training also taught Scott how to actually move forward underwater while inside the suit, as well as the logic of buoyancy. He found it very demanding. He said it required a considerable human effort just to begin the challenge and to go on with any confidence.

At the start of his underwater marathon, he slipped into the water at Fort Augustus, where the Caledonian Canal meets Loch Ness, with a plan to complete a set distance of three miles each day, but two weeks later, when he emerged from the water at Lochend, at the opposite end of the loch, close to Inverness, he had completed a true 'marathon' effort. Conditions were far from ideal on the bottom of the loch, visibility was limited and Scott simply had to endure the whole experience. He was not permitted to go deeper than 10 metres below the water surface or to spend more than the maximum time of four and a half hours in the loch without a break. He also injured his shoulder when he fell 15 feet off a ledge, while he was veering away from his guide rope when attempting to walk across rocks. He was less than halfway through the marathon at this time, but he was fortunate that the eight-man support team, which followed him in a boat with GPS technology, was able to come to his rescue before he fell any further down a 294-foot drop. The current of the water, which was strengthened by strong winds, also hampered his progress.

'It was almost like a success getting to the start line. Then we had the matter of trying to get from one end of the loch to the other,' Scott said. 'It wasn't in the deepest point. I wasn't allowed to go more than 10 metres deep because of the decompression and the amount of time I was able to spend underwater. It was difficult because I had to contend with the pressure of the water, very limited visibility, it was very suspect underfoot – mud, silt, clay, rock, it was very irregular, it was cold, isolated, the airline kept getting caught and for a number of reasons it was far more difficult than I imagined. If it was a good day, we tried to "make hay while the sun shone" and crack on as much as we could, and some days were short. We hoped to do two or three dives a day, but sometimes we could only do one.

'If I came up, it would have to be another hour and a half before I could go back down again so I tried to stay under and tried to get as much done in one hit. The longest I did was four and a half hours in one dive. The idea was to do a certain amount each day, but it depended on what it was like underfoot. I spent two days literally crawling on my hands and knees because I couldn't see where I was going and the guys actually laid a line down for me to follow. But there was a problem finding it because I couldn't see. The best visibility was when it was rocky, but it was very slow getting over the rocks. They were very slippery. It was all different conditions and they all posed their own problems.'

Problems of all sorts, it seemed. These included the problem of deciding where and how to answer a call of nature while trudging across the bottom of Loch Ness in a diving suit with some very amusing and bubbly consequences. 'When you were underwater, you couldn't go to the toilet, although we did have a zip in for when I was on land,' he said. 'A couple of times, I got caught short and had to let nature take over . . . Well, after a couple of days, the suit ponged! It had a life of its own. It already had mould growing in it. So I took it back to the lodge where we were staying and ran a bath and put the suit in the bath with a whole bottle of bubble bath to try to cover up the smell. The following day, I put the suit back on and as they lowered me into the water, because it contained a huge amount of bubble bath, it all started foaming up again. So, as well as claiming the world's first underwater marathon, we are also going to claim the world's biggest bubble bath in Loch Ness!'

Many individuals have failed in a challenge of a different sort at Loch Ness: to catch a glimpse of the famous monster 'Nessie'. Scott had one experience when he thought he was going to come face to face with the elusive beast. 'I got my foot caught,' he said. 'I wondered what it was because something was grabbing my foot and as hard as I pulled I couldn't release it. I had to get the rescue divers down,' he explained. 'I couldn't see what it was because I couldn't turn in the suit and helmet.' The explanation was just about as unexciting and prosaic as anyone could have feared: no monsters, not even a small water creature. 'I had actually put my foot through an oil drum,' Scott explained. 'So, it wasn't the encounter we had hoped for!' Having spent two weeks in his own Atlantis, completing his first underwater marathon, Scott achieved his goal. He overcame the obstacles, injuries and the pressure of expectations. The first underwater marathon was added to his growing list of unique achievements.

8. HISTORY 4 – ESTABLISHING THE DISTANCE AND THE RULES, IN LONDON AND STOCKHOLM

The marathon race at the 1908 London Olympic Games was run on 24 July on a hot and muggy afternoon that began in front of the majestic sight of Windsor Castle, in Berkshire, and finished in front of Queen Alexandra in the royal box at the vast 90,000-capacity Olympic Stadium in Shepherd's Bush – later known as the White City Stadium – in west London. The full distance of the course was 26 miles, with a further 385 yards added for the final lap of the stadium track. It was a significant last lap for many reasons, but once run it was established and the distance was respected later as the official one for any race to be called a marathon. Yet this historic statistic, important as it may be to the students of the modern marathon, has already been overshadowed by other events on that famous day: events that led to an Italian being immortalised in the lyrics of a song written by the famous American Irving Berlin, the same man being decorated by British royalty for his gallantry if not his athletic success and the actual race winner, an American called John Hayes, who was a counter assistant in the famous Blooming-dale's department store in New York, allegedly earning promotion to become head of the sports goods section of the shop on his victorious return to the United States. If it was anything, this marathon was the first to command remarkable global interest and deliver the kind of stories that kept the media satisfied on both sides of the Atlantic.

While the Paris race had been condemned as chaotic, the St Louis event as little more than a domestic American contest decorated with gimmickry and cruelty and Athens as a throwback to the sport's foundations, this one took the challenge of progress in its stride and delivered something that was satisfying and memorable, even if some of the images that lingered were worryingly unfortunate. Typically, as those who criticise British pomp, ceremony, uniforms and pageantry might say, the hosts were somewhat over-attentive to their own liking for rules and regulations and, at times, overlooked more important matters. The Americans, in particular, felt uncomfortable living under British conditions. Having inherited the Games from the Italians after Rome had failed to convince the IOC that it had the organisational skills to deliver on time following the powerful eruption of Mount Vesuvius in March 1906 (more than 2,000 people died), the British Olympic Organising Committee, led by Lord Desborough, chose to stamp their character on affairs, even if the Americans did not always like it. Unfortunately, the American flag was not flown at the opening ceremony and from then on the visitors from the United States decided to complain whenever possible. In retaliation, it seemed, the American shot-putter Ralph Rose did not dip the American flag he carried when he passed King Edward VII in the royal box. This acrimony was present as much on the track as among the officials and it was manifested at its worst in the final of the 400 metres. The race featured three Americans and an English-man, whose sprint on the final lap to pass an American was baulked by his rival who deliberately ran wide to obstruct him. The British officials broke the tape, announced that the race was void and declared that another final should be run. This happened two days later. The Americans boycotted the race (so showing the potential for using Olympic events as a platform for political or other demonstra-tions) and as a result the sole British runner, Wyndham Halswelle, ran on his own and duly collected the gold medal. It was a bad day for sport, a bad day for any kind of sportsmanship. By the time of the long-awaited marathon, relations between the two nations were more than strained.

Thus, when it was known that the marathon would begin at Windsor so that the British royal family could enjoy a birthday party at home for one of their children and so that both King Edward VII and Queen Alexandra could see as much as possible, the Americans were not much impressed. By 2.30 p.m., when the race began, the weather was oppressive as 56 runners, from 16 different nations (31 of them from 12 European countries), lined up in four rows at Windsor, in the castle grounds, close to the east terrace and under the windows of the royal nursery. The Princess of Wales gave a signal and Lord Desborough fired the starting gun. Over the opening miles, the pace was quick and the race took an early toll on some runners. Ted Jack of Scotland, an early leader who was clearly keen to delight the British crowds, had to stop at a refreshments stand. He continued, but was no further threat. Various other runners challenged during the middle part of the contest until, after eighteen miles, the dominant figures were the South African Charles Hefferon and the little Italian, whose name was to be immortalised in song, Dorando Pietri. Learning from the anguish he suffered in 1906, he had paced himself more carefully.

Like many Italians, Pietri had been a cyclist as well as an athlete in his career. Born on 16 October 1885, in Mandrio, in Reggio Emilia, he worked as a confectioner in Carpi. He had been an inconsistent runner, but he had managed to qualify for the London race by setting an Italian record for a forty-kilometre race less than three weeks earlier. He ran in a white shirt and baggy red shorts, wore the number nineteen on his chest, and oozed private determination. His story, his attempt a glory, was to be one of the greatest in the history of the modern marathon and certainly one of the most popularised. One example of his gutsy determination was recorded by Emanuele Carli, in his book *Dorando Pietri, Corridore di Maratona*. According to him, Pietri was making pastry one day in 1904 in his shop in Carpi when the town was visited by the great distance runner, Pericle Pagliani, who gave a demonstration run. Seized by an urge to compare his talent to Pagliani's, Pietri dropped his work, ran off and followed the Roman wherever he ran. Apparently, he was fast enough to run with him right to the end and this fired his enthusiasm.

In London, however, even when he attempted to calm himself and keep his urges to chase under control, he was still in danger of burning himself out before the finish. When he caught Hefferon, he was consumed by a desire to lift the pace and run on. He caught the South African at Old Oak Common Lane. Hefferon was fading and the little Italian began to pull clear. It took a huge effort, but he found the resources and did so. Despite a much-improved organisation for drinks and refreshments (the famous English Oxo Company was appointed official caterer and supplied flasks to all of the competitors as well as managing four stations en route), he also had to pay a price. As he came closer to the stadium, among the crowds, he began to feel faint. He leaned from side to side, lost his bearings briefly and yet he staggered on. When he entered the stadium, he made his first mistake and turned right instead of left. As officials ran to correct his error, he fell down. A group of doctors and assistants ran to his aid, worked to help him and brought him back to his feet. The huge crowd roared appreciation, not knowing, as few among the group did, that their actions would render Pietri disqualified from the event. It seemed not to matter to anyone at the time. The Italian staggered on and fell again. He was helped up and continued. This happened five times in all before he reached the finishing line where he was assisted in completing the distance and taking the tape. His time was 2 hours, 54 minutes and 46.4 seconds. The crowd, taking to the underdog, had given him noisy vocal support, cheering his every wobble, slip and stagger. But it was all to no avail. The doctors who had run to his assistance and chosen not to leave him lying on the track exhausted and spent, had instead confirmed his disqualification in arguably the most dramatic finale to any marathon. It was the race organiser, Jack Andrew, the general secretary of the famous Polytechnic Harriers, who was identified afterwards as the man who had literally helped him over the finishing line, following, he said, the instructions of the race's medical officer Doctor Bulger.

Behind him, by around half a minute, was the American, John Hayes, the man from Bloomingdale's. He ran unaided to the finish where, as the Italian flag was raised on the victory pole, another American protest began, justifiably, and resulted in him being declared the rightful winner. Hefferon came in third, to be promoted to second. He knew, of course, that had he not succumbed to temptation, absurdly, in the closing stages when he was offered and accepted a drink of champagne from a spectator, that he might have done better. Instead, he staggered in suffering from stomach cramps and dizziness. Hayes, however, was a worthy winner and a worthy pioneer for New York's special relationship with the marathon. He had finished second in the Boston Marathon three months earlier and had won the Yonkers Marathon the year before. He had also trained well and prepared properly. To most unbiased observers, Hayes was a worthy Olympic champion, but he was never to be the hero of this dramatic story.

Pietri's collapsing finish, in front of the British royal family, aided by a group of doctors that was claimed to have included the famous writer Sir Arthur Conan Doyle, who created Sherlock Holmes, made certain of that. Wearing a straw boater, Doyle may have been one of the men who rushed to the Italian's aid, or it may have been someone else altogether. The evidence is thin. The next day, Queen Alexandra began initiating arrangements, supported by Doyle, for Pietri to receive a replica gold cup to that awarded to Hayes for winning. When Pietri left London, by train from Charing Cross station, huge crowds turned out to cheer him farewell. In the United States, Hayes was fêted for his victory, but songs were penned for the losing Italian. Hayes was photographed being carried shoulder-high on a table by his American team-mates, while Irving Berlin composed his first major hit song named 'Dorando'. The tune was catchy and it helped marathon running catch on in America rather more than the feat of the successful, but unsung, Hayes. It was said that Bloomingdale's had laid a running track for him to train on the roof of their store and had given him leave to compete on full pay. When he returned, he was promoted; but his real fame and pleasure came later when he and Pietri raced again in their prize-money marathons contested as professionals in New York. The marathon race in London was also captured on film for the first time, so adding to the growing interest in this battle of physical defiance run over great distances. Pietri earned well for a time, but his fortune was not to be enjoyed. His brother, who came and worked with him, disappeared with his money, leaving the long-distance runner to return to Italy and work as a taxi driver before his death on 7 February 1942.

Four years on from London, the 1912 Olympic Games were held in Scandinavia for the first time with Stockholm selected as the venue. It was due recognition of the growing enthusiasm shown by the people of northern Europe for athletics in general and, so far as this book is concerned, for the marathon in particular. The Finns, for example, later to emerge as one of the greatest nations for long-distance running, had organised their first national marathon championship race in 1906 and had discovered the extraordinary Kolehmainen brothers, three of them, all capable of running marathons in astonishing times, but all set to go in different directions. Stockholm built an impressive red-brick Olympic stadium complete with a clock tower that remained in use long afterwards and welcomed the Games and the runners with warmth and efficiency. Unfortunately, their marathon was to be the one that will be remembered for producing the most tragic statistic in the history of the Olympic marathon – its first and only death. The runner who died was Francisco Lazaro of Portugal, who was reported to be running in eighteenth position after a third of the 24 miles and 1,723 yards distance. Although little documentary evidence exists to explain how and why he collapsed and died, it is believed that he was suffering from sunstroke and heart problems.

Had all three of the Kolehmainen brothers chosen to do so, it is quite possible that they could have entered this marathon together and taken the top three places – under the Russian flag, however, for Finland was occupied and controlled by Russia at this time. Instead, they went in different directions: Taavetti 'Tatu' was fast enough at the right time (he was 23) to have run in London, but was overlooked despite finishing second in the Finnish trial and then, sadly, retired while running in the Stockholm race. His brother Hannes, five years Taavetti's junior, was to win the marathon in Antwerp in 1920, having opted to avoid it in Stockholm where, instead, he won the 5,000 metres, the 10,000 metres and the cross-country race, setting records along the way. The third brother Viljami opted for professionalism and clocked a world record of 2:29:39.2 at Vailsburg, New Jersey, in 1912, the year in which he could, of course, have been running in Stockholm. After winning his great 5,000-metre duel with the Frenchman Jean Bouin, Hannes reflected his country's feelings when he said, 'I would almost rather not have won than see that flag [of Russia] up there.'

The Stockholm marathon that Viliami missed was, like so many, run in great heat again on 14 July. More than half of the 68 starters did not finish and most wore white hats or handkerchiefs on their heads to protect themselves from the sun. The Americans, coached by the 1908 winner John Hayes, believed they had a very strong team, including Joseph Forshaw, the bronze medalist in London, and Clarence DeMar, a Boston Marathon winner and record-breaker. None of them, however, was to shine this time on a course cleared of traffic, swept clean and watered before the start at two o'clock in the afternoon.

Tatu Kolehmainen led after three miles and stayed there to the turnaround point on the course that went from the new stadium out of the city to the village of Solentuna and back. Behind him, running comfortably, were the South Africans, or perhaps more accurately South African representatives, Christian Gitsham and Kenneth McArthur. Gitsham, who was born in Pietermaritzburg, took control at the front soon afterwards and, as rival runners began to retire or call for a bucket of water to be thrown over them, he and the other two leading men began to pull clear. The South Africans then raised the pace and, after twenty miles, even the fancied Finn could take no more and dropped out. The two leaders, more used to running in high temperatures than many of the others, stayed together and stuck with their special agreement – struck before the race – that if one paused for a drink, the other would wait. That was until it became serious . . . and clear that they were actually racing for the gold medal. Hence, when Gitsham stopped for some water, instead of waiting, McArthur carried on and opened up a lead of such comfort that his compatriot had no chance of closing it. In the stadium, he was given a victory wreath on his last lap before finishing in 2 hours, 36 minutes and 54 seconds. Gitsham finished less than a minute behind him, but took silver and joined his compatriot in celebrating a double South African success. McArthur, however, was not a 'pure-born' South African. He was born in Dervock, County Antrim, Northern Ireland.

The death of Lazaro, 24 hours after the marathon, in hospital, cast an unhappy and dark cloud over this race, however, leaving Stockholm's name forever associated with that tragedy as much as the happier note delivered on the track. Lazaro's death was not forgotten, or ignored, by the organisers afterwards and it is to their great credit that they sponsored a special display at the stadium and raised a substantial sum of money for his family in Portugal. In another unusual postscript to Stockholm, as reported by Lovell, one of the race's other sunstroke and heat victims, Shizo Kanakuri, of Japan, recovered to swear that he would return one day and complete the distance. Eventually, he did: 54 years later, in 1967 when he returned to the Swedish capital and ran a final lap of the Olympic Stadium. His final finishing time may have straddled six decades, but he had responded to the spirit of the Olympics that was established beyond doubt in that hot summer of long ago. It was good that he did. Those Games, in another age, had confirmed their worth and ensured that they, and their marathon, would survive the violent interruption of the First World War.

9. BERLIN – THE TEARS OF AN ANONYMOUS HERO

The old marathon man wept. And with him another 88,000 people, his countrymen, his fellow Koreans, wept too. Rarely, at an opening ceremony for any Olympic Games, had there been so much emotion in public. Never before had there been so many tears. This was no show in front of a partisan crowd, choreographed by fear and bullied into submission. This was not the Nazi exhibitionism of 1936, when few dared not to raise arms in salute to a detested dictator. Nor was this the pride that is tangible among the athletes and people of Greece, with its ancient traditions. No, this was the scene in the grand Olympic Stadium in Seoul, in 1988; a lifetime away from those dreadful days of repression and horror in Germany, on a day when Korea's most famous and badly treated runner, Sohn Kee Chung, had been forced to run under a Japanese name and, after winning, take his gold medal to the strains of the Japanese national anthem while the Japanese flag was raised. Then, in 1936, he hung his head in shame and protest. Now, in 1988, he lifted his face to the world, wiped away the tears and erased the pain.

Berlin, the city that was heading towards war in a dazzling blaze of wanton effervescence and permissive, desperate celebration, as the Nazis rose and swaggered, had left him wounded – in his heart, in his mind and in the very core of his being. A proud man, he was crushed by the actions of the organisation that failed to recognise his true nationality and his real achievement. And that is why, when he carried the Olympic flame, that eternal symbol of hope, harmony and peace, into the vast bowl of Koreans, to mark the start of the Games in his homeland, the tears rolled forth. He was wiping away that treachery in Berlin, a great city of bad memories.

In Berlin, Sohn was made to run under the Japanese name Kitei Son. The Japanese were then occupying and ruling Korea. 'At the time, it was impossible for a Korean to gain fame, but sport was the only exception,' he explained later, when asked why he agreed to run in the Japanese team in Berlin. 'I wanted to let the world know I was a Korean by winning the Olympics.' Sohn refused to sign his name in Japanese during the Berlin Games, where the African-American Jesse Owens claimed four gold medals and wrecked Hitler's dream of witnessing a parade of superiority by a blond Aryan master race. Sohn also told all interviewers that Korea was his mother country, not Japan. And Sam Sung-Yong, another Korean who finished third in the Berlin marathon, under the Japanese name of Shoryu Nan, also bowed his head during the medal ceremony in a silent protest.

In the Berlin race, on 6 August 1936, the runners went from the Olympic Stadium out through the Grunewald forest, alongside the Havelsee (Lake Havel), onto the Avusrennstrecke, the Avus race circuit, which was used for motor racing at the time, before returning through a tunnel into the stadium to complete the distance. Argentine Juan Zabala led until he fell and retired and Sohn, or Son as he was in the Japanese colours, led home British runner Ernie Harper, and Nan, to take Japan's first gold medal. He could not celebrate. His pride was assaulted by his own shame. The losers were the cheats, those in Japan who had hijacked his talent and those in Berlin who turned a blind eye to the events that followed. For the Germans, oblivious to the truth, their Berlin marathon hero was a Japanese, not a Korean, and they, too, had to wait a long time to cleanse their memory banks.

In 1981, seven years before the scene of tears in Seoul, the old marathon man, the winner of the race at the 1936 Games, made a harrowing trip back to Germany to visit Berlin. He was the guest of honour at the first Berlin Marathon to take to the streets of the city since the event was launched in 1974. The people of Berlin knew their history. They knew, in particular, who this great man of the past was – and when he went there to the start line, he was recognised and given overwhelming applause. It was another moment for tears, but these were the tears that signalled how much had changed in Berlin since 1936.

Then, the Hitler Games had been close to being boycotted. Both Britain and the United States were offended by Hitler's ideology and claims about an Aryan master race but, despite protests, discussions and threats, they backed down and took part. In many consciences, they may have felt it was a mistake. But Jesse Owens proved that Hitler was wrong with his four gold medals on the track and Sohn demonstrated, in the marathon, that repression and prejudice cannot succeed against talent and self-belief. Afterwards, there were many more tears in Berlin. For many long years. And for many, far more serious, reasons.

Sixteen years after the modern Berlin Marathon was run for the first time in 1974, a significant chapter of its history was written. On 30 September 1990, the chosen course for the 25,000 competitors, from 61 different countries, took them through das Brandenburger Tor (the Brandenburg Gate) for the first time – three days before Germany was reunified after 29 years of political separation. The marathon was the first sporting event to run on both the East and West side of Berlin, which had been separated by the Berlin Wall since 1945. As they ran, these marathon men and women, many of them wracked with painful and special emotions passed on to them from the years, and decades, of guilt that had followed those 1936 Games and the Second World War, wiped away tears. Their faces were soon stained as they cried and ran and the pictures of that day are harrowing yet uplifting images of mixed feelings, relief and release, freedom and pain and exhilaration. The physical act of running from West Berlin, through the wall and into the East was heavily symbolic in Germany's healing. It was far more than any ordinary marathon, far more even than any normal Berlin Marathon. Three days later, the reunification of the city and the nation was complete when, on 3 October a unification treaty was signed, consigning 45 years of separation of people, families, lives, politics and sport, to history.

The Brandenburg Gate was the only one of Berlin's eighteen original city gates that had survived. It was an evocative and symbolic part of the wall built, in 1961, by the East Germans when they were under Soviet occupation. When the marathon runners streamed through it in 1990 it was a final confirmation of the end of the 'cold war' that had separated East and West. And it came as a celebration of the freedom demonstrations that had seen manifestations in Leipzig, in East Germany, the previous year before an organised exodus, through Hungary and Austria, to reach the western side. The wall was unable to stop them and, soon afterwards, it came down. The marathon in both parts of the city confirmed the Berliners' freedom again and acted as a symbol to the world that, like Sohn, everyone should stay faithful to their principles.

*   *   *

Australian Steve Moneghetti won that historic and emotional 1990 Berlin Marathon. More significantly, however, a 25-year-old former East Berliner, who had been raised under the Communist regime and given little chance to shine, recorded a notable victory in the women's race. This woman was Uta Pippig and the 1990 triumph was to be the first of three famous Berlin Marathon victories for her, the others coming in 1992 and 1995. Her maiden win was delivered with a kick, too, in a course record time of 2 hours, 28 minutes and 37 seconds; but it gave her a kick, also, as she gulped with relief and confused feelings as she ran through streets from which she had previously plotted a daring escape.

That Berlin Marathon win was also Pippig's breakthrough to the international athletics stage. Pippig, who ran to success in the colours of the Stuttgart Kickers, switched to the vest of Charlottenburg-Berlin just a few months later. She had joined the East German Army Sports Club, in Potsdam, in 1983, to further her career as an athlete and it was there that she met her coach Dieter Hogen. He did his best to train her to realise her potential, but they struggled within the difficult political system and it was not until the wall came down that she was able to break free and leave her home in January 1990. The marathon, her win, the fall of the Berlin Wall and her decision to move helped turn her into one of the world's top women marathon runners. But she knew that, like so many who ran that day, it was the unique significance of the Berlin Marathon that mattered.

'The most difficult run I have ever attempted was not in the Olympics, or in the World Championships, or at the New York or Boston Marathons, or in any of the races that I have won,' said Pippig. 'No, the most challenging race of my life was the one that began in East Berlin, early one January morning, in 1990, and ended in West Germany – where freedom and opportunity awaited. Most runners have to worry about the "wall" that comes at the twenty-mile mark in a marathon, but the wall I faced was fifteen feet high, made of steel-reinforced concrete and topped with barbed wire. It was also manned by troops armed with machine guns, in watchtowers, with guard dogs by their side. The decision to leave my home and the country that I loved was the most difficult decision of my life. But with the heavy weight of a Communist regime on my nation's shoulders, I knew I was incapable of realising my dream as both a runner and a person.

'Every effort to broaden my athletic horizons were met with the restrictions of a bureaucratic wall. It made me feel like I was held in a kind of prison. I was not allowed to travel, race or pursue the type of training my coach wanted me to. I was desperate to seek challenges outside of those walls that held us in East Germany. We decided to risk the consequences of violating my responsibilities, as a member of the Army Sports Club, and to flee the country. If caught, I would have been considered a deserter, but the potential rewards were worth the perils of failure. So, on 5 January 1990, without a dollar between us, Dieter and I drove off in a small car loaded with just three suitcases and a great deal of hope. Fortunately, our odyssey was successful. It allowed us to reap the benefits of a free world.'

That freedom came in a rollercoaster after 1990 and Pippig chose to leave Europe and move to the United States where she has studied for a medical degree and continued her athletic training. She knows she was lucky. She could face her fears less than a year after her frightening Berlin experience in running to the West. Others, like Sohn, waited a lifetime to banish their ghosts.

'Three months after our escape, the political situation in East Germany eased,' she recalled. 'I felt alive in my whole new world. It was easy to make the transition, because I got so much help from wonderful people. For years, I had so often dreamed the dream of freedom that it felt like I had already lived in this new world for such a long time. Despite my many days of frustration, worrying and sleepless nights, finally my vision had come true.'

That dream was realised with her victory in the Berlin Marathon, or the Unification Marathon as it was later to be described. It was an emotional day that she, and the other 24,999 who competed, will never forget. 'It remains one of my most emotional and gratifying victories. It was during that race that I was able to partake in the extraordinary experience of running from West Berlin through the Brandenburg Gate into East Berlin. It's a moment that I will cherish for as long as I live and I feel fortunate to have shared that special occasion with so many. That race served as a symbol of freedom to the millions who dreamed of a day when liberty would become a reality. When I ran through the Brandenburg Gate into the East, I got goose pimples. A shiver ran down my spine, a chapter was coming to an end. I realised it was time to look ahead and stop looking back. For me it was a new beginning.' Two years later, in 1992, South Africa's David Tsebe won the race, not long after the Apartheid regime was lifted and athletes were permitted to compete in worldwide competition.

The Berlin Marathon, organised by SCC-Running, was first run on 13 October 1974, when Günter Hallas and Jutta von Haase raced to victory in the respective male and female categories. The race, the brainchild of Horst Milde, who remained as race director in 2003, had started at the Mommsen Stadium, the home of the Sport Club Chartlottenburg (SCC Berlin), and the 286 who started ran primarily along the AVUS Highway, which leads into the centre of Berlin, on a route next to the Grunewald, the West Berlin wood. In 1981, Milde persuaded the local authorities to allow the course to take in parts of the city centre and persuaded police to shut off roads in order for the finish line to be on the Kurfurstendamm, a two-mile long boulevard of shops, boutiques, cafés, restaurants, bars, cinemas and hotels. The route also passed 'Checkpoint Charlie', one of the few places in the old divided city where it was possible to cross through the Berlin divide. Police believed it was impossible for the marathon to travel past the checkpoint, but Milde contacted the United States military forces and John Kornblum, who later became the United States ambassador, granted permission.

Two years later, in 1983, the start was moved and the marathon began in front of the Reichstag, the centre of the German government and the symbol of the new Germany. This move marked the tenth anniversary of the marathon and confirmed it had survived its infancy. However, it needed to overcome a bizarre event in 1984, before it grew steadily through the following years. The strange incident came when Danish runner John Skovbjerg won the marathon in torrential rain, but almost had his win taken from him because he had committed the heinous crime of bending his starting number with the result that the logo of the race's sponsor was no longer recognisable. After talks and protests, he was reinstated as the winner.

The start was moved again in 1987, to the front of the Brandenburg Gate, before 1990's reunification took the competitors straight through it. The modern marathon course, which winds through 10 of Berlin's 23 districts, starts on the six-lane Strasse des 17 Juni (the Street of June 17). The street is a continuation of the Unter den Linden, a tree-lined boulevard on the east side of the

Brandenburg Gate, and was renamed to commemorate the uprising of the East Berliners on 17 June 1953 against Communist rule. The date, 17 June, was established as a national holiday in West Germany and was also a day of commemoration, before the reunification.

Given all of its history, including the famous marathon run during the 1936 Olympic Games, and the proliferation of great athletes and runners in Germany, it is no surprise that the annual modern Berlin Marathon is a great success. More than one million people usually fill the streets to witness it and, in that atmosphere, with decent weather, it is also renowned to be a fast race, partly thanks to the flatness of the course. Indeed, many would say it is the fastest marathon race in the world to be run on a regular basis.

After all the alterations, too, the Berlin Marathon is considered to take the runners through one of the prettiest courses in Europe. Some have called it the 'picture postcard marathon', but others prefer to think of it more as a long-distance speed trap. In 1977, for example, West German Christa Vahlensieck set a new women's world record with a time of 2:34:48 on the old route. Then, in 1998, on the 25th anniversary and in the largest German sports event of all time, Brazilian Ronaldo de Costa shattered the eleven-year-old men's world record held by Ethiopia's Belayneh Dinsamo with a time of 2:06.05 and, in doing so, became the first runner to reach an average speed of more than 20 kilometres per hour.

Tegla Loroupe, the diminutive Kenyan, lowered her own world record by four seconds in 1999, before her time was trimmed, in Berlin, by Japan's Naoka Takahashi. In breaking the record, in 2001, she also became the first woman to break the 2:20 barrier as she set a new best of 2:19:46. Takahashi said she had deliberately chosen Berlin for her first marathon after winning gold at the Sydney Olympics, but put her speed down to an unexpected source of help – an exclusive drink made of giant killer hornets' juice that she had consumed at every opportunity during the marathon. 'It tastes like any other sports drink,' she said. 'But you can get it in shops everywhere in Japan.'

Given the women's heroics on the streets of modern Berlin, it was likely that the men would find it a good venue for assaults on their marathon record too and no surprise that Loroupe's compatriot Paul Tergat became the first man to run under 2:05 when, in September 2003, he spectacularly fulfilled pre-race predictions for a new world best by out-sprinting his own pacemaker Sammy Korir through the Brandenburg Gate and in the run to the finish line to record a time of 2:04:55.

It was a spectacular effort, and one that the old marathon man, Sohn, might have appreciated. He had held the record himself in 1935, when he ran in Tokyo under his Japanese name. Yet it could have been even quicker still if Tergat had not run through the wrong pillars, at the gate, when the lead cars filed away to allow him to take the finish line. Luckily, Korir followed him through the central columns instead of the right ones, where the finish line was located. 'There was nobody there to show me,' was Tergat's response at the end. It hardly mattered. The brilliant Kenyan had just become the fastest marathon runner of all time . . . on the streets of marathon-mad Berlin.

10. HISTORY 5 – FINNS FLY IN ANTWERP AND PARIS

After the heat of the Swedish summer, and the long years of suffering with the First World War, the next Olympic Games were held in cooler conditions in 1920, at Antwerp, in Belgium. They had been scheduled for Berlin, in the summer of 1916, but the conflict made that impossible and that proposed event was cancelled on the outbreak of hostilities. In 1915, as another result of the war, Pierre de Coubertin made the unilateral decision to establish permanent headquarters for the IOC away from the theatre of conflict at Lausanne, in Switzerland. Until then, the headquarters of the Olympic movement had moved every four years with the Games. Berlin had been offered the 1916 Games originally because de Coubertin believed that, in spite of their growing militarism, such an event would help persuade the Germans to avoid any war, but this rather naive view was soon rendered futile. Indeed, it was during the IOC Congress, in Paris, in 1914, when de Coubertin was unveiling his plans for an Olympic flag and the Berlin Games, that, on 28 June, a Serbian assassin shot Archduke Franz Ferdinand, the heir to Austro-Hungarian throne, in Sarajevo, thus sparking the chain of events that saw Austria-Hungary declare war on Serbia and then Germany declare war on France and Russia. Germany invaded Belgium, which was neutral, and Britain joined the Belgians and the French in an alliance to repel them. The outbreak of war resulted in upheaval within the IOC and this triggered the cancellation of the Berlin Games. When the time came to consider who might host the 1920 Games, it was felt that Germany and Austria-Hungary had acted as aggressors, so plans to hold them in Budapest were also abandoned. Instead, the IOC chose to award them to Antwerp.

This final decision was taken in 1918 after consideration also of Lyon, in France. The Belgian city was selected, however, because of its accessibility by ship and rail for people coming from all over the world, as it was hoped they would, to the war-ravaged continent of Europe. The Olympic Games, and the famous Olympic marathon, were seen to be symbols of recovery and hope in this difficult time;

but the Germans, Austrians and Hungarians and Turks were not invited to take part, it being deemed inappropriate by the Belgian organising committee to include them so soon after the war had ended.

The Olympic ideal remained alive, flickering like the eternal flame, prompting faith in the future for a continent that was wounded and stunned and devastated. Antwerp built a new stadium, with a capacity for 30,000 spectators, and with six lanes. Invitations were sent out, 29 nations brought teams and the 2,607 athletes were accommodated in schools and homes all over the city. When they competed, they were driven to the venue for their event in open-topped trucks and cheered by crowds on the streets. At the opening ceremony, the Belgian fencer Victor Boin became the first athlete to utter the Olympic oath, to abide by fair play, and these Games also marked the first appearance of the flag with five entwined rings. De Coubertin had first had the idea for a flag in 1913.

In competition, Antwerp was to be notable for many things. It had been eight years since the last Games and that, obviously, was a long time for any of the previous champions to have maintained their condition and form, let alone during a period of war. Conditions had changed and so, too, had the identities of the nations. Finland, for example, having produced promising runners for Stockholm, was now independent of Russia and celebrated by winning as many gold medals as the United States. One of them, famously, came in the marathon with Hannes Kolehmainen, the star of Stockholm, proving that he remained a great athlete; his success, however, was tinged with sadness. He had survived the war, but his two great rivals from the 1912 Games' 5,000-metre race, George Hutson of Britain and Jean Bouin of France, had died in action during the war. Finland's success, winning 34 medals in all, would have warmed his friends' hearts.

The rise of the Finns as great athletes, Olympians and runners was the story of Antwerp where the great Paavo Nurmi emerged as a national hero for the first time. Though he lost his first Olympic final, the 5,000 metres, in which he was defeated by Frenchman Joseph Guillemot, who had survived being gassed in the trenches, he went on to collect nine gold and three silver medals in a remarkable career that stretched until the Helsinki Games in 1952. His dedicated training set a new example that accelerated athletic development for everyone. His work, his attitude and his success announced that the Finns had arrived and they were to be taken seriously.

The marathon of 1920 took place on a cool and damp Sunday afternoon on 22 August, starting soon after four o'clock, and the conditions – it was the first time the Olympic marathon had not been run in blistering heat – produced much faster times in spite of the fact that the course distance of 26 miles and 991 yards was the longest ever to be run at any Games. The race, from the stadium, now known as the Beerschot Stadium, home of the Belgian soccer club Beerschot, out into the country and then back again, in a wide circle, had forty entrants from seventeen nations, officially, and eighteen unofficially (one of the 'British' runners, Eric Robertson, was in fact from a colony, Newfoundland). The early leader was South African Christian Gitsham, the man who finished second in Stockholm. After nine miles, he was caught by Kolehmainen who ran with him, at the head of the field, for some way before he eased clear. Hannes, his name created from the abbreviation of Johannes, had run his first marathon aged only seventeen and he had no fear. Born on 9 December 1889, he was the youngest of the three brothers and he had great experience not only of the very long distance races, but also, as we know from his performances in Stockholm, the shorter ones, the middle-distance races. In the decade from 1909 to the end of the war, he ran only one marathon, in Boston, in 1917, and from 1913, in this period, he lived in the United States where he was successful in all kinds of middle-distance events. He married in America too – in Brooklyn, in 1914 – and was therefore settled in his life by the time he ran another marathon in New York in 1920, to qualify for the Finnish Olympic team.

Kolehmainen had strength to spare in this race and after the seventeen-mile mark he was virtually able to dictate the pace until an unexpectedly fast finish was required. Gitsham struggled to stay with him and then retired with foot problems, a torn shoe causing him severe discomfort. The Estonian Juri Lossmann worked hard to close the gap, but the Finnish champion won by 70 yards to record the fastest time known in an Olympic marathon of 2 hours, 32 minutes and 35.8 seconds over the longest distance. It was also the closest finish, but to a middle-distance-trained man that was nothing even if Lossmann later blamed lack of support and information from his teammates for his failure to make his late surge any sooner. Hannes's time was also the world record for the marathon then, by more than three minutes. Remarkably, it has been suggested that, had the course been measured correctly and run over the 'normal' distance, then he might have been the first man to finish a marathon in less than two and a half hours. This was a feat that was not to be officially achieved for another fifteen years.

Eric Robertson's entry, mentioned earlier, also deserves further explanation. He was from St John's, Newfoundland, and he was invited by Canada to be their fifth and reserve runner, even though he was not Canadian, but British (Newfoundland did not join Canada from the British Empire until 1949). As all four Canadians were fit, and ran, it meant there was no place for him. However, the British team had four places, but only three runners – and Robertson, who was in Europe after fighting in the Battle of the Somme during the First World War, where he was wounded, was offered the fourth spot. Robertson had gone to London after the war where he joined the famous Polytechnic Harriers running club (a long-time breeding ground for Britain's best runners and many marathon specialists). When in 1920 he travelled to Antwerp, he found his friends from London and was invited to join the British team. He finished 35th in a time of 3 hours and 55 minutes. Afterwards, the Harriers gave him a silver medal inscribed with the words 'The Polytechnic Sports Club, awarded to Eric Robertson, Olympic competitor, 1920.'

Another interesting point to arise from the Antwerp Marathon was the performance of another Finn – Hannes Kolehmainen's brother Taavetti, who finished tenth – and the fact that the top six were all Europeans. The American domination of the distance appeared to be waning. The first and tenth finishes of the two famous Finns from the same family was also unique; no other family combination has emulated this feat. But if anyone thought this show of potential by Finland was just that, and only a one-off wonder, they were wrong: four years later, in Paris, the Finns really showed the world they were flying!

The return to the French capital (instead of Amsterdam, which switched to 1928 to accommodate Paris) was a gesture to please Pierre de Coubertin, who was soon to retire. He wanted to show the world that the French could organise the Olympic Games properly, to his and the athletes' satisfaction, and that France would enjoy a great event that earned international prestige. This time, he struck good fortune even if the weather for the marathon, again, was so hot that, after discussions had taken place and common sense prevailed, the start was delayed from three in the afternoon to five. By now, too, people understood the Olympics and knew what it was all about. The organisers provided a 'village' with accommodation for the athletes for the first time. The crowds were bigger and better behaved and these Games were followed with interest.

The organisers had delegated much of the responsibility for planning to the individual international sport federations that had developed in the previous years, including the newly created International Amateur Athletics Association (IAAF), formed two days after the Stockholm Games in 1912. When the IAAF held its fifth congress, in Geneva, in 1921, it made clear that it would be 'strong' in arrangements for the athletics competitions and also agreed to standardise the marathon distance at 26 miles and 385 yards. The Paris Games, therefore, signalled in many ways a new and modern era for the Olympics. They became famous afterwards for many things, of course, not least the running of the two Britons, Harold Abrahams and Eric Liddell (as illustrated with some considerable artistic licence in the Hollywood film *Chariots of Fire*), but more so for the sheer brilliance of the Finns and their greatest athlete of all, Paavo Nurmi. His achievements, however, also served to hide the excellence of certain other individuals, not least the 1924 marathon winner Albin Stenroos, a sewing-machine salesman from Helsinki, who ran his race to perfection and won by six minutes.

The marathon course went from the Colombes Stadium in Paris to the town of Pontoise, and back to the stadium. The build-up to the race, on Sunday 13 July 1924, was not good for the Americans whose star runner, Clarence DeMar, winner of his third successive Boston Marathon earlier in the year, objected to the group coaching that the squad were forced to endure. DeMar was America's most famous runner of the 'roaring 20s' and had a long and successful career from 1909 to 1954 during which he is reported to have run a total of more than 100 marathons. Born in Madeira, Ohio in June 1888, he was dubbed the 'king' of the Boston Marathon, was known for his individualism, for rumours that he suffered from some kind of 'heart murmur' that kept him away from athletics for a time (subsequently dismissed by medical experts who said his cardiovascular stamina was 'incredible') and who, eventually, died, aged 70, of cancer. In

France, unhappy with arrangements, however, he made his feelings known; he, therefore, trained alone and morale was poor.

Elsewhere, there were high hopes for the French, the British and the Finns. When the race began, finally, a Frenchman, Georges Verger, and a Greek, Alexander Kranis, set the pace, but neither was to finish and Stenroos, sixteenth through most of the early miles, worked his way forwards, took the lead and ran clear. DeMar, third early on as the competitors, with handkerchiefs knotted to their heads to protect them from the sun, pounded the streets, pushed up to second, but could not compete with a late surge by the Italian Romeo Bertini who secured the silver medal, leaving the American with bronze. The three medallists were old men by Olympic marathon standards, but enjoyed their hours of glory: Stenroos was 35, Bertini 31 and DeMar was 36. It was a testament to their fitness and preparation that they succeeded; 28 of the 58 starters failed to finish. As Stenroos came home, all alone, the Finns, including Nurmi and Vilho Ritola, who took every gold medal in all distances from 1,500 to 10,000 metres between them, cheered him to the echo. Stenroos's triumph meant that Finland's runners had won every distance race in the Games.

11. HELSINKI AND OSLO – UNNATURAL HEROES AND NATURAL ATHLETES

Nordic Europe is different to the south, a land of almost schizophrenic seasons, lives and natures: a place where the summer is virtually without darkness and the winter virtually without light; dazzling for months of outdoor fever, excitement and sport in the sun; gloomy and dismal for months of frustration when it takes iron discipline for many to avoid the easy distractions fuelled by alcohol. Yet from these lands, and particularly from Norway and Finland, have come many great athletes and many great long-distance runners. The contrasts of night and day are greatest in Finland's vast tracts of forested land heading to the north, beyond Helsinki, the capital. The escapism is outdoors. There, they can ski, skate, snowboard and slide in the winter and swim and run in the summer, often sprinting across clear landscapes unpolluted by the excesses of more heavily industrialised societies elsewhere. It is the same in Helsinki itself, a place where there is always a sense of freedom and decent oxygen, even when it is at its busiest. They know, understand and love their athletes and their athletics, too, in Helsinki. These Finns, who run, learn also to run long distances, to sustain high speeds and to test their nervous, physical and mental systems to the limits. They are introspective, self-controlled and calm natured. Physically, they are often tall, slim and languid; they can run without excessive waste of energy and they can remove emotions to ensure that they can produce strong performances without distractions. In many ways, the Finns have a natural inclination for long-distance running and, thanks to the exploits of their earliest great runners, they have developed a tradition and, sometimes, unwanted expectations.

It began, more than anything, with the three superb Kolehmainen brothers who were the first supremely talented long-distance running beneficiaries of their countrymen's love of athletics. This love of running was first demonstrated when Finland was one of the first countries to organise its own national marathon race, in September 1906, at Oulunkyla, just to the north of Helsinki. Kaarlo Nieminen won the inaugural event and did the same in 1907 when the course was moved to Viipuru. In 1908 he won the Olympic trial race, held at Helsinki, proving beyond doubt that he was the top marathon runner in Finland at the time. He won seven of the first nine marathons to be run on Finnish soil.

But Nieminen's eminence, at this time, served only to hide the emerging talents of perhaps the greatest runners Finland was ever to produce. At Viipuru, for example, he came up against two of the talented trio: Taavetti 'Tatu', who was 22, and finished second, and his brother Johannes 'Hannes', who was only seventeen, but fast enough and strong enough to finish third. In the Olympic trial, Tatu finished second again, this time twelve minutes behind Nieminen, and he was not taken to London in 1908. The selectors, it was said, did not think he was sufficiently fit to be worthy of the trip. Yet, just a month before the London Games took place, Tatu ran 40.2 kilometres at Viipuri in a record time for the distance of 2 hours, 39 minutes and 4 seconds. It was, if nothing else, a clear signal of the talent that was available to the Finnish selectors.

The third of the three remarkable Kolehmainen brothers was August William 'Viljami' Kolehmainen who was said to be just as talented as the other two, but opted for a professional career. This decision meant it was the others that claimed the acclaim, but it should not be overlooked that he ran a marathon at Vailsburg in New Jersey, in the United States, in 2 hours, 29 minutes and 39.2 seconds in October 1912. This effort lowered the professionals' world record at the time and made sure that Finland was known across America for the stamina and speed of its long-distance runners.

In the same year, at Stockholm, of course, Johannes 'Hannes' Petter Kolehmainen was demonstrating his talents to the full at the Olympic Games, fulfilling his obvious talent and blazing a glorious and golden trail across the history of long-distance running on his way to winning the Olympic marathon gold, eventually, at Antwerp in 1920. But at Stockholm, it was Tatu who rightly picked to run for Finland in the marathon (Nieminen having emigrated to the United States and turned professional to make a living out of the craze for prize-money distance contests) while Hannes was selected for the 5,000 metres, 10,000 metres and cross-country. In the preparations, Tatu, who had not run a marathon for three years, recorded a time of 2 hours, 29 minutes and 7.6 seconds to surprise many observers in the trials race at Oulunkyla, in May, on a part-road and part-dirt course. It was to be a more notable result than he recorded in the marathon itself.

The Finns, however, were more than compensated by the efforts of Hannes who took three gold medals in his events, demonstrating that he was arguably the greatest of them all. In a performance of staggering virtuosity, he foreshadowed the later efforts to follow of Zatopek. Hannes, of course, had been running distances with speed for years. In 1909, he ran three marathons in eighteen days, two of them at track events where he showed great resistance to injury and competitive drive. This was not endurance running, à la Fiennes, but high-class distance running; the combination of his three events in Stockholm, furthermore, added up to 42,000 metres run between 9 and 15 July. He virtually did a marathon anyway, cut into three golden slices.

Eight years later, he claimed the first Finnish victory in an Olympic marathon, in Antwerp, breaking a seven-year-old record time for the distance by nearly four minutes. His brother, Tatu, finished tenth this time. Born in Kuopio, on the edge of Lake Kalki, in central southeastern Finland, surrounded by lakes and forests, Hannes was rightly acclaimed at home and around the world for his feats. By the end of the Stockholm Games, he had held world records at 2,000, 3,000 and 5,000 metres and at the next opportunity he had added the marathon. Even the man who stands guard over Lac Leman can't claim to have bettered that. Oddly, however, Hannes had left Europe to go and live in America after Stockholm, running successfully and living in New York. He became a naturalised American, but for Antwerp was told he must run not for his adopted land but only for his native land, for which he had already been a representative. It must be recalled also that the interval between his two great Games efforts was a full eight years, straddling the First World War.

His brilliance at marathon distances faded after this, but Hannes had been a credit to his family and his country over the long run. His throne, as the Finns' greatest of all, was to be challenged, and some would say taken from him, by others as the years unfolded. The biggest and best claim was to come from the man originally dubbed as the 'Flying Finn', Paavo Nurmi, who went out and won twelve Olympic medals in the 1920s (including a silver in the 5,000 and gold in the 10,000 metres on his Olympics debut at Antwerp), but who never won the Olympic marathon, that honour going to another Finn, at Paris in 1924, the 35-year-old Albin Stenroos, a carpenter known for his inconsistency over long-distance races. For Hannes, however, Paris was a disappointment and he joined that elite club of men who could claim to have followed a gold medal triumph in one Olympic Games marathon with a dismal unfinished race at the next. Hannes was the first man of four in the opening hundred years of the Games' history to experience this kind of glory followed by disappointment. He died in 1966.

Stenroos, however, deserves further mention. In an age when he was up against distance men like the Kolehmainen brothers and Nurmi, he ran some excellent races and produced great results. Notably, in July 1909, in a non-Olympic marathon race, he was the only man to separate the trio of brothers when he ran 3:03:54 and finished third, eight minutes ahead of Hannes, but behind the victorious Tatu and second-placed Viljami. In all, Stenroos, who also emigrated and ran in the United States, competed in eleven recorded marathons, but won only once. It was this one that mattered, however, in Paris on 13 July 1924. Despite many great runners, many great marathon men, it was also to be the last time a Finn won an Olympic marathon in the twentieth century.

The taciturn, some would say morose, bearded policeman Lasse Viren emerged in the 1970s as, perhaps, the next of the truly great Finns with a chance of emulating his countrymen's earlier feats, but failed. He won the 5,000 and the 10,000 metres in Munich and then again in Montreal (a 'double' double that established his enormous class) where he decided to enter the marathon. He wanted to emulate Zatopek; this was no easy task. Not even for a great man like Viren who, like Zatopek, had never run the distance previously. His victory in the 5,000 metres had been achieved only the previous day, a signal that he may be too tired to be competitive, but there was a sense that he could repeat the feat of the great little Czech runner and so he tried. Alas, for him and for Finland, he did not and it is the achievement of Zatopek that remains unique. The Finns, however, had proved again that they remained the nation to watch at any time when it came to the production of great long-distance men capable of winning a marathon.

Two years after Viren's brave run to fifth on the banks of the Great St Lawrence seaway at Montreal, another Nordic athlete with designs on the marathon was to emerge. Watching the tall, bearded and insular Finn's vain bid for splendid glory in North America, from her home back in Oslo, was a girl who was to become one of the marathon's truly great runners and record-breakers, Grete Waitz. It is enough to say that she won the New York City Marathon nine times from 1978 to 1988, but if you add that she also won a silver medal at the 1984 Games, in the marathon in Los Angeles, and that she broke and held the world record for the women's marathon four times (in 1978, 1979, 1980, all three in New York, and then, in 1983, in London), thus reigning supreme from October 1978 to April 1983 (when American Joan Benoit took it away from Norway for the first time in nearly five years), then it is clear that Waitz was both unique and extraordinary. She was the first of the truly great women runners and she put women's running 'on the map'.

Born on 1 October 1 1953, three weeks before the usual date of the New York City Marathon, Waitz not only overcame the elements (Norway is a severely cold country and in Oslo, as in Helsinki, there is a winter to avoid), but she also overcame the prejudice, or utter indifference, that made it difficult for her, as a girl, to be noticed as an athlete at all. As a teenager, she had to fight her family, too, because they believed she should concentrate on supporting her brothers, who were identified as the athletes, rather than pulling on her own running shoes and seeking to enter races for herself. It was not until 1970, by which time sexual equality and equal opportunity were expressions that were establishing themselves in the English lexicon of human history, that Grete's parents took her seriously and started to offer any support.

Two years later, Waitz made Olympic history as one of the first women ever to run in the 1,500-metre race at the Munich Games. By 1975, she was breaking records for the 3,000 metres and discovering that her true talents lay in longer distance running. All her training paid off. All the long days, when she attended her teachers' training college and maintained an average of 75 miles a week outside student hours, had proved to be worth the effort.

By the mid-1970s she was running longer distances, but it was not until 1978 that she established herself as a marathon runner, entering her first marathon in New York that October. She was hardly well prepared but, at 25, she was full of energy and ambition, though underestimated and little known. She was entering the unknown with her mind set on retiring from athletics that year so that she could concentrate on her teaching. She had never run more than twelve miles before, but she went out and not only won the race, but also set a world record. It was a spectacular start and a spectacular breakthrough for her, for Norway and for women. Soon she was to abandon teaching and carry on running, living off the prize money.

Her record-breaking time was 2 hours, 32 minutes and 30 seconds. She was an overnight star in the Big Apple and around the world. Her hot face, her blonde hair in pigtails to keep it out of the way and her sheer determination were the features that burned her into the world's consciousness. 'I remember that first New York marathon,' she recalled later. 'They didn't have bottles for the elite runners. There were just paper cups and I couldn't drink from cups while I was running. I'd get water all over my face.' The established practice for the best runners was to give them a private, set aside table on which their pre-prepared fluid bottles were left standing.

In Gail Kislevitz's book *First Marathons*, Waitz revealed that she was originally rejected from running in New York, in what proved to be such a spectacular debut marathon, because the organisers were not impressed by her application or her European short-distance and middle-distance results. She was quoted saying,

> The first time I called the New York Road Runners Club, to get an invitation to the 1978 marathon, I was turned down. I had never run a marathon before and when they asked for my records, I gave them my track and field accomplishments, but it was all in short-distance events. I wasn't terribly disappointed, but I was looking forward to a holiday in New York with my husband . . .

Waitz had been encouraged to try for an entry by her Norwegian team-mates, knowing that she could not afford the flights. When she was refused an entry, it seemed her trip to the United States was off. But, as is so often the way, fate took a twist. 'I was getting ready to retire from my ten-year track career and thought this would be a fun way to go out. After all the years of teaching full time, training twice a day, and racing almost every weekend, I was tired,' she explained in Kislevitz's book.

> The New York City Marathon was going to be my last race, but it didn't seem as if it was going to happen. Then I received an

unexpected call from Fred Lebow, the New York Road Runners Club president and race director, asking if I still wanted to come. Fred was familiar with my European records and knew that I was fast. Although he never thought I would complete the race, he needed a "rabbit", someone who would go out strong and set a fast pace for the elite women. With that as his only premise for inviting me, Jack and I found ourselves on a flight to New York City. For us, it was a second honeymoon.

The teacher and her husband did not know what lay ahead, of course. To them it was going to be a nice weekend away from home in a city with a reputation as one of the most exciting in the world. The city that never stops, according to some of the publicity of the time. Waitz was not worried by the marathon at all.

'I didn't think about the marathon, I had no idea how to prepare for one,' she admitted. 'I thought my longest run of twelve miles would get me through. The night before the race, we treated ourselves to a nice restaurant, complete with a four-course meal of shrimp cocktail, filet mignon, baked potato, red wine, and ice cream!

'The next morning, along with 13,000 other runners, I stood at the front of the line, looked around, and didn't know a soul. At the start, I went out fast and continued that pace for quite a while. In fact, I was having such a good time, I increased my speed. I was getting too comfortable and, after all, this was a race. By mile nineteen, though, I stopped feeling so great. I knew my body had reached unknown territory, never having run so far. My biggest problem was not being able to convert the miles to metres, my measurement system. And since I didn't speak English that well, I was too embarrassed to ask where the heck I was. My quads were beginning to cramp, too, so I decided to try and drink water, but I had never experienced this quick form of drinking before and kept spilling the water all over myself. It is definitely an acquired skill, something to be practised beforehand.

'I continued running strong, but having no idea what mile I was on or where this place called Central Park was, I began to get annoyed and frustrated. Every time I saw a patch of trees, I thought, "Oh, this must be Central Park," but no. To keep motivated, I started swearing at my husband for getting me into this mess in the first place. I started sucking on oranges for nourishment, since I had given up trying to drink anything. This was definitely harder than any track course I had run. I knew I was out of my league and hadn't trained properly. Finally, exhausted and hurting, I crossed the finish line.' Little did she know what she had achieved.

Immediately, a throng of reporters ambushed her. She felt tired and irritated and wanted nothing else but to find her husband and go for a rest. She was exhausted. 'I was swarmed by the media, pushing microphones and cameras in my face. I didn't understand what they were saying and tried to run away from them,' she recalled. 'All I wanted to do was find Jack and go home. I didn't like this marathon racing. The rest is history. I had no idea that day that I had set a course and world record. In fact, I had registered so late that my entry number, 1173, wasn't listed in the pre-race entries. No one knew who the girl in pigtails was.

To be suddenly a hero on a world basis was hard for me to understand. I was a runner. That was my job. I was uncomfortable with all the fuss Americans made over my victory. God gave me a gift and I had used it wisely, since I was a little girl. By the time I was twelve, I had participated in handball, gymnastics, and track. I liked all sports, but running became my focus. My two older brothers set a wonderful example for me and since we were always in friendly sibling competition with one another and I tended to follow their training habits, other girls found me tough to beat. That's probably one of the reasons I made the 1972 Olympic team at eighteen years old. I didn't expect to set any records back then, just appreciated being there and viewed it as a learning experience.

The teacher was a good pupil. Her outward enthusiasm for running and her love of athletics changed her life. In Munich, she tasted something fresh and enjoyable and she was happy. 'Actually it was lots of fun – I received free clothes, there was very little pressure, and it was like being at camp for three weeks with my best friends,' she said.

But when I returned to the Olympics in 1976, it was a different ball game. I now knew what to expect and, more seriously, knew what was expected of me. The 1984 Olympics was a highlight in my career as it was the first time women were allowed to compete in the marathon event and I brought home a silver medal for Norway.

'I always took my training very seriously, getting up at five in the morning for my first workout of the day. Then it was off to my teaching job and at the end of the day, back home for my evening run. I don't like to cook and spend as little time in the kitchen as possible, so I didn't have to worry about some of the household responsibilities.

Remarkably, she also found a husband who did not mind his wife jumping out of bed at unearthly hours, declining to do the preparation of meals and spending most of her spare moments running around in ever-increasing circles.

Jack has always been very supportive of my running career,' she said. 'I was probably the first female athlete to realise the benefits of twice-a-day training. I am a firm believer that track training is crucial to any running programme. It's where you develop the speed. Distance makes you stronger, not faster. If the training isn't tough enough, it won't work. I prefer to train in the dark, cold winter months when it takes a stern attitude to get of bed before dawn and head out the door to below-freezing weather conditions. Anyone can run on a nice, warm, brisk day. That's fun, but there's no sense of sacrifice, no great accomplishment.

'It takes strength, courage, commitment, and many days and nights of sacrifice to win. Looking back on my career, and thinking that I almost retired in 1978, except for that famous New York City Marathon, I am glad I got a shot at a second distance-running career. That's where women's focus seems to be these days. I finally did retire in 1990, but only to start my third life's career, as a spokesperson for women's sports. There is so much that still needs to be learned about women in sports and, more important, getting the right information out to women. When I was running, back in the seventies, and was about twenty-three, my period stopped. When I went to the doctor, he wasn't concerned, said don't worry, it will come back. Now we know that amenorrhoea (not menstruating) is a serious condition. There are other things that affect women that we are just learning about. '

Her long and fabulous career finally over, Waitz became a sports consultant and a commentator and, most importantly, an inspiration to other athletes, particularly women, all over the world. 'It is very important to keep this flow of new information circulating to running clubs and women's groups,' she said. 'Entry numbers are on the rise in road racing, mostly due to the number of female applicants. Whether walking or running, slow or fast, women are out there competing. When most people decide to start a running programme, they start up too fast and get discouraged. It is a big step from being inactive to starting any form of exercise. I always suggest to walk first. Start at a level that is comfortable and slowly increase from a walk to a jog to a run. The first steps can be very intimidating.

'As long as you don't have any form of physical illness, your goals can be achieved. Novice runners often fail to recognise how much a part of their training is dedicated to mental energy and concentration. Those also have to be incorporated into the overall exercise programme. Two of my most memorable marathons were ones I didn't win. My 1992 run with Fred Lebow, in remission with brain cancer, was very emotional. I didn't think I could run for five hours, but he gave me the strength. It went by so quickly . . .'

Lebow and Waitz were very good friends. When he was fighting the cancer, that later claimed his life, their run together, in a finishing time of 5 hours, 32 minutes and 35 seconds, said much about the wider meaning of the marathon. 'He was one of the old-fashioned guys,' Waitz recalled with fondness. 'He was human. He really wanted to treat his clients, his runners, the best way.' His legacy to the New York event was matched in her generosity in response.

'My other memorable moment was in 1993, when I promised Achilles Marathon runner Zoe Koplowitz, crippled with multiple sclerosis, that I would be there for her at the finish,' Waitz explained.

'It took her twenty-four hours to complete the course and when she crossed the finish line at six-thirty a.m. the next morning, I was there. No one had a medal for her, so I rushed back to my hotel to get my husband's medal for her. I don't have half the struggles in life she does. It puts my own life in perspective. My two brothers and husband have carried on the New York City Marathon tradition for me. One of my brothers has run it fourteen times. Now I enjoy being part of the scene. I like to watch my favourite marathon and be a part of running history.'

Waitz is not only a nine-times winner of the New York City Marathon, but also a five-times winner of the World Cross-Country Championships and was a gold medal winner at the 1983 World Championship Marathon in Helsinki. Since her retirement, she has become an accomplished author and a leading health and fitness advocate. She also does a great deal of charity work on behalf of CARE International and the International Special Olympics. But her reputation, as the 'patron saint' of the New York City Marathon and the pioneer of women's marathon running, still reigns supreme. She was the first woman to break the 2:30 mark, she secured her place in the hall of fame, she became the queen of the marathon and the inspiration for women all over Norway and the world. Once a year, the streets of Oslo are filled by around fifty thousand female joggers. It is a demonstration of their recognition of her achievements. The event has been dubbed the Grete Waitz race. It is a warming tribute to the girl with the pigtails. But she is remembered well, too, by those who stroll towards the famous Bislett Stadium, Oslo's athletics landmark. Just outside, there is a statue that marks her out among the greats: Grete Waitz, the woman from the Nordic lands who became the first queen of the women's marathon.

12. HISTORY 6 – SPANNING THE WORLD: AMSTERDAM TO LOS ANGELES

The 1928 Olympic Games were held in Amsterdam. Having been given several years to prepare, the Dutch organisers did their utmost to ensure the facilities were first class, embarking on a major building programme. This was mainly around a drained lake at the south-western edge of the city where a 40,000-capacity stadium was built with the first 400-metre track laid down in the history of the Games. Unlike Paris, there was no village this time and the 2,724 athletes were accommodated all over the city, apart from the American team, for example, which chose instead to live on the *SS President Roosevelt*, on which it had sailed to Europe from New York. There were other novel innovations: these were the games at which a torch was lit to signal the eternal flame for the first time, women were included (though not in the marathon, as it was considered too difficult for them at this time) for most track and field events and Pierre de Coubertin was absent. Having retired as president of the IOC, he was also unwell and he sent a message of farewell to be read out at the opening ceremony. His anticipation of the worst was premature, however, as he lived on for a further nine years.

The marathon race, held on the damp and chilly Sunday afternoon of 5 August, turned out to be a famous one for several reasons. It produced the first African-born winner (although he ran for France) and a very close finish; it also produced one of the first tragic stories surrounding a triumphant Olympic hero as the marathon victor's later life unfolded. The course was mostly flat, inevitably. It began in the Amsterdam Stadium, passed out through the Olympic gate into the countryside and then followed towpaths by the Amstel River and its dykes, circled back and returned to the stadium. All runners were given a set of rules allowing them to wear a watch and a vest, as always, but they were warned that competitors were 'not allowed to run in to the Amstel for a bath'.

Joie Ray, of the United States, was an early pacesetter ahead of Martti Marttelin of Finland and Kanematsu Yamada of Japan. At the half-distance marker, Ray still led, but the Japanese soon passed him followed by his compatriot Seiichiro Tsuda. These three ran at the front through most of the second half of the race, but were gradually reeled in by a little-known Algerian-born Frenchman, Boughera El Quafi, and Miguel Plaza Reyes of Chile. Plaza, reportedly a newspaper delivery boy from Santiago, had stuck to El Quafi as a tactic in the previous Olympic marathon, without much reward, but this time his effort paid off. As the finish approached, in the final three miles, they began passing the leaders and entered the stadium in first and second places to take the leading places. El Quafi won in 2 hours, 32 minutes and 57 seconds, some 26 seconds ahead of the Latin American. Marttelin finished third, Yamada fourth and Ray, from America, fifth. These five different nations reflected the growing international nature of, and enthusiasm for, the marathon. The cool weather helped everyone too. Of the 69 starters, 57 finished. Afterwards, in the post-race recovery room, El Quafi was reported to be relaxed and chatty as he drank water and requested a cigarette. Other runners were in agony with cramp and dehydration.

El Quafi's win was a historic triumph for him, for France and for Africa, but it did not have a happy ending. Born near Biskra in 1899, he grew up as a date farmer who enjoyed running. At 23 he set an Algerian one-hour record for track running. Then he moved to France where, it was reported, he applied to join the French Colonial Army. He was also said to have worked in Paris as a garage mechanic at the time of the Olympic Games held there. Afterwards, for a time, he went back to Algeria where he worked as a despatch carrier for the French Colonial Army, at last. This gave him a chance to run long distances in the hot and dry conditions and explains why it appeared that he had given up running seriously before 1927 when he started training again for the 1928 Olympics. He had won the 1924 national marathon trials in France and he did the same in 1928 to ensure he was able to take part in the Amsterdam Games. After winning, he turned professional and in one famous indoor race beat a field including Antwerp silver medallist Juri Lossman, Briton Arthur Newton and Joie Ray at Madison Square Gardens in New York, a race reminiscent of the old prize events involving Hayes and Pietri twenty years earlier.

Thereafter he was forgotten until, years later, in 1956, in Melbourne, when another Algerian-born runner in a French team triumphed in the marathon. This man, Alain Mimoun O'Kacha was asked about his predecessor and revealed that El Quafi was back in Paris, unemployed and living in poverty. Immediately, French reporters and sportsmen launched a fundraising effort that helped him briefly before he died, three years later, aged 61, following a family quarrel. His end was brutal: on 18 October 1959 he was shot and killed while sitting in a café. Some said it was a random killing, others that he was involved in a simmering dispute. It did not matter. His early death, his bloody ending, may have been savage, but it could not eradicate his triumph from the record books or hide the obvious signal that the Africans were on their way.

The explosion of interest in marathon running around the world had included not only Africa and Asia, but also South America, in addition to Europe and North America. It was, therefore, no surprise that the Latin-American nations began to emerge as strong contenders, nor that they would supply a winner when the 1932 marathon was run at the Olympic Games in Los Angeles. The win, by Juan Carlos Zabala of Argentina, was hardly easy, however, as he laboured heavily on his final finishing lap, losing the lead and then regaining it before collapsing across the line with four other runners in the stadium. It was a great feat for him, and for Argentina, after the team had been involved in serious in-fighting against the way their team was being run and had gone on strike in the athletes' village. Later, it was reported, they came to blows on board their ship on the way home. According to David Miller, the ringleaders, including Santiago Lovell, the heavyweight boxing champion, were later sent to prison in Argentina.

Perhaps most remarkable of all about this entire episode is that Argentina could afford to send a team to Los Angeles at all. California, and the rest of the world, was in the grip of a great depression and twenty of the teams invited could not attend because of financial problems. Yet these second American Games were a great success, the organisation was excellent and a wonderful stadium, the Coliseum, was built with a capacity of more than 101,000. It was good enough to be refurbished for use again in 1984 when the Olympics returned to California. As in Paris, a village was used to accommodate the athletes and it worked successfully; so much so that the idea remained a fixture for future Games. The victory podium was also introduced. The happy atmosphere, probably generated as much to forget the general air of disillusion, was helped, too, by the enthusiasm of the big crowds and their warmth towards their guests. These Americans had made it clear they wanted to offer real hospitality.

Unfortunately, such generosity was not on offer from the IAAF and, therefore, the organisers in the run-up to the Games. In a move that deprived the long-distance events, and the marathon, of the presence of the great Paavo Nurmi, the IAAF decided to disqualify the Finn just three days before the opening ceremony. The IAAF said that Nurmi, 35, had received compensation in excess of his expenses while he was racing in Europe and ruled that this made him ineligible to compete as an amateur. He had been talked of as the favourite to win the Los Angeles marathon after winning nine gold medals, and twelve medals altogether in the previous three Games. Without him, it was set to be a race between Zabala, who was strictly trained by his coach Andrew Stirling from Scotland, and American Albert Michelsen, according to the experts. But Zabala, only twenty, had retired with a foot problem after leading a trial race over the course by more than eight minutes earlier in the summer and his fitness was questionable.

Only 29 runners from 15 countries lined up for the start of the marathon in near-perfect mild conditions at 3.25 p.m. on Sunday 7 August. That did not matter to the local Californians and a crowd of an estimated 80,000 was in the stadium. The course began and finished in the Coliseum, in between taking the runners out on a roughly square tour of the suburbs of Los Angeles, mostly on concrete-based roads. Zabala, whose career as a runner had really started when he was discovered by Stirling as a thirteen-year-old, had predicted he would win. His confidence came from years of preparation. Stirling had virtually adopted him, trained him to become a world-class athlete, and before he was twenty had guided him to winning the South American 10,000-metre title. In October 1931 he set a world record for thirty kilometres, so he knew he had the speed and the long-distance endurance to succeed.

Zabala took an early lead, but this was to be a race in which the lead changed hands many times, the tough little Latin American fighting back each time he was passed. He had most of the leadership for the first twenty miles until, predictably enough given their eminence at the time, a Finn, Lauri Virtanen, stole into the lead and pulled away. It looked as if another Finnish triumph was being sketched out, but instead several other runners responded. Briton

Duncan Wright fought back and took the lead. Virtanen, exhausted, dropped out. When Wright tired and faded, Zabala regained the front position, chased by another Briton, Sam Ferris, from Northern Ireland. Unluckily for Ferris, the vast crowds around the course made it virtually impossible for him to identify an advertisement for milk, which he had decided to use as his marker for making a final kick to win, and so he left it too late. It was a tough end for Ferris, a veteran, at 31, of many gruelling runs, a man who had put together a series of exceptional successes in the famous London race known as the 'Sporting Life' marathon, organised by that newspaper and the Polytechnic Harriers. (This marathon was run from 1909, following the London Games marathon of 1908 and run over much the same course). Ferris won it eight times in all between 1925 and 1933 and was making his third Olympic Games marathon appearance in Los Angeles, having finished fifth in 1924 and eighth in 1928. However, despite his longevity and his spirit, luck deserted him this time in California. By the time he entered the stadium, he realised his mistake in missing the milk advertisement, and ran as fast as he could.

Zabala, however, although having difficulties, had enough of a lead to survive and win, collapsing on the track as he did so. Descriptions of his last-lap agony on the way to glory movingly added that the 75,000 crowd, or bigger, was kept enthralled. Trumpeters on top of the roofs of the stadium had announced his imminent arrival. Wearing a white vest, pale blue running shorts, edged in white, and wearing the white handkerchief on his head to prevent sunburn, he looked tired and close to collapse. Ferris, another Finn, Armas Toivonen, and Wright were also in the stadium and chasing hard at the time, too, providing a dramatic scene that sent the spectators wild. Zabala's win, at the classic distance, was completed in an Olympic record time of 2 hours, 31 minutes and 36 seconds. For him, it was a magnificent victory. The following day's *Los Angeles Examiner* newspaper carried a report by Damon Runyon. He wrote: 'In spirit, in heart, and in endurance, Juan Zabala, a slim young son of Argentina, was the modern reincarnation of Pheidippides of old.' It was poetic nonsense, of course, but it summed up the mood. The boy from Buenos Aires, who had been orphaned as a child, who needed help to put his legs back into his tracksuit bottoms after his victory, had made a big impression. The gold medals for marathon winners were being shared around the world.

13. SEOUL AND TOKYO – MEN OF PRIDE, WOMEN OF COURAGE

In the summer of 2002, a great sports event took place in Japan and South Korea. Yes, it may have been won by Brazil, but it was a triumph, too, for the hosts. For once, the two nations were unified in spirit, for a month, by co-hosting the soccer World Cup finals. Millions danced in the streets, but rarely supporters from the two nations together, because their teams remained in their homelands. But each became more aware of the other, and learned to appreciate the other through watching their national team's performances on television. For visitors from Africa, Europe, or the Americas, it was a moving experience; to see the passion of the Japanese and South Korean fans for their teams and to share the event with them. Even if, at times, the historical dislike between the two rose to the surface, it was unable to disturb the unique atmosphere enjoyed in both countries and it could never disguise the love of sport that pumps through the streets of each nation's crowded, excited and dazzlingly lively capital city. Tokyo twinkled as Seoul sizzled, both brought to the boil by sport, just as they have always simmered with delight whenever a famous Japanese or Korean runner has stormed the record books. Both of these extraordinary cities can boast a passion for the men and women who have run great marathons, too, and both nations have shown their delight, and excellence, in the event for decades.

As we know from the tale of Sohn Kee Chung in Berlin, the marathon meant much to him and his people, and we know, too, that he was ashamed, as a Korean, to be made to run in the colours of a nation that was then an occupying power in his country. He hated being thought of as Japanese, a nation that was in so many ways an ancient enemy to the Koreans – in sport and in life. Sohn Kee Chung was born on 29 August 1912, in Sinjiju, a small and poor agricultural village that also produced timber, on the River Yalu, in what is now part of North Korea, close to the Chinese border. He ran and completed his first marathon in 1931, before setting a world record in November 1935 of 2 hours, 26 minutes and 42 seconds at Tokyo, in an Olympic preliminary, to qualify for the Berlin Games.

This record-breaking run saw his effort recorded as performed by Kitei Son of Japan, making him, on paper at least, the third successive Japanese to have broken the world record for the marathon between March and November 1935. (The record he set was to stand for twelve years before it was broken by a Korean, Bok-Suh Yun, who clocked 2:25:39 in April 1947, in Boston).

Sohn had been educated at Yangjung High School and the Meiji University before he ran and won his gold medal, aged 22, in Berlin. It was a phenomenal achievement as he became the first Korean winner of a marathon gold medal, a feat that was not to be emulated by another Korean until the Barcelona Games in 1992, when Young-Cho Hwang also 'struck gold', so maintaining the Koreans' dedication to the distance and their devotion to excellence. Sohn, in his Berlin victory, also seemed to be setting a new standard for survival after running the race in shoes that were split at the front. This, however, missed the point of the story as he later revealed with a smile. 'Oh, that was just a fad,' he said. 'It gave me neither an advantage nor a disadvantage.'

He had previously performed at 800 metres and 5,000 metres before trying the classic long-distance race, but then he went and won all of his first three marathons, in Seoul. Heading to Berlin, he was the clear favourite to win and both Japan and Korea recognised this. He did not disappoint either adoring nation, but stood with his head bowed on the podium. Korea, under the colonial rule of Japan at the time, revelled in his success as 'one of their own'. This inspired one local daily newspaper, *Dong-a-Ilbo* (East Asian Daily) to print a photograph of Sohn standing on the victors' podium after winning his gold medal, but with the Japanese flag that had been sewn on to his shirt deliberately removed. As a result, the Japanese government arrested and imprisoned eight members of the newspaper's staff and halted publication for ten months.

It was Sohn's finest moment. He had set a new Olympic record but then took his record of ten victories from thirteen marathon starts into an early retirement. He went on to take a role as manager of Korea's marathon athletes, but he had to wait until the end of World War Two, in 1945, for the country to regain its independence. He finally had his opportunity to celebrate as a Korean when he ran into the stadium in Seoul, with the flame, and four years later when he was in Catalonia for the Barcelona Games and saw Korea's first 'official' Olympic champion achieve gold. Sohn, who wrote an autobiography entitled *My Motherland and Marathon*, also enjoyed coaching success when his protégés Bok-Suh Yun and Ham Kee-Yong won the Boston Marathon in 1947 and 1950 respectively. He died on 15 November 2000, at the age of 90, after battling with illness and pneumonia. His achievements had earned him Korea's Citizen's Merit Award and posthumously the Cheongryong Medal, the highest award of sport merit, and Blue Dragon Order. A Sohn Kee Ching Memorial Park stands in his memory in Seoul.

His life attracted much interest from Olympian historians and several interesting stories emerged to add to the tapestry of colour and drama that had surrounded him since 1936. In one, reported by Charlie Lovett, he developed his stamina, strength and speed by running each day to collect the bread for his family. In another, also noted by Lovett, he met and befriended Jesse Owens in Berlin during the Olympic Games of 1936. 'He was the first black man I had seen with my own eyes,' said Sohn. 'And though, at first, we couldn't understand each other, we practised together every day and we became friends.' It was something that the Japanese could not understand at that time, but later worked to develop when they hosted the World Cup finals. Sport, after all, has a way of healing wounds, aiding communication and bringing people together. And the marathon, so popular that it is regarded by many in Japan and Korea as the most important and popular discipline in sport, was regarded as the best way to their hearts in both countries.

In Korea, in particular, the marathon is seen to be the epitome of sport. There, Koreans believe there is a Korean spirit in the event. That is why the marathon has become the most loved and supported sport in Korea. From their Olympic Games stars of the 1930s to their modern men of the marathon, all are acclaimed. The Koreans themselves are intrigued by this love affair. 'Is this the production of a strong spirit, or a physical superiority?' they ask themselves, at least according to some of the introductory text presented to runners making enquiries about participating in the Seoul Marathon. In answer, the Seoul Marathon publicity machine responded, 'It is not the sort of question that a scientific theory can provide an answer [for], like mythical legends (as in Greece).' The explanation went on, via an occasionally rudimentary translation to throw light on the background to the Koreans' fascination with their running.

Anyhow, there was overflowing energy from the beginning (sic) when the marathon started for the first time in Korea. As it was placed as a national sport from the start, it gathered interest of all the people and the Korean marathoners surprised the people around the world, as well as the Japanese, by winning the gold medal in marathon in its early history. The heat for marathon (sic) among the Korean people was initiated and reinforced by the active support from the media like the *Dong-A Ilbo* and schools like Yangjunggobo. It has passed seventy years since the starting-gun fired in (sic) Kyoungsung-Youngdungpo Marathon, the matrix of Dong-A Marathon. Now, here is a brief look at the history of Dong-A Marathon, which reflects the glory, frustration, joy and the rage of the Korean people . . .

The explanation is worth including. It exudes Korean pride in their love of the marathon and their success in the event. It continued,

The first Dong-A Marathon – March 21, 1931 . . . The great ambitious race started with the siren informing the noon. The marathon, with the circular road [round track] of Seoul-Youngdu Ngpo, a measured distance of fourteen and half miles, was the beginning of Dong-A Marathon. It was organised by Koryo Track Sports Association and co-sponsored by the *Dong-A Ilbo* and Chosen Athletic Association under the title of "The First Marathon Game". The course was the circular road [a round track] passing Kanghwamoon, Taepyeongtong, Namdaemoon, Han River Iron Bridge, Noryangjin and Youngdungpo Station. Among the fourteen competitors were Sung Kun Lee who was known as the Marathon King in the country, Yong Whan Byoun who was the best runner in the long distance, Eun Bae Kim and others from Yangjungkobo. At that time, The *Dong-A Ilbo* ran an article under the title of 'The race in the bright and sunny day: who will be the first man to pass the finish line?' Chosun Athletic Association, under the leadership of chairman Eekk Youm Yoo and other executives, prepared for the event. The event drew keen attention from people in Seoul.

Eun Bae Kim, who was the top racer of Yangjungbogo, won the first glorious victory with a record of 1 hour, 22 minutes and

5 seconds. Hae Boong Yoo from Yangjungkobo, with the one hour, 26 minutes and 22 seconds record, followed him and Sung Kun Lee who had been the best athlete at that time became the third winner with 1 hour, 27 minutes and 22 seconds. Young Whan Byoun, Kyoung Lark Choi and In Sang Cho followed them. Thousands of people came out and gave cheers for the runners throughout the course.

The second Dong-A Marathon, 21 March 1932 . . . The same course with the (as for, in a clearer translation), first event and 29 competitors. Even though Eunbae Kim, the winner of the first game, gave up the race because of his illness, a new face, Kijung Son, from Shinyiju, came into the spotlight in this race. Yong Whan Byoun from the government won the race setting a new record of one hour, 21 minutes and 51 seconds and a 20-year-old man, Kijung Son, was ranked second with one hour, 25 minutes and 25 seconds. Kyubok Baek followed him as a third winner.

The third Dong-A Marathon, 1933. The course was changed into the circular road from Goangwhamoon through Chunryanglee, Mangwoolee, with the measured distance of 15 miles because of the repairment (sic) of Seoul-Inchun road. In very bright and sunny spring weather, on 21 March, 35 competitors, who started from the starting line in front of the *Dong-A Ilbo* building, did their best to set a new record and win the race. Kijung Son finally became the winner by putting on a spurt at the end of the course after he had close race with Haeboong Yoo. His record was new in 1 hour, 24 minutes and 3 seconds. Haeboong Yoo was ranked the second with the record of 1 hour, 24 minutes and 30 seconds, lost to Son by 27 seconds. And Sungyong Nam followed him with the record of 1 hour, 26 minutes and 46 seconds. At that time, Son was scouted by Yangjungbogo, which had the main racer, Sungyong Nam.

Marathon running has grown into a boom sport for Korea, and Japan, following those formative affairs leading towards the 1936 Berlin Games. For the 2004 Seoul International Marathon, the details show that very attractive prize money is on offer and the organisation is, apparently, first class. The 2004 race was scheduled to take place on 14 March, starting at 8 a.m. at the city centre Sejong Cultural

Centre and finishing at the Jamsil Olympic Stadium. The elite male runners were seduced to take part by offers of 50,000 American dollars to the winner, 30,000 to the second-placed runner, 20,000 to the third and prize money to all the runners finishing in the top ten. Time bonuses were offered, too, with 100,000 dollars available for a world-record-breaker (winner only), and sums of 30,000 to 5,000 for other fast times inside 2 minutes and 10 seconds. The top woman, however, was offered only 20,000 dollars, a figure that, in comparison with the men's, was palpably unattractive. The field, undoubtedly, reflected the prize money.

In Japan, women are encouraged to run marathons in a more general way, particularly since the success of Yuko Arimori in winning the silver medal at the 1992 Barcelona Games, and have been successful. This is, perhaps, most notably demonstrated by the fact that Naoko Takahashi won the gold medal in Sydney at the 2000 Games and broke Kenyan Tegla Loroupe's world record in Berlin in September 2001, so becoming the first Japanese or Korean woman to hold the marathon world record. In the men's progression of world records for the marathon, two Japanese have held the ultimate time since the achievement of Bok-Suh Yun of Korea, in 1947: Toru Terasawa, who took the record with a run in 2 hours, 15 minutes and 16 seconds at Beppu in Japan, on 17 February 1963, and Morio Shigematsu, who clocked 2 hours and 12 minutes in London on 12 June 1965, taking the record from Abebe Bikila who had established his in winning the 1964 Olympic Games marathon on 21 October in Tokyo. The great Ethiopian was, thus, at least handing his title back to the land where he had taken it!

Curiously, Japan's infatuation with the marathon, as strong as Korea's in most minds, has produced more great women runners. It has also produced an insatiable interest in them as heroines, so much so that their lives are conducted under a microscope of public and media interest. This was encouraged further by turning the 2003 Tokyo International Women's Marathon, the 25th event, into an open festival as well as using it as the selection event for the 2004 Athens Games. It was marketed as the first marathon for women to be held in the heart of the city that was open to more than 3,000 people.

The success and popularity of women's marathon running in modern times grew dramatically, too, with the success of Arimori. It was understandable. Her silver-medal-winning performance at Barcelona was the first such success by a Japanese woman for 64 years. And, on top of that, she cut a glamorous, almost scandalous, figure in the media, too, as publicity surrounding her marriage threatened to overshadow her athletic achievements. In 1998, she shocked the Japanese media by announcing that she had married American Gabriel Wilson, 32, a teacher from Colorado who'd previously lived in Japan. The couple had kept their relationship out of the public eye, but failed to stop the media discovering the wedding plans. Speculation was rife that Arimori was only marrying to obtain a 'green card' and would, therefore, run for the United States in the Sydney Games. If this was not bad enough for a Japanese public that worshipped its beautiful star marathon runner, matters took a turn for the worse when the couple split up within a month and further revelations followed. These included the extraordinary statement by Wilson that he was a homosexual, a comment that instigated an immediate rush of reporters to Shinjuky ni-chome to search for more sleazy material. Wilson said that he had told Arimori, and her parents, of his previous sexual inclination before the marriage. He added, by way of explanation, that it had no bearing on the break-up. The situation appeared to back up the green-card theory and did little for Arimori's vehement denials of any intention to abandon Japan for America.

Finally, it was revealed that Wilson was heavily in debt, sparking further in-depth reporting of the couple's chaotic partnership. Arimori hinted that divorce was probable but, after a few weeks, the furore died down and, quietly and away from the public eye, the couple reunited. According to later reports, Arimori joined the board of directors of Wilson's dance school, the Andana Academy in Colorado, kept a low profile and attempted to make a marathon comeback without rediscovering the form that swept her to fame and, briefly, infamy.

Born in Okayama, Arimori was a graduate of the Japan Physical Education University and she was virtually unknown before winning the Osaka 1990 International Women's Marathon, setting a new national record in the process. A year later, she came fourth in the World Championships in Tokyo and in 1992 produced her silver-medal-winning run at the Barcelona Games. Following an operation on both heels in 1994, she was out of action for more than a year before resuming her training in the United States, at Boulder in Colorado. Surprisingly, it was not the first time she had suffered with injuries. It was reported that she had been born with a congenital dislocation of her joints, a problem that was corrected with a cast.

In 1995 she made a comeback and won the Hokkaido Marathon before going on to take the bronze medal at the Atlanta Games in 1996. Afterwards, according to reports, she said, 'jibun de jibun o homete agetai' (I want to praise myself), a statement that caused further uproar because Japanese athletes do not usually indulge in self-esteem. Following the Olympic Games, she turned professional, the first athlete to achieve such status by the Japan Amateur Athletic Federation, and wrote an autobiography, Animo, in which she described her turbulent life as an athlete. In 1999, in Boston, she set her personal best marathon time of 2 hours and 26 minutes.

As with so many great marathon runners, she also demonstrated a selflessness as she grew older that echoed the career of Grete Waitz. She exploited her celebrity status, inaugurating the 'Hearts of Gold' charity, which manages the Angkor Wat Half Marathon in Cambodia, raising funds for landmine victims. In Sydney, she failed to realise her greatest dream of winning a gold medal and, afterwards, chose to move on by concentrating on a television career – and passing the baton, or perhaps poisoned chalice, of being the queen of Japanese marathon running to the new star, Naoko Takahashi.

Another iconic figure in Japanese athletics, Takahashi achieved enormous fame with her victory in Sydney on 24 September 2000, eclipsing all others' efforts by becoming the first woman from her country to have a marathon gold medal hanging from her neck. She might have retired there and then, if she knew what Arimori had been through – but, instead, she ran on and became the first woman to break the 2:20 mark at the Berlin Marathon in 2001. She seemed invincible. Japan loved her but by 2003 it seemed she, too, was struggling under the pressures of fame and expectation as she suffered a series of injuries including a fractured rib. When the rumours started to circulate, as they so often do, it was said that she trained too hard and pushed herself beyond reasonable limits. These accusations were put to her in an interview in the Japan Times in 2002 and she gave illuminating answers that help in the understanding of any great marathon runner's predicament as they strive to improve their performances under some duress.

'For the Olympics, I had five months to get myself ready for the race, but this time I had little time to prepare,' she told the newspaper.

For the Berlin Marathon, I had basically two months to get myself conditioned. After a while, I start to calculate backwards from the day of a race, counting how many days I have to go until the start. When I look at my practice schedules, and how fast I am running, and what distance I am running at this stage, I feel the desire to quickly get to my best condition – to jump the four months of training that I would usually do, although I don't even have those four months.

And, because I don't have that period, I try to do more within the limited two months, training harder, even if I am hurting, whereas if I have the four months I could take a few days' rest and see how it goes; but I can't afford the two days to rest, so I just do more and more training and by doing so, sometimes, I can put the injury behind me, but it could also lead to further injuries. There is a big gap between these outcomes and this time it led to a bad result. I don't feel any pressure from other runners, but I have this will to want to be ready to run a certain time at a certain stage [of preparation] and so I draw the line for myself.

It was reported that prior to the Berlin Marathon of 2001, when she set the world record, Takahashi ran up eighty kilometres daily at high altitude in Colorado, in the United States. When this was put to her as being too much running, she said, 'Well, I don't always run that much every day. There would be days when I would run seventy kilometres and then there are days I would run twenty or so. I just mentioned that figure to state that there are days I would actually run up to seventy or so. The fact that I can run that far gives me confidence and makes me believe I am doing a good job.'

The following day, she said, when most mortals would be curled up in a hot bath in an attempt to ease the agony, she would reduce her workload to around forty kilometres – twenty in the morning and twenty in the afternoon. The *Japan Times* asked her to describe an average training day. She replied,

We get together at 6.30 a.m. for morning training and, in America, we have like five of us training together, so for that I wake up around 5.50. We finish training so we can eat breakfast around nine. Then between 2.30 and 3 p.m. we resume training until about seven. Between those two [sessions] we are free. At 7.30 p.m., we have dinner and then wrap up the training, with stretches, and by 9.30 or 10 p.m. we are fast asleep. Breakfast, and dinner, are prepared by a cook, but for lunch we decide what to eat – and when, according to the amount of training we do. We would usually make a light meal, bread or something. The people who cook our meal want to serve us the world's best food, so they really take care of us well. By the best food in the world I don't mean expensive food, but well-balanced meals centred on healthy food like hijiki [seaweed] and natto [fermented soybeans] – good for your body.

Asked about her lifestyle changes, she said she felt that Sydney may have changed her life, but not her. 'I think I am an ordinary girl,' she said. 'I don't have anything unusual going on or anything like that. The reaction of the people isn't so overwhelming any more. I can walk the streets fine and I can even go out in Tokyo.'

Predictably, given the public furore surrounding women marathon runners and their love lives in Japan, she was asked to explain her own philosophy for life and how she copes with training for the top and staying normal. 'Everyone wants to get to the top and we all start at the same line,' she responded.

I try to remain strong, but am a weak person really, and so that's why I feel I have to try hard. Because of that, I don't want to compromise. Whether it's training or the real race, I don't want to not give it everything. Whatever the result, I want to do everything I can day by day for my goal. Each day is precious for me. I believe how you approach each day mentally will show in your result. So what is most important for me is not to think I have to try and stay at the top, but to make sure I don't make any compromises.

In the old days there used to be a sort of taboo, like 'track and field athletes should not be involved in romance,' and I don't think that way. I believe if there could be a person to support you then I think being supported is a good thing. As a runner, I don't like being distracted. When I am in the States I don't want to make calls to friends or even family, and I am in a state where I can't think anything about romance. For the last two years especially, I really haven't thought about or been involved in things like romance, and I sometimes feel: 'Is this right? Am I really satisfied with this life without romance?' I used to think that I wanted to be married by 28, but now I think, maybe being single isn't so bad, or as long as I am successful maybe this isn't so bad. I now think, well, maybe it isn't so embarrassing to be single. Once I began to think like that, I didn't have any sort of longing to feel 'I want to be married like that' any more.

As with Waitz, of Oslo, the girls of Tokyo who train in America appear to possess iron resolve to overcome all difficulties and a desire to give back to their people and their sport all that they can. In both Seoul and Tokyo, the passion for marathon running provides the energy that carries their Korean and Japanese athletes to records and medals. It is a lonely road, but one fuelled by selfless determination, a history of long-distance running and a mystical intrigue with the event that is entwined in their lives.

14. HISTORY 7 – FROM NAZISM TO PEACE, ASIAN RECORD-BREAKERS OPEN UP THE WORLD

After the emergence of the fast Finns and a Latin explosion detonated by young Zabala in California, it was those islands associated with the land of the Rising Sun on the other side of the planet that next stunned the marathon-running world. The Japanese, and the Koreans, were proving more than adept at meeting the challenge of great distance running and by the mid-1930s they were proving to be a match for anyone. Europe, or the United States, were still seen as the traditional benchmark environments for setting standards and records, and the sporting communities of both continents were shocked in 1935 when it was announced from Tokyo that, on 3 April, an athlete called Yasuo Ikenaka had completed the classic distance in a time of 2 hours, 26 minutes and 44 seconds. The previous known record at the time was believed to have been set by Albert Michelsen who had recorded a best time of 2:29:02 at Port Chester, in New York, nearly ten years earlier on 12 October 1925. Prior to him, the marathon record belonged to Hannes Kolehmainen of Finland following his triumph in Antwerp in 1920. However, little known to many, another Japanese runner, Fushashige Suzuki, had lowered that mark by more than a minute only a few days earlier, on 31 March, also in Tokyo, when he clocked a time of 2:27:49. That the Japanese could produce two world-record marathon runs in a matter of days was astonishing enough, but when a man known as Kitei Son, in Japanese colours, but a natural-born Korean, trimmed the record by two-hundredths of a second later in the year, on 3 November, in Tokyo, astonishment turned to open-mouthed amazement. This man was really Sohn Kee Chung, born at Sinjiju, in Korea, on 29 August 1914, and he was to be one of the greatest marathon runners of his or any other age. In 1936, while Europe was preparing for another marathon of military conflict, the axis of athleticism was also on the move. By New Year's Day 1936, seven of the all-time top ten fastest marathons were run by Japanese athletes, or at least runners in Japanese colours.

In 1933, of course, Adolf Hitler had begun his rise to supreme power after being appointed Chancellor of Germany on 30 January. The Reichstag was set ablaze on 27 February, events began to accelerate towards inevitable military conflict and the scheduling of the Olympic Games for Berlin, in 1936, was trapped in this black decade of world history. Assassinations followed assassinations as the Nazis marched across Europe, Hitler became Dictator in 1934, Italy began war with Abyssinia, the League of Nations began ineffectual economic sanctions, all in 1935, and, in 1936, while Edward VIII came to the throne and then chose to abdicate after reigning for only 325 days, Addis Ababa was occupied by the Italians, the Rhineland was remilitarised and Spain was split by Civil War. It was inevitable that the Olympic Games of 1936 would be strained by these events. In fact, they were the most politically charged in history, grasped by Hitler, who allowed the organisers and the IOC a free hand in making the administrative decisions as a propaganda opportunity the like of which had never been seen before. He wanted to demonstrate the physical and athletic superiority of the 'master race', the Aryans.

The IOC had granted the Games to Berlin, long before Hitler's rise to power and infamy in 1931. By 1936, much had changed beyond recognition. Spain's Olympics team had to be recalled because of the Civil War. Japan had invaded Manchuria, Italy was marching across North Africa, Hitler was spreading anti-Semitism and Ayran supremacy everywhere he went as he led a Nazi assault on virtually anything in his path. The IOC insisted, against Hitler's personal wishes, that Jews be allowed to compete in the Games and the fascist dictator complied, concentrating instead on showing off the talents and strengths of the 'master race'. Little was spared in this. Hitler had a massive Olympic development built, a stadium for 110,000 spectators, and planned for the eternal flame to be carried by a relay of runners from Athens to the vast auditorium. It was the first time this had happened. In another act that was both thrilling and horrifying to lovers of the marathon, the great, now 64-year-old, Spiridon Louis, winner of the first Olympic marathon in 1896, offered the Fuhrer an olive branch from the sacred grove of Zeus at Olympia. Worse still, for those who loved the tradition of the classic marathon and Greek mythology, but who hated all that Hitler and the Nazis represented, Louis graced the episode further by wearing the same costume, a traditional Greek uniform, that he had worn to the King of Greece's breakfast all those years before. How utterly horrendous it was to learn in the years that followed that not only did Hitler show nothing but contempt for Louis's olive branch, but he also massacred many Berlin Olympic Games medal winners in the Holocaust that was to follow.

If Louis' misplaced gesture was to be lost, however, the Games as a whole and the marathon in particular managed to produce another reflection of the way in which the unquenchable spirit of humanity could overcome all kinds of political and military repression and shine through. It was planned, by Hitler, to be the Games for his chosen demonstration of supremacy in a stadium filled with Germans, with superb organisation, facilities and atmosphere. (In the village, Martin and Gynn reported, there were saunas for the Finns, steam baths for the Japanese, separate kitchens to specialise in different cuisines and even wine on the dinner table for the French.) But instead of blond Ayrans dominating, and gleaming, it was the visitors of other colours and creeds whose exploits championed the claims of the underdogs, the victims of repression and tyranny. And, in the marathon, above all other events, this glorious echo of uprising against evil was manifested by the running of the great record-breaking Korean Sohn Kee Chung, the man who was forced to wear Japanese colours and uniforms. Sohn's marathon triumph was as great a signal of defiance and triumph as was the unforgettable sprinting and jumping of the black American athlete Jesse Owens, who won four gold medals.

The marathon was run, in hot and sunny afternoon conditions, on Sunday 9 August, starting and finishing in the Olympic Stadium either side of a trail out into the countryside on a course that followed the shaded asphalt roadway known as the Havelchaussee, next to Lake Havel . There were 56 runners entered from 27 different nations. The favourites included the defending champion, Zabala of Argentina, most of the Finnish team as always and the great, but as yet little-known or understood, Sohn.

There, in Germany, in the Nazi amphitheatre created by Hitler, he was made to run under a false Japanese name, Kitei Son. This was placed on the official entry list though Sohn himself, when he signed the Olympic register, according to Lovell, used his real name and added a sketched map of Korea next to it to ensure people knew who he was and where he was from. He also became friends with Owens.

The great man was his greatest supporter when the starter's gun was fired. Zabala, who had been training in Berlin for three months, ran into the lead. Content to bide his time, Sohn fell into last position and worked his way forward gently. After six miles, he ran with the elegant British runner Ernie Harper, whose contorted face was in contrast to the rest of his appearance.

Zabala, who built up a lead of more than ninety seconds, began to struggle after nine miles and, though he recovered by the fifteen-mile mark, he found it more and more difficult in the later stages. After seventeen miles, Sohn and then Harper passed him. Zabala, exhausted by his own pace, fell, recovered, ran on, but was unable to sustain a competitive speed. Soon afterwards, he retired, leaving Sohn to ease away at the front, run quickly into the stadium and complete his marathon with a sprint that saw him finish the final 100 yards in 12 seconds. Harper finished two minutes behind him, his own shoes filled with a blood from the wound left by a burst blister. Sohn's time was an Olympic record: 2 hours, 29 minutes and 19.2 seconds. Another Korean, Nam Sung Yong, was third, after resisting the efforts of the Finns. This meant two Koreans stood, in Japanese colours, on the podium, and they both bowed their heads to signal their private protest and shame when the Japanese anthem was played and the Japanese flag was raised in their honour. For Sohn, it was torture, an experience he could barely tolerate; but he was to return to the Olympic arena again in 1948, after the war was over, when he carried the flag of South Korea in the opening ceremonies in London; and, again, in 1988, when he was a member of the local committee that helped take the Games to Seoul. By this time aged 76, he carried the eternal flame of the Olympics on its final leg in the stadium in front of a worldwide television audience and thousands of emotional, weeping countrymen. In that final lap, he helped erase a personal nightmare that had lived with him for 52 years.

For the rest of the world, the nightmare was just beginning too; the outbreak of war between Britain and Germany was finally declared from 5 p.m. on 3 September 1939, but it had been clear for months and years that military conflict was inevitable. The 1940 Olympic Games had been given to Tokyo, but by 1938 it was apparent that the Japanese were much too occupied with their war in China to dedicate any energy, time of investment, let alone men, for the purpose of hosting the Games. They declined and, instead, the Games were awarded to Helsinki. By 1940, the Finnish capital's plans were also cancelled as World War Two made all contemplation of sport impossible. The 1944 Games, scheduled originally to be in London, were also called off, but a year later, when the fighting finally ended, the IOC met and agreed that the next Games, for 1948, should be held in the British capital city. It was agreed that this was an appropriate decision as the Games would signal for London, as they had for Antwerp in 1920, the restoration of peace in the blitzed remains of the English spirit's home city.

The old Olympic stadium, the White City Stadium, had been destroyed by German bombs, there was controlled rationing and little money available (but abundant goodwill) and the weather was as dismal as so often can be the case in an English summer. Yet London still managed to stage a memorable Games event lit up by the unforgettable running of the thirty-year-old Dutch mother and housewife Fanny Blankers-Koen, who won four gold medals in nine days. Wembley Stadium, converted to be used for the athletics events, housed 85,000 keen spectators, including King George VI at the opening ceremonies, and a village for the athletes was hastily created in the barracks of the Royal Air Force. German and Japanese teams were not present: they had not been invited because of their aggressor status in the war. The conditions were imperfect, the recent history sombre, but the enthusiasm of the participants and public ensured that even in such times of austerity there was a place for the Olympic ideals and for life to go on. For marathon fans, too, there were two special reasons to remember these London Games: the first sighting of a young man called Emil Zatopek, 27, a lieutenant in the army of Czechoslovakia who was to go out on the track and win the gold medal in the 10,000 metres and the silver in the 5,000 metres; and the marathon race itself, in which the bronze-medal winner Etienne Gailly, 21, from Belgium, a former paratrooper who was involved in the final triumphant assaults on Germany in the war, was cheered to the line as he staggered and fell, reviving memories of that famous Italian Dorando Pietri from the fables of the 1908 Games, forty years before.

Gailly, one of the 41 starters from 21 nations who went to the line that cloudy and windy Saturday afternoon on 7 August 1948, had never previously run a marathon. Yet such was his confidence that he took an early lead and then ran as if he knew what he was doing. He had made a promise to himself before the start that, if he was still standing when he reached the finish, he would win a medal. This, therefore, meant he had to run relatively fast to be competitive on the looping out-and-back run from Wembley Stadium to Elstree and Radlett. After fifteen miles, he led comfortably by nearly a minute, but then he hit what long-distance runners describe as 'the wall'. By twenty miles, he was being passed by Yoon Chil Choi of Korea and then Delfo Cabrera, a 29-year-old fireman from Argentina, also in his first marathon, keen to emulate the feats of his compatriot Zabala in Los Angeles in 1932. He had won at 1,500 metres and at 10,000 metres, but was untried at the longest distance of all. Another Argentinian, Eusebio Guinez, ran in fourth place and closed on the staggering Gailly, the spectators' favourite.

As the race wore on, the drama intensified. Choi retired, Cabrera led, Guinez was passed by a Welshman, Tom Richards, 38, and the crowd was enthralled. As they approached the stadium, Gailly summoned energy from somewhere to regain the lead and pull fifty yards clear. But the Belgian was running on empty, close to collapse and seemed utterly exhausted as he reeled around his final lap. Carbrera, still moving with consistency, entered the stadium and closed the gap, agonisingly for everyone involved; and then he passed the poor Belgian and won. His was to be the first of three successive Olympic marathon victories by men running at the distance for the first time, Zatopek achieving the feat in 1952 and Alain Mimoun in 1956. Richards, who worked as a nurse, arrived next and did much the same, to take the silver medal, leaving the staggering Gailly to call upon only the energy supplied by the crowd's vocal chords to move on and on. With 50 yards remaining, however, he fell, but somehow fought back and made it to the finish whereupon he was surrounded by medical assistants and taken away on a stretcher, too dehydrated to attend the subsequent ceremony. He had a bronze medal and the memories of Dorando Pietri, who was disqualified after receiving assistance in 1908, were at least partially expunged.

The Times of London reported the entire episode the following day. The article described how

a figure fully as tragic as Dorando's emerged from the tunnel. It was the Belgian, Gailly, so sore of foot and weary of leg and soul that he could hardly make any progress at all. Suddenly, quite close behind him, appeared another figure, that of the strongly built Cabrera, who doubtless was tired, too, but looking a fresh and lively sprinter by comparison. The Argentinean passed his man in a few strides and set off to complete a lap that must have seemed like five miles or more to the poor tottering Belgian. No more than twenty seconds later came the loudly and justly cheered arrival of Richards – a pleasant surprise indeed for most people. Richards had little pace, but he easily passed poor Gailly in the back-stretch and lessened by a little the original fifty yards between himself and Cabrera. Richards finished only sixteen seconds behind the winner. Gailly once very nearly pulled up dazed and hopeless with the appalling distance of sixty yards still between him and the tape. Already other gallant runners were appearing, and it was in no grudging spirit that one breathed again when Gailly at long last staggered into third place. He then collapsed and was carried off on a stretcher.

Exhausted, yes, but proud; he had done what he set out to do.

he running man: Emile Zatopek on his way to winning the 1952 Olympic marathon.
Empics

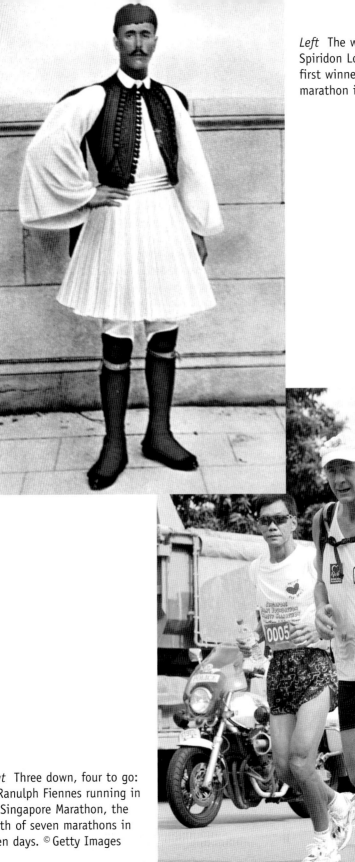

Left The water carrier: Spiridon Louis of Greece, the first winner of the Olympic marathon in 1896. © Empics

Right Three down, four to go: Sir Ranulph Fiennes running in the Singapore Marathon, the fourth of seven marathons in seven days. © Getty Images

Above A royal farewell: spectators at Windsor Castle watch runners set off in the marathon in the London Olympics in 1908. © Popperfoto

Right Running in shackles: Korean Sohn Kee Chung was forced to run under the name Kitei Son by the Japanese occupiers of his country in the 1936 Berlin marathon. © Empics

Left Record-setter: Englishman Jim Peters broke the marathon world record in London in 1951 with a time of 2:20.42. © Getty Images

Below Sportsmanship: Australian Ron Clarke, seen here lighting the Olympic flame at the 1956 Olympics, and his compatriot John Landy were immortalised in a statue that stands in Melbourne. © Getty Images

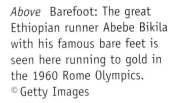

Above Barefoot: The great Ethiopian runner Abebe Bikila with his famous bare feet is seen here running to gold in the 1960 Rome Olympics.
© Getty Images

Left Gold collectors: Mamo Wolde a compatriot of Bikila cements Ethiopia's achievement in long-distance running with gold in the 1968 Mexico Olympics. © Empics

Strength in numbers: Norway's dominance of women's running was confirmed when Ingrid Kristiansen broke the women's world record at the London Marathon in 1985. © Empics

Left Good times: London has seen several world record breakers including the current holder of the men's record, Khalid Khannouchi.
© Getty Images

Below Golden girl: Bedford's Paula Radcliffe, seen here setting the women's world record in London in 2003, is set to try her luck at the Athens Olympics.
© Getty Images.

15. PRAGUE – SOURCE OF STAMINA, HOME OF HEROES

Few visitors to Prague, the capital of the modern Czech Republic, can possibly stroll unmoved through the ancient streets of delightful architecture and brooding atmosphere that have made it a popular destination for modern low-price, no-frills tourists. After the attractions of the beer and the beautiful buildings, they enjoy the place for what it is: an intriguing and historic city, filled with art and redolent of another age. These days, of course, most of the visitors enjoying the trappings of a rapidly expanding tourism industry that serves the city will be aware of the darker days that preceded the present mood of optimism as they look down at the River Vltava, enjoy the picturesque scenery and soak up the culture of a place beloved by its inhabitants, but few will understand them. The Czech Republic, after all, is one of those countries locked away in eastern Europe, a landlocked republic bordered by Germany, Poland, Slovakia and Austria, a place that was for too long perceived to be just another state buried in the impenetrable tracts of Europe that lay beyond the Iron Curtain.

Today, as the new Europe celebrates the freedom that has come with the twenty-first century, the Czechs are happy too; their land, which comprises the former provinces of Bohemia, Silesia and Moravia, became free and independent in 1993 when the former Czechoslovakia, created in 1918, was dissolved. The Czechs threw aside their inhibitions and chains and regained their identity as an indigenous race with a population of around eleven million people. Economic freedom followed, prosperity beckoned, as did the European Union. The end of the twentieth century, for the citizens of Prague and the people of the Czech Republic, was very different from its core, the years after the Second World War when, as the Czechoslovak Socialist Republic (CSSR), their nation was under the heel of a wider military power.

Then, suffocated by socialism, the Czechs were impoverished and restricted, unhappy and repressed. They could not live as they pleased, but had to go out and find their freedom and personal exhilaration in the oldest senses available. For Emil Zatopek, this meant playing in the streets, acting as the family messenger and running: chasing the geese, fetching sandwiches and racing his friends. He did not know he was the fastest boy around. Nor that he was to become the greatest long-distance runner of all time. Nor would he know, in the future, that a statue of him was to stand above the lake and guard the gates to glory. Zatopek, winner of the 1952 Olympic Games marathon in Helsinki, was born in the small northern Moravian village of Koprivnice on 19 September 1922. His wife, Dana, also an Olympic gold medallist in Helsinki, was born on the same day. The coincidences that existed in their lives together were as extraordinary as the story of the man himself and his achievements. Zatopek, making profit from his talents, rose to exemplify all the best qualities of sport and the Olympic ideals, using his gifts to inspire others and give joy. He was a man of humility and greatness.

His achievements came from within him, from his own hard work. He was the son of a carpenter, from a poor family, and he expected nothing from life. Instead, he gave all he could. He worked in a shoe factory as a young man before joining the Czech Army. He enjoyed the discipline and opportunities for sport in his military life and rose to take the rank of lieutenant colonel. He adored running, a fact he discovered in his childhood; his talent, he found more accidentally. By the time he won the marathon at Helsinki, at his first attempt at the distance, within days of winning both the 10,000 metres and the 5,000 metres, he was already a supreme distance athlete; he held records at 10 miles, 10,000 metres, 20 kilometres and the 'one-hour run'. In all, he set 17 world records at different distances from 5,000 metres to 30,000 metres. Between 1949 and 1952, he built up a series of 69 successive victories in races over 5,000 or 10,000 metres; he was invincible. Only the original Flying Finn Paavo Nurmi can stand next to him in that special hall of fame known as the home of the greatest runners of the twentieth century.

In *Athens to Athens*, his comprehensive history of the Olympic Games and the IOC, David Miller wrote, 'Zatopek was a phenomenon not just for his records and medals, but also for his extreme modesty. His willpower burned intensely, yet outwardly he was throughout his life so unassuming that it was difficult to correlate the man and the athlete.' His life reflected this; a great man of huge athletic achievements, he was as modest as any passing everyman in his civilian and daily life. The reasons are manifold and yet difficult to fathom; in short, he was an exceptional human being from an unexceptional background.

'In our family,' he told Miller,

I had a good reputation – as a fast messenger. Even my teacher knew that and used to send me to bring him a ham sandwich. I also have happy memories of our grey Chinese geese, which were wonderful house-guards. Our postman dared to deliver the mail only to our garden gate. Once he had his trousers almost torn off by them when he overstepped the boundary. I became very friendly with the geese because they used to love to run and to fly. I used secretly to open the gate to let them out and then start to run like mad down the road, calling them after me. They joyfully followed me and I could hear the patter of their feet, a humming sound overhead and, suddenly, with necks outstretched, there they were airborne. Like this they accompanied me for several hundred metres to the end of our street and they must have enjoyed the fun as much as I did because they made a habit of waiting at our garden gate for me to return from school. My mother was worried that the geese were not fattening quickly. When she heard about our fun and games, she soon put a stop to it, saying: 'Geese are for fattening and for laying eggs, not taking part in athletic events.'

So began the brilliant career of Zatopek – racing geese for fun in the streets. His speed was to be discovered soon afterwards, while he was still a child, when his friends measured out a racing circuit of approximately a kilometre around their homes. The challenge went out to anyone who could run the distance, at speed, without stopping. By the time Zatopek was completing his third lap, there were no rivals left standing, or moving. 'The boys stared at me,' he told Miller. 'And then one of them said, "You were running like Nurmi!" It was the first time that I had heard his name.' It was prophetic, too.

By the time he was fourteen, Zatopek was working in the Bata shoe factory at Zlin. He was alone and often lonely. It was there, to while away the hours, that he began to run more in earnest. It was running for pleasure and he disappeared for two or three kilometres to wipe away the hours. He built up speed. By the time he was eighteen, he was an unknown runner of great potential who had never even seen an athletics track. Then, in 1941, aged nineteen, he was requested to run in a race through Zlin. 'I did it with reluctance, but I finished second,' Zatopek recalled. 'People applauded during the race, too, and that affected me. All of a sudden, I felt more important than normal and that is how it all started for me.' His use of the word reluctance is almost ironic; according to various reports, he tried his utmost to avoid this race, which was more of a mass cross-country than anything else. He even went to see the doctor claiming he had a dislocated knee, an idea he had dreamed up with unsuccessful results.

The runner in Zatopek took over his life. He joined a club, he ran regularly, he trained and he competed. Success followed. By the end of the Second World War, he was the Czech record-holder of 5,000 and 10,000 metres and eligible for the London Games in 1948. 'I didn't want to lose this chance,' he told Miller. 'I was practising even during the night with interval running, which at that time was a very unusual schedule. I was driven by the thought that I would meet the best in the world, but my main motivation was not to make a disgrace of myself.' His fears were ungrounded, of course. He won a gold and a silver medal in London and found doors opening to a wider world, a different public with different opportunities. His win in the 10,000 metres made him the first Czech ever to win an Olympic gold medal. He awoke, too, to the Olympic ideals that he found suited his own and an ambition to continue and succeed again. In Helsinki, of course, he did that emphatically, revelling in his supremacy, but with modesty and a marvellous grasp of the spirit of the event. Shortly before the Olympic Games in Sydney in 2000, the year in which he died, Zatopek echoed his feelings of earlier times when he said, 'The Games in Sydney will be the gateway to the new century. Let's hope that this marvellous world event will sustain sport's motivation, the principles of fair play and the warmth of worldwide friendship.'

Zatopek the athlete was, of course, also Zatopek the soldier and a man of great principle. He was also a man of iron discipline and resolve, someone who not only felt and thought strongly on many issues, but obeyed his heart and acted upon it. When the Soviet

Union's tanks trundled into Prague in the spring of 1968 to quash the democratic uprising led by Alexander Dubcek, the premier of the time, and the student martyr Jan Palac, who burned himself to death, Zatopek protested. He signed the 2000 Words Manifesto, supporting freedom. He felt he had to, but the price he paid was heavy. He was dismissed as a senior army officer, expelled from the Communist Party and sent to the Bohemian uranium mines for six years. He had suggested that the Soviet Union should have been barred from taking part in the Mexico City Games of 1968. It was an act of typical courage and principle from Zatopek, and not his first. In 1952 he stood up for a point of principle and almost did not make it to the Helsinki Games, an act that might have deprived the marathon of its greatest winner of all. As it happened, he and Stanislav Jungwirth, whose father was a political activist and opponent of the Soviet Union, were both able to travel after Zatopek had protested that 'if he does not go, then nor do I'. It was a timely and sensible decision by the authorities.

Zatopek stood firm when he felt it was necessary. He expected nothing for it but the satisfaction of doing what was right and the pleasure he gained from helping others. Modest, almost to a fault, he admitted that he was 'not very talented' and, as a boy, 'never imagined he would succeed'. His running carried him to freedom and made history. By 1944, during the ravages of the war, he had to borrow tennis shoes to run. Cynics in Prague, later to be so proud of their compatriot's achievements, found it difficult to believe that a Moravian runner was breaking the records that were so revered in Bohemia.

In 1952, the Helsinki year, Zatopek had to overcome ill health at the start of his running season before he went on and completed the dazzling treble of 5,000 and 10,000 metres and then the marathon. His win in the 5,000 metres came on the same day that his wife Dana won gold in the javelin. This magical day was the one that helped create the story in which, it was said, Zatopek chose to enter the marathon only because he wanted to re-establish male superiority in his home. Those close to Zatopek always said it was a forlorn hope. Dana was always in charge. To those who had questioned his ability, earlier in his career, Zatopek's win was a lesson in astute observation. Often, it was said that because he ran as if in agony, or on the edge of collapsing, his head rolling, his face contorted, his body and his shoulders hunched (but his legs flowing perfectly across the ground), he was not capable of becoming a great champion. They were wrong. It was just the Zatopek style. Asked many years later about this, it was reported that he replied, 'I was not talented enough to run and smile at the same time.'

His clever use of language and his sense of humour could not disguise an intelligent man, adept at languages who, after his banishment, was recalled by the Ministry of Sport in Prague and asked to translate sports periodicals in a search for tips from foreign coaches that would improve their domestic runners. He was effectively a sports spy, as said by David Wallechinsky. He stayed in this job until he retired in 1982, leaving a legacy of love and goodwill behind. His rivals, his competitors and his many friends all spoke with one voice when the man from Czechoslovakia was mentioned. His nicknames were forgotten. He was a sincere and genuine sportsman, a great Olympian and a true champion. To call him 'the beast of Prague' does him and the city a disservice. His feats are now recalled in reverence by any athlete and every runner. In 1990, following the fall of communism, Zatopek was reinstated in the Czech Army and the defence minister apologised to him for the way he had been treated 22 years earlier. Prague, where he lived for so long, deserves to be remembered, too, as the home of the Czechs' great man, whose statue stands proudly over Lac Leman in Switzerland.

When he died, aged 78, on 22 November 2000, in a military hospital in Prague, following a virus complicated by pneumonia and a weak heart, according to the BBC, there were tears around the world. He had been taken into hospital after suffering a stroke on 30 October. Lamine Diack, president of the International Amateur Athletic Federation, led the tributes. 'Emil Zatopek was one of my youthful heroes and still today his story stands as an example for all those who start a career in sport,' he said.

'I wanted to win every time I was on the track,' Zatopek told his biographers, in quotes attributed to him in the many obituaries that followed. 'At Helsinki, I was tired after the 10,000m race, but I still shattered all my rivals.' Diach added, 'Emil Zatopek knew the greatest triumphs and the greatest suffering and that is what will keep him as an eternal symbol of athletics.' It is no surprise that Prague is now home to one of the warmest of all the big international city marathons in the world. On the website, the home page spells it out.

'Welcome to the website of Prague International Marathon – the world's most international marathon, with two-thirds of runners coming from 55 different countries. PIM's marathon course is also the seventh fastest and one of the most beautiful in the world.' Friendship through sport was always one of Zatopek's great beliefs, for everyone in the world. It is a fitting tribute to him that the Prague marathon works on the same principle.

16. HISTORY 8 – A NEW WORLD ORDER, HELSINKI TO MELBOURNE

What if the man who guards the gates of glory had never kept his most famous rendezvous? Emil Zatopek came within a hair's breadth of not going to the 1952 Olympic Games. Approaching thirty, the Czech Army officer was not only iron willed in his running, but a man of some moral steel as well. When a fellow athlete, scheduled to compete in the 1,500 metres, was omitted from the Czech team on the grounds that his anti-communist father was a political prisoner, Zatopek opted to make a stand and stay home with the man he believed should be his Olympic team-mate. Faced by a public backlash over the possible non-appearance of Czechoslovakia's greatest medal hope, the authorities capitulated 48 hours later. Emil Zatopek was free, after all, to go running into history.

Zatopek would later describe the marathon at those Helsinki Olympics as 'the easiest victory of my career'. The words were not meant to sound arrogant, for the man who spoke them never had an arrogant bone in his body. They were a simple statement of fact. That Zatopek's first-ever marathon was also the blue ribbon event of the Games of the XVth Olympiad in Helsinki in 1952 merely underlines the magnitude of the Czech's achievement. The man who would become known as the 'Human Locomotive' surprised all and sundry with his gold medal in the 10,000 metres in the London Games of 1948, to which he added silver over half that distance. But in Helsinki, home to perhaps the greatest long-distance running tradition of the twentieth century, Zatopek, who was, in Tom Callahan's memorable description, 'a balding Czech about the size of a parking meter', performed the feat that sent a seismic rumble through the running world.

There could have been no more fitting stage for Zatopek's finest hour. The Finnish capital was the smallest city ever to host the Games, its population well under the 400,000 mark at that time. But it was a perfect venue for its day and hosted a record 69 nations, including the Soviet Union, taking part for the first time since the Russian Revolution in 1917, and 4,925 athletes. The wonderful

70,000-capacity stadium that had been built in the forests north of the city was finally put to use, twelve years after it had been built for the cancelled 1940 Games. Fears that the Games would be over-shadowed by the 'cold war' tensions of the time were utterly unfounded as the athletes all mixed happily, the Soviet participants going so far as to invite the Americans into their separated Olympic compound, away from the village and close to their military base. It was a small triumph for the enlightened decision to take the Games to Finland, the nation from which had come two of the finest runners of all time. One was the 'Flying Finn' himself, Paavo Nurmi, a two-time winner of Olympic gold in the 10,000 metres and favourite for the marathon in Los Angeles in 1932, until he was suspended days before the event over an alleged infringement on his expenses. The other was Hannes Kolehmainen, winner of the Olympic Marathon in Antwerp in 1920 in a then-world record time of 2:32:35. It was a wonderful prelude to Zatopek's performance when Nurmi ran into the stadium as the last man in the torchbearers' relay, and handed it to Kolehmainen to ignite the flame that signalled the start of the Helsinki Games.

Inspired, perhaps, by his surroundings, and fuelled by his own insatiable appetite for running, in an eight-day spell Zatopek first retained his 10,000-metre title on Sunday 20 July by a comfortable margin; in the middle of the first week of the Games he then improved on his London effort by claiming a second Olympic title in a sprint finish to the 5,000 metres. This meant he had equalled the great Kolehmainen's performance in the Games of 1912, also staged in Scandinavia. (It meant also that, in a mood of elation and generosity, he could afford to lend his cherished gold medal to his wife Dana who was about to take part in the javelin competition; she took it from him, put it in her bag and then set an Olympic record of her own with her first throw and won her own gold medal on the same day.) But that was not enough. On the second Sunday in Helsinki, a warm afternoon on 27 July, Zatopek ambled to the start line to try his hand at the supreme distance alongside such giants of the marathon as then-world-record holder Jim Peters of Great Britain. Peters would go on to win undying sympathy from a stunned audience at the 1954 British Empire Games in Vancouver, where his dehydrated, exhausted frame tottered desper-ately in search of an illusory tape. On Sunday 27 July 1952, sympathy was in short measure, especially from the running machine who set off at his side.

So innocent of marathon technique was the man from Czechoslovakia that he had decided the best course of action was to shadow the best – at that time unquestionably Peters, whose world-best mark of 2:20:42 had been achieved in London just six weeks earlier. Finding the great man's running number in the newspaper, Zatopek ambled over, introduced himself and stuck with Peters over the first half of the course, another out-and-back run into the countryside to the north. The exact words that passed between them are unclear. Some sources say that Zatopek, concerned at how easy this all seemed, asked Peters if the pace was too slow, and that the Englishman, perhaps stunned by the question, was so taken aback he tried to pull a fast one on the upstart by agreeing that it was. 'Too slow?' repeated Zatopek, seeking confirmation. When it came, he went, leaving Peters in his wake, eventually to retire with cramp. The only man to try and stay with Zatopek was Sweden's Gustaf Jansson. Zatopek watched with interest as Jansson paused to eat a lemon on the way. 'If he goes faster, I will eat two at the next drinks stop,' he told himself. No need: the Swede ran out of steam while a zestful Zatopek cruised home to victory in a new Olympic record time of 2:23:03.2, the cheers of a wildly enthusiastic crowd ringing in his ears as the scale of his unprecedented achievement hit home.

Zatopek may have spurned those mid-race lemons, but when the second man eventually made it into the stadium the Czech was waiting for him at the line with a refreshing slice of orange. It was Argentine Reinaldo Gorno, gallantly following in the 1948 footsteps of his marathon-winning compatriot Delfo Cabrera, who would finish sixth in Helsinki. Zatopek had destroyed Cabrera's 1948 Olympic gold-winning time by almost twelve minutes, and Sohn Kee Chung's existing Olympic record, established in Berlin, by more than six, so Gorno's feat in being just two and a half minutes adrift of the new champion comes into startling perspective in its own right. Third, a further 32 seconds behind, was the plucky Jansson.

'It is at the borders of pain and suffering that the men are separated from the boys,' Zatopek once claimed. His grimacing features, the head rolling from side to side as if in agony, the pumping action of his arms as his legs produced the relentless pitter-patter of his short but unstoppable stride, meant Zatopek more clearly than any other man epitomised the pain and suffering inherent in great athletic feats. 'My running was very simple,' he insisted. 'It was out of myself.' Self-taught, discipline drilled into him by incessant cross-country work in Nazi-occupied Czechoslovakia during the war, Zatopek simply ran. And ran. And ran. In stiff combat boots, part of his Czech Army issue, that meant his feet would feel lighter when he actually came to the track. Zatopek put to his own use some of the interval-training methods Nurmi himself had employed. A typical routine would involve five 200-metre sprints at an average 34 seconds; twenty – sometimes more – 400-metre dashes in a window between 75 and 90 seconds, all with a 200-metre recovery jog between, and he would log up over 100 miles a week. As Christopher Chataway, who famously fell in Helsinki, would later say, 'Zatopek was invincible. His training was a world away from what we were doing . . .'

Emil Zatopek claimed world records at distances from 5,000 to 30,000 metres. In 1951 he became the first man to run twenty kilometres inside an hour, a landmark from which he drew encouragement for his 1952 assault on Olympic marathon gold. 'The marathon is not a very difficult race,' he later maintained. 'Other races are all about speed. The marathon is all about rate of recovery. Having the one-hour record, I thought I might do all right.' Never, surely, did the art of understatement come so naturally to any man. Small wonder, then, that the man who guards the gates of glory drew glowing tributes on his death in 2000. Lamine Diack, IAAF President at the time, summed it up in one short phrase when he referred to Zatopek as 'an eternal symbol of athletics'. Small wonder, either, that four-time gold medalist and first-time marathon winner Zatopek himself said, 'The Olympics are the one true time.'

Zatopek's Helsinki achievements did not go unnoticed by the visiting Australians, Percy Cerutty – Herb Elliott's famous coach – among them. So impressed were they, and so dismayed by the absence of a marathon tradition in their native land, that they set up the Victorian Marathon Club to remedy the situation. One of the men to benefit was future Olympian Ron Clarke. As we shall see, Clarke shared some of Zatopek's views on the development of the sport. In 1990, for example, Zatopek looked back on his own time. 'If there is luxury,' he observed, 'there is the danger of degeneration. Sit behind the wheel of a car and a man gains time, but loses condition.

There was no car. I ran instead. Look at the distance champions today: they are mostly Africans, runners from underdeveloped countries. They are not softened by luxury.'

So concerned was Zatopek about becoming soft in his advancing years as a runner that he decided he must up the rate of his strength work. The Locomotive took on a passenger – literally. Desperate to build up his legs, Zatopek ran with his wife Dina on his shoulders. The inevitable happened: before the 1956 Olympic Games, the reigning triple champion had to undergo surgery for a hernia. But he was determined to run in Melbourne. For one thing, he had another rendezvous to keep.

In 1946, as travel became marginally less difficult in post-war Europe, Zatopek had made a visit to Algeria. There he met and befriended a local athlete by the name of Maimoun Okacha. A decade later, the two were due to enjoy their latest meeting, on the marathon course in Melbourne. By then the Algerian had become officially French. His name was now Gallicised to Alain Mimoun. They were old adversaries: had Zatopek not beaten Mimoun to Olympic gold on three occasions already? But in 1956, as the Olympics left their northern-hemisphere sanctuary and went 'Down Under' for the first time, Zatopek's days of running into history were over.

He nearly didn't keep this rendezvous either, this time through no action of his own. In the first place, Melbourne had won the right to break new Olympic ground by just one vote from Buenos Aires. In the second, there was a small wave of political protest in that momentous year for international politics: the Soviet Union's invasion of Hungary saw nations like Spain, Switzerland and the Netherlands stay away from the Games, as sport once more became the whipping boy for failed diplomacy; the crisis over the Suez Canal meant Egypt, Lebanon and Iraq also boycotted the Games in protest over British intervention in the region; and the People's Republic of China stayed home in a huff because the Republic of China, otherwise known as Taiwan, was going to the Games.

If there was a false start to the Games of the XVIth Olympiad, there was another one in the marathon as the 46 competitors from 23 nations lined up. Two factors seemed to operate in Mimoun's favour, even though he, like Zatopek, was making the Olympic marathon his first. One was the searing Melbourne heat: 102 Fahrenheit, or almost 39 degrees Celsius: surely a man from North Africa would fare better than most in such extreme conditions? The other was his strategy, which was beautiful in its simplicity: start fast and keep accelerating. The plan worked. Mimoun first kept pace with the front runners, then made the decisive break just before half distance as the course took the field uphill. Soon he was almost a minute ahead; by the end he was 92 seconds in front of the then Yugoslavia's Franjo Mihalic, who in turn had a comfortable 75-second cushion over bronze medalist Veikko Karvonen. The latter had improved two places on his Helsinki run, though his pace was a minute slower than on his home soil. Runners from eight different nations filled the top eight spots, Zatopek coming home a rather dazed sixth – four and a half minutes behind the man he had so often beaten for Olympic gold. And thereby hangs a tale, which Ron Clarke will tell us in the chapter that follows. Of the man who was such an inspiration to him, Clarke also said, 'I loved his personality, his willingness to help: he was enthusiastic, he was cheerful – all virtues that rank very highly with me.'

Alain Mimoun went on to become a semi-permanent fixture at the head of French marathon running, capable of 2:34 even as a quinquagenarian. When Paris was making her bid for the 2008 Games the proudly patriotic little man from Algeria was a central figure, happily waving the *tricolore* whose lustre he had enhanced half a century before. Mimoun had to overcome pain and suffering of his own, inflicted not by a punitive schedule like Zatopek's, but by enemy forces at Monte Cassino in World War Two, his legs still showing the scars. Mimoun, the man who changed his name, had managed to reinforce one marathon tradition and begin another: a sequence of French successes going back to turn-of-the-century Paris and Michel Théato and continuing with El Quafi in 1928 in Amsterdam, and the North African record, no less impressive, that would span the decades from his own great victory to the next great Olympiad 'Down Under', when Gezahgne Abera won the marathon for Ethiopia. For now, though, another Olympic phenomenon was just over the horizon. His name was Abebe Bikila.

17. MELBOURNE – 'THE PAST IS A FOREIGN COUNTRY . . .'

There is not one running man, but two, in the sports precinct at the heart of the great sporting city of Melbourne. They, too, are sculpted to perfection, and the statue has a close link to the man who guards the gates of glory in Lausanne. To be accurate, at the moment captured by sculptor Mitch Mitchell, neither man is actually running. For one has fallen and the other, fearful that he may have caused him injury, has turned back to help him to his feet. The stricken runner is Ron Clarke, who on that March day in 1956 was already world junior record-holder for the mile. The man assisting him is John Landy: yes, the same Landy who had famously lost the 'Miracle Mile' in the Empire Games in Vancouver two years before, looking over his left shoulder for Roger Bannister as the Englishman surged past him on the right to claim the gold.

In Melbourne's Olympic year of 1956 Landy and Clarke were out front in the Australian Championships, a world record clearly in their sights. Then, as the third lap ended, Alec Henderson tried to force his way through on the inside. Clarke caught his heel and stumbled to the cinder track. Hurdling his fallen rival, Landy raked Clarke's shoulder with his spikes as he went past. Within a few yards Landy stopped, turned back, helped Clarke to his feet, dusted him down and apologised. With the field now 60 yards away, Landy, the man they said had no finish, produced a searing sprint that carried him through the tape in first place in a time of 4 minutes, 4.02 seconds. What if he had not given up those precious seconds? No matter: both men, Clarke and Landy, were running into history in other ways.

The statue of the two of them is called 'Sportsmanship'. A few months after the incident Landy, who is now Governor-General of the State of Victoria, took bronze in the Melbourne Olympic Games. Carrying the torch on its final journey into the Melbourne Cricket Ground, the Olympic stadium that year, was Ron Clarke. At those same Melbourne Olympics Clarke was to witness what he still calls one of the greatest acts of sportsmanship he has ever come across.

As we have just seen, the 1956 Marathon gold medal went to France's Alain Mimoun. The Algerian-born Mimoun had finished second to the great Emil Zatopek – the man who guards the gates of glory – a heartbreaking number of times, three of them in the Olympic Games: in the 10,000 metres in London, at the same distance and again over 5 000 metres in Helsinki. The first of December 1956 was the day the French runner turned the tables. But the gold medal was not the ultimate prize.

Zatopek struggled home in sixth place, more than four and a half minutes behind Mimoun. Recalling the men who inspired his own record-breaking career, Clarke quickly homed in on the 1956 Olympic marathon winner. 'I remember another guy who is often forgotten,' he said, 'and that's Alain Mimoun. Zatopek made a tremendous gesture in 1956. Mimoun had won the race, and stayed around till "Zato" arrived, helping him to the finish. When Emil had crossed the line he raced over and shook him by the hand, saying, "Emil, I won, it is me, I am the victor!" But all Zatopek did was smile, step back and salute him. I asked Mimoun about it years later on an anniversary trip down here, when Alain spoke much better English than he had in 1956. "That was my proudest moment," he said, "even better than running through the tape, because I respected him so much." It was the pinnacle of his career, because that's the type of person Emil was. He could have pulled out of that marathon, but he kept on struggling through.'

'Struggling through' might seem an apt way to describe Clarke's own marathon career, if, that is, we are to take the man himself at face value. Clarke, who annexed no fewer than seventeen distance-running world records in his wonderful career, never won Olympic gold, nor in the marathon did he win a medal of any kind. But he was the first Australian to make any impact on that event, and in many ways he started what has become an Aussie tradition. After the high-profile performance as torchbearer at the Melbourne Games (heightened even further by the fact that he suffered burns from the molten torch), Clarke dropped off the athletics scene for some years. Athletes speak often of the need to put miles in the bank – their legs – over the years, so what must that gap have cost Clarke at such a formative stage? 'It probably cost me an Olympic gold,' is his straightforward answer. 'What happened was that I got married, finished my studies, got established in business – I did all the "normal" things. I came back in 1963 because we moved back to the city; I went for a run with [well-known Australian coach] Les Perry and a man called Bob Horman. I was 24 at the time – and they were waiting for me up the hills. I thought, "This is ridiculous . . ." Shortly after that I turned twenty-five. Les said if I wanted to get fit again I should train at Caulfield Racecourse.'

Caulfield is one of the major venues in racing-mad Melbourne, a superb inner-city course which stages several of the nation's most important horse races. Little may the colts and fillies have realised that for some years they shared their hallowed turf with some other thoroughbred runners. Clarke joined the Glenhuntly Athletics Club in Melbourne, and duly trained at Caulfield. 'We ran fifteen yards out from the inside fence,' Clarke recalled, 'to miss the hoof-marks. I was an accountant in the city at the time; at six o'clock I would jog back and meet the others; we'd run eight to ten laps (a mile and a quarter plus 110 yards), I'd leave for home about seven-thirty to eight and arrive at about a quarter to nine, have a meal then work on some tax returns because I was a tax agent in my spare time to earn some extra money. I had never dreamed of running internationally. But then we won the State titles, got thrashed in the Australian titles, but began to run better and better. I still wasn't serious about my running, even by the time of the 1962 Commonwealth Games when I ran second – we had been water-skiing the day before! I beat Bruce Tulloh and Bruce Kidd, but I didn't get Murray Halberg.'

Seeing Halberg win Olympic gold in Rome persuaded Clarke what could be done with apparently minimal talent, though the freakish example of his compatriot Herb Elliott and his unforgettable Rome victory in the 1,500 metres served as an eloquent counterpoise. Convinced he was 'a journeyman who didn't have much talent', Clarke nevertheless got back down to serious business in his own right. But ask him how, when and why he started marathon running, and he will tell you that he never really did. 'My first marathon came when I was just starting out again, and I did a 2:51 or so. A guy called Alf O'Connor, a solicitor about fifty-four or fifty-five, was President of the Victorian Marathon Club at the time. There weren't many marathons around in those days, and Alf had just won the South Australian title. My plan was to use this one as a training run, find Alf and stay on his pace. But it was just boring as hell, it was far too slow. So I trotted off ahead of him. In the marathon, near the twenty-mile mark or so I always really suffered because of my high knee action: I would run from lamppost to lamppost, on each stride I would use my hip to bring the leg through, then the other one, I was in so much pain. That day I was struggling to finish, then I looked up and in the distance I could see Alf. I thought if I got to him I'd be able to jog in at his pace. But when I did get to him I quickly realised that what had seemed so slow now felt like a fast 100-metre sprint, and I just let him go. But the next year I won the Australian marathon title in 2:23.'

Returning to the theme of 'struggling through', Clarke is utterly candid in assessing his own marathon performances. 'In fact I have never run all the way in a marathon,' he admits. 'I always ended up walking at some stage in the last three or four miles, and despite that in Tokyo in '64 I ran 2:22. Had the money been around then that there is these days I might have found a way round that problem. I ran another one in South Australia in 1966 and went in as favourite because by that time I had several world records and what have you. But it was terribly hilly; it was Derek Clayton's first marathon, and he just went streaming past me around the eighteen-mile mark. I take credit for discovering and encouraging Derek, who became not only a great mate but an outstanding marathon runner. In fact I would say it was Derek who really made it into a special event. Up till then it was a distance runner's event that you could retire to or play around with, but once you start going under 2:09 it really does become a specialist event.'

As we shall see, Derek Clayton formed a bridge between the pioneering Clarke and the man who was to become arguably Australia's greatest ever marathon man, Robert de Castella. But Clayton himself remains something of an enigma. As one writer has suggested, he was born in Lancashire, raised in Northern Ireland and then came to Australia – and in his character he combined the worst traits of all three. National pride and personal humility were not among them. 'I don't run for other people,' he is quoted as saying. 'I don't run for my country. I'm not very nationalistic. Derek Clayton comes first in my book.'

Derek Clayton also came first in a number of very important races, though like Clarke he could never win an Olympic marathon. An ungainly six-foot-two-and-a-bit (188 cm), his was an unlikely physique with which to combat some of the marathon's smaller men.

But a punishing training schedule put Clayton at the pinnacle of marathon running through the late 1960s and early 1970s. A weekly average was 160 miles (256 km), often composed in 10-week cycles for supposedly optimum performance. By his own admission, Clayton perfected a running style that was based on an almost total absence of style, barely lifting his legs off the ground in contrast to the high-stepping Clarke. Awkward and self-centred as he apparently was, perhaps for those very reasons, Clayton became the first man, not just the first Australian, to break the 2-hour, 10-minute barrier for the marathon. It came about in Fukuoka, Japan, in 1967 – Clayton's fifth marathon, and his first overseas sortie. En route to a time of 2:09:36, Clayton recorded the first half-marathon in under one hour. Before that Japanese epic, his PB was 2:18.28. In fact Derek Clayton retained the marathon world record for fourteen years, breaking it himself in 1969 in Antwerp, where he also became the first man to crack the 2:09 barrier, lowering the mark to 2:08:34.

In 1967 Derek Clayton was ranked number one marathon runner in the world; between then and 1973 he remained in the top ten. And yet he never won a major competition. Why? The answer comes from the man who succeeded him as world-record-holder, compatriot Robert de Castella. 'Derek was mad as a meat-axe,' says 'Deek'. 'He used to train himself into almost annual surgery [in fact Clayton underwent major surgery seven times]. He had an amazing ability to push and punish his body. He was a contemporary of my coach, Pat Clohessy, so we were often entertained by crazy stories about Derek. But he never got his timing right for the major championships: he was always either injured or he had overtrained.' In the Mexico Olympic marathon of 1968 Clayton could do no better than seventh; four years later he was thirteenth in Munich, an event de Castella later described as a watershed in marathon history. Clayton also dropped out of the Commonwealth Games races of 1970 and 1974. 'Even that second world record he set in Antwerp was actually a lead-up to another event,' de Castella recalls. 'But at the time Derek took the marathon on to another level.'

Clayton's own analysis of how he did that is simple in the extreme. 'The difference between my world record and many world-class runners is mental fortitude,' he claimed. 'I ran believing in mind over matter.' Sadly, as he later acknowledged, he might have done better to heed the warnings those injuries represented.

A decade after Clayton, it was de Castella's turn to fly the Australian flag on the marathon battlefields of the world. If Clayton was still fresh in his memory, Clarke, too, had a hand in shaping his career, albeit indirectly. 'Ron Clarke is one of my heroes,' de Castella frankly admits, 'but his career was a bit before my time, so I never saw him compete while he was at his peak. He was another contemporary of Pat Clohessy's, so I knew of him; Ron and I were also members of the same Glenhunty club, so I enjoyed our conversations and our runs together.' De Castella's tale of how he came to the punitive pastime called the marathon is rather less brutal than Clayton's. 'I thought I could be good at it,' is all he says. 'I started running as a kid in school, and the longer the runs got, the better I was, relative to my peers. So I thought there might be a future in this. My first marathon, in 1979, was a part of the lead-up to my attempt to make the 1980 Olympic team. And after that, I guess, the romance and mystique of marathon running took hold. It's a personal challenge, pitting yourself against yourself as well as against the clock, and following in the footsteps of others like Bikila or Derek Clayton.'

If Clayton, as an individual, had elevated marathon running to new heights, an altogether new and collective phenomenon was about to bring it to the attention of the world. It really began, in de Castella's view, with the Munich Games of 1972. 'That happened with Shorter winning and the marathon being televised. It produced some very powerful footage. At the same time there was the start of the mass-participation running boom in the United States: you had Bill Rodgers running in the Boston Marathon, and that fuelled the whole road-running scene. I came along in about 1980–81 and raced these guys in the USA when they were on the downhill curve.' There was every reason to believe that de Castella's own career was on a steep uphill curve that had no reason to end.

He did achieve Olympic selection in 1980, the boycotted Games in Moscow, where he ran against reigning marathon champion Waldemar Cierpinski, the great Lasse Viren, hero of Montreal, and the rest of them. 'It put me at a level way above where I'd previously been. And a tenth-place finish – to make the top ten was just wonderful. Yes, those were the boycotted Games, but that didn't matter to us, as a team we were all very united in our resolve.' That same resolve carried de Castella to unprecedented heights in the opening years of the 1980s. Like Clayton, he chose Fukuoka to announce his presence to an astonished world. Still just 24, he produced a startling 2:08:18 to succeed Clayton as world-record-holder. On home soil, at the Brisbane Commonwealth Games of 1982, de Castella caught and passed the pre-race favourites from Tanzania to win in 2:09:18. In 1983 came two more spectacular triumphs: in Rotterdam he destroyed Alberto Salazar, in Helsinki he became World Champion. As the decade unfolded Robert de Castella would become the leading figure, literally, in some of the great city marathons, Boston in particular, where in 1986 he recorded his own PB of 2:07:51; he would take Commonwealth gold again in Edinburgh, also in 1986. But this former Australian of the Year, like Clarke and like Clayton, could never win Olympic gold, despite four tries.

Events between Moscow and Los Angeles had made him favourite for the 1984 Olympics, as he readily admits. 'Unfortunately I overtrained a bit,' he explains. 'I thought the Olympic Games were more important, so I thought I should train even harder. I put myself in a hole six months previous to the Games. I was coming out of it, but I couldn't recapture the sparkle to put me up there on the dais. Looking back, that is one of the disappointments of my career: it's easy to see the mistakes I made at that time. But to me, not winning gold is not failure: to me, failing is not trying. I always gave 100 per cent, even 101 per cent – maybe that extra one was my undoing!' By the time Seoul came around, other factors were beginning to take their toll. 'Yes, I was having back problems and injuries. In fact I was fortunate to finish where I did. My preparation had been very interrupted, so eighth was a good, solid performance.' And then on to Barcelona. 'By that time I was working full time at the Australian Institute of Sport and trying to cram my normal training routine into a long, demanding work schedule. Maybe I could have run a bit better . . .'

The sentence may tail off, but there is no hint of false regret. Quite the contrary: Robert de Castella treats those famous impostors, triumph and tragedy, with the same equanimity. Quizzed on the pride he must have felt about being unquestioned world number one, he says, 'I always went back to something Dave Bedford said in answer to a similar question: "I train so bloody hard I expect to be good." It's not as if you wake up one morning and you've gone from being a hacker to a champion.' De Castella's training routine scarcely varied across a long marathon career. He trained twice a day, seven days a week, which included two long runs: Wednesday, two hours or eighteen miles, relatively flat, with a steady 3–5 miles in the middle, and Sunday 21–22 miles, maybe 2:20 or 2:25 over a hillier course. Monday and Friday were easy recovery days, 3 miles on one, 5–6 on the other. On Tuesday and Thursday, quality hill or track sessions, and Saturday was a fartlek hill session. About 120–130 miles a week. 'I was fortunate to have a good coach,' he insists, 'and I started at a young age. I avoided major injuries.'

Since he retired over a decade ago, 'Deek' has remained active, working principally on weights and martial arts, and has gained some eighteen kilos, a fair bit of which is muscle. 'That gives you some indication of how emaciated I was,' he points out, 'because I was fighting against my natural physique, which was not ideal for a marathon runner. I ran at around 68 to 70 kilos. But I was always very grateful for the opportunity that my physiology gave me. There are so many different paths in life, paths we may or may not cross, for example meeting my coach Pat Clohessy. Pat was an athlete himself. He was one of the first Australians to go to the US on an athletics scholarship; he had also travelled in Europe with the Lydiard athletes (Halberg, Snell), and he had seen the American interval approach as well. He is one of the most selfless, generous men I have ever come across, and one of the most positive and motivating. Whatever you had done, he always had a positive word. He gives people an opportunity to develop as individuals, he never occupies the foreground. I owe him an enormous debt, not only in physical preparation but in the philosophy he adopted.'

More recently Steve Moneghetti, another outstanding Australian, has 'failed' in the Olympic Games when the rest of the world had succumbed to his relentless rhythm. 'A family man from Ballarat', a gold-mining town in rural Victoria, is how 'Mona' describes himself, but in 1994 the country boy was king of the world. Steve Moneghetti ran his first marathon at a fairly high level: the Commonwealth Games in Edinburgh in 1986. Moneghetti had already competed at 10,000 metres, coming fifth. 'I had a long run scheduled anyway,' he said as an aside after taking the bronze in the best-ever time for an Australian in his debut marathon. Boston Marathon winner in 1990, 'Mona' had to wait until 1994 for his next major success. But victory in the Tokyo Marathon and a gold at the Victoria Commonwealth Games sealed his status as world number one. And yet, no Olympic success ... In 1988 in Seoul, Moneghetti was fifth, three places ahead of de Castella, a performance he described as 'the realisation of a twelve-year dream'; at Atlanta in 1996, the closest Olympic marathon finish of all time, he was seventh. And by the time the Sydney Olympics came around 'Mona' was 38. The honour of being captain of the Australian athletics squad was compounded by a creditable tenth-place run in the marathon. Already, three years earlier, 'Mona' had started to read the writing on the wall. It appeared, of all places, in Athens, scene of the 1997 World Championships in which Moneghetti claimed bronze. It was his eighteenth marathon. 'My body is saying I have to stop this,' he admitted. But when he added, 'I have all I ever wanted,' the true measure of the man shone through. His stated ambition on officially retiring from competition: to get a real job.

Australians, in the title of one of their most famous books, are a weird mob. Such is the national preoccupation with sport that 'not winning' has become one and the same as 'failing'. Not in Ron Clarke's eyes. Like de Castella, he spends a lot of time talking to young people. Curiously enough, he uses the same phrase as Deek: 'To me, the failure is in not trying. Unfortunately the media here, and everywhere for that matter, concentrate so much on success, they don't look at people who have performed above themselves but not won. I suppose I spend most of my life telling schoolkids the only way you fail is not getting out there. The main thing is to enjoy yourself and make the most of life.'

Which brings us back to the man who guards the gates of glory, a man revered by Clarke. 'Emil Zatopek, of course, was very inspirational. I loved his attitude. He won, I lost – but we enjoyed our running for running's sake. We went out and put it to 'em. I didn't like the style of competition where everybody sat around and then they all did a fast last lap, I liked putting it out there. I loved his personality, his willingness to help: he was enthusiastic, he was cheerful – all virtues that rank very highly with me.' What better way to remember Australian distance runners at their finest, paradoxically, than by looking at the statue of the two men whose race has stopped? 'I hope it's a reminder of everything that sport stands for,' said Clarke at its unveiling in 2002. 'It's the game that's the most important thing, not the triumphs – the winning and the losing.' Sportsmanship? L.P. Hartley was right, in that oft-quoted opening line of *The Go-Between*: 'The past is a foreign country, they do things differently there.' And the way they do them meant those two Australian men were running into history.

18. HISTORY 9 – 'EX AFRICA SEMPER...' ROME AND TOKYO FALL TO THE FIRST DOUBLE WINNER

Two black athletes captured the world's attention at the Games of the XVIIth Olympiad. One did it with his hands, the other with his feet. The first would achieve sporting immortality as Muhammad Ali, perhaps the greatest boxer ever to walk the earth. The second emerged, barefoot, from little-known Ethiopia to win the marathon – not once, but twice. Abebe Bikila was the first black African to win Olympic gold; he also became one of the most tragic figures who ever ran into history.

The Olympic Games were over half a century late in arriving in the Italian capital. Pierre de Coubertin wanted to grant the Games of 1908 – the year the marathon was first run over the famous 26 miles and 385 yards – to Rome, but another big noise on the world stage deemed otherwise. Its name was Vesuvius, whose eruption before the planned Olympics was untimely to say the least. No matter: there were fireworks aplenty when the Games made their belated appearance, televised for the first time to the whole of Europe. An audience of millions would share the privilege of witnessing one of the crowning moments of Olympic history.

The relatively scant material on Abebe Bikila tells us he was born in 1932, at Jato, near Debre Birhan to the northeast of Ethiopia's capital city, Addis Ababa. The legend of Bikila is merely enhanced by the fact that his birth date, 7 August, coincided with the running of the 1932 Olympic marathon in Los Angeles. A shepherd who enjoyed only a basic education, at twenty he was recruited to the Imperial Bodyguard surrounding Emperor Haile Selassie. It was in the military that Abebe Bikila was first exposed to running and was, apparently, impressed by seeing the name of his country emblazoned on the kit of his countrymen who had returned from the 1956 Olympics. Like Zatopek at Helsinki, it seems the future king of the marathon came close to missing his own date with Olympic destiny. Conflicting reports of his initial prowess suggest, on the one hand, that he was a surprise winner of his first marathon and that Olympic selection was a foregone conclusion; on the other, some stories circulate of his failure to finish in the first four in the event in Ethiopia's military championships. Only a bizarre decision by one of the men who beat him came to Bikila's rescue: the elated runner decided not to catch the team bus back to the start, opting instead to run – all forty kilometres. When physical exhaustion ensued, in stepped Bikila.

Another myth surrounds the barefoot black man. He is quoted as having said, when asked why he ran barefoot, 'I wanted the world to know that my country, Ethiopia, has always won with determination and heroism.' That may be true of Ethiopia, but it does not explain the barefoot phenomenon. The Rome Olympic marathon was run on 10 September. In July and August, Bikila had already run marathon distances; his shoes were somewhat the worse for wear. New ones provided by the Ethiopian Athletic Federation proved too tight. Ordering a different pair, Bikila opted, in the meantime, to try running barefoot. When the next shoes proved just as unsatisfactory, the decision was taken that led to Abebe Bikila having the most famous feet in athletics history.

The bare feet were not the only 'first' thrown up by that September day. For one thing, the start and finish of the marathon were outside the stadium. The race was to end at the celebrated Arch of Constantine, willed into being by a Senate grateful for the emperor's victory over Maxentius in AD 312 for which they called him 'liberator of the city, bringer of peace'. If anything, the choice of finishing point should have served as an inspiration to the great man's namesake, Konstantin Vorobeyev of the Soviet Union, who started the Olympic event as one of the favourites along with compatriot Sergei Popov. At the time Popov was the marathon world-record-holder with a time of 2:15:17, established in Stockholm in August 1958. Another threat was Moroccan Rhadi ben Abdesselem.

As events unfolded it was not the Russians, but the man from Ethiopia who drew inspiration from the past. Running over the cobblestone streets of Rome, the field had to pass close to the spot where the Fascist dictator Mussolini ordered Italian troops to embark on their 1936 invasion of Ethiopia. Less than two kilometres from the finish line stood an obelisk plundered by those forces. By a happy coincidence it also marked the spot where the course began a slight incline: the perfect place for the man with no shoes to attack.

Another first for that Rome marathon meant the race began at dusk on 10 September and ended in a spectacular blaze of light from torches held by more friendly Italian soldiery. The Russians dropped, Bikila kept pace with Rhadi ben Abdesselem almost until the end, then relentlessly headed for home. If the Arch of Constantine loomed over that marathon finish, the words of an even older Roman, Pliny the Elder three centuries before, might have been ringing in their ears: 'Ex Africa semper aliquid novi' – 'Always something new comes out of Africa.' Little did those watching millions know that the something new, this time, was laying the foundations for one of the greatest distance-running empires the world has ever seen. Before he reached the tape, Bikila had another, much more contemporary hazard to negotiate: an Italian on a motor scooter let his enthusiasm run away with both him and his machine as Bikila closed to within sixty yards of the line, forcing him to take swift evasive action.

Bikila's time of 2:15:16.2 was a new world best and, to underline how quickly marathon running was evolving, it was a good eight minutes faster than the legendary Zatopek's Helsinki mark eight years before. Bikila's kick for home had carried him over 200 metres or 25 seconds clear of the Moroccan, who in turn had a minute and a half and more in hand over third-placed Barry Magee of New Zealand. As a note in passing, Magee's fine effort in taking marathon bronze combined with the gold-medal runs of his compatriots Peter Snell in the 800 metres and Murray Halberg in the 5,000 metres to make the Rome Olympics a memorable tribute to the 'Lydiard' athletes. The Soviet Union duo completed the top five, Vorobyev ahead of Popov. Another sign of the times was the seventh-place finish for another Ethiopian, Abebe Wakgira.

Abebe Bikila did – and didn't – repeat his Rome triumph four years later. Yes, he became the first athlete in history to win the marathon at successive Olympics: but at the second time of asking, in Tokyo, he did it wearing socks and shoes. Aptly enough, the first man to break Bikila's Rome time was a Japanese runner, Toru Terasawa, in February 1963. By the time they came to Japan for the Games of the XVIIIth Olympiad it had been lowered twice more and stood at 2:13:55, set by the great British runner Basil Heatley in June of the Olympic year. If Rome had waited a long time for its turn to stage the Games, Asia had waited even longer: these were the first Olympics to grace that continent and Japan embraced them with all the fervour of a nation still in rebuilding mode. As a sign of how the world had changed, the final torchbearer was a man born on 6 August 6 1945 – the day his home town died. His name was Yoshinori Saika, born that fateful day in the tragic city of Hiroshima.

That Tokyo field was, at the time, one of the strongest collections of marathon runners assembled for one race. Australia's Ron Clarke may have started as a marginal favourite, given the apparent ease with which world records were falling to his relentless pace, and especially as the great Ethiopian had endured an appendectomy a mere forty days before. Clarke certainly set off with every intention of breaking the rest of them, maintaining a sub-five-minute mile pace despite what many observers felt was a punishing schedule of running, a Zatopek-like week of four races culminating in the longest of them all. 'It wasn't punishing!' he insisted, looking back in 2004. 'I thought racing was the best way to train. Fitness is a combination of two things: how fast you run from point A to point B, and how quickly you recover. You have to put the two together. The fitter you are, the better you're running, the quicker you recover. I always ran as hard as I could and as often as I could, sometimes racing three days in a row. In fact my best recovery ever was after the Olympic marathon: three days later I won for the British Commonwealth in a match against the USA.' The man who had the world-best mark, Basil Heatley, was also there, as were Irishman Jim Hogan and another former holder of the world-best time, American runner Buddy (real name Leonard) Edelen.

As Clarke and Hogan headed off into the distance, Bikila got back to them around the seven-kilometre mark. Well before half-distance, the man who now wore shoes had broken Clarke. 'Just knowing Bikila was behind me was intimidating,' Clarke acknowledged four decades later. 'He ran so lightly you could not hear him, but you always knew he was there.' Shortly after half-distance, Hogan, too, was beaten, later to drop out altogether. Abebe Bikila strode into the Olympic stadium with one of the most commanding margins in the history of the Games, winning by four minutes and seven seconds and having time to indulge in some warm-down calisthenics before the other two medal places were decided. They lay between Japanese favourite Kokichi Tsuburaya and Heatley. The Englishman was not short of pace: had he not, in 1961, annihilated the great Zatopek's 10,000-metre world record? He had been only eighth at the 30-kilometre mark, improved to third at 40-kilometres but was still over a minute behind Tsuburaya in the closing stages. Entering the stadium, though, Heatley sensed silver was there for the taking, applied the pressure with a sprint finish and relegated the Japanese runner to bronze.

Some men would have handled that 'defeat' a little differently. Clarke himself, run out of Olympic gold yet again in Tokyo, took it all philosophically: 'Olympic gold has to be a chain of circumstances,' he says. 'Despite what's claimed by the press, Olympic gold doesn't make you a world champion in my book. My first lesson in that respect was Helsinki 1952, when [Luxembourg's] Josy Barthel took gold – that 1,500 metres was just about the only race he ever won. I think we overdo the Olympic Games and underdo the year-in, year-out competition. I don't regard Clayton, de Castella or Moneghetti any the less because they have not won Olympic gold; but I wouldn't regard them any more highly had they won it either.'

Not so Kokichi Tsuburaya. An injury-plagued preparation for the Olympics in Mexico in 1968 culminated in his realisation, early in that new Olympic year that, despite doctors' insistence, his body was telling him he could not reach his peak again. Perhaps the keenly honed Japanese sense of 'failure' or 'losing face' had become just too much – in 1963, before the Tokyo bronze, Tsuburaya had broken Zatopek's record of twenty kilometres in an hour, but had still come second in that Auckland race to New Zealander Bill Baillie. Whatever the final reason, poor Tsuburaya ended his own life before Mexico came round, a last note saying simply that he could not run any more.

Alas, he was not the only member of that Tokyo top three to meet a tragic end. Hailed as a national hero, Abebe Bikila was promoted to sergeant in the Imperial Bodyguard after his Rome success, and Lieutenant after Tokyo. What rank was waiting for him if he could complete the hat trick in Mexico. Sadly he could not: a leg injury reduced Bikila to a shadow of his former self and he withdrew before that race had reached two-thirds distance. A grateful government had also awarded him a car, a Volkswagen, in recognition of his sterling efforts in his country's service. In March 1969 Bikila lost control at the wheel and lay trapped for hours in the wreckage. His neck broken, spinal cord severed, the barefoot runner suffered the cruellest of all fates for a man like him: he would never walk again.

Haile Selassie himself was behind Bikila's transfer to the famous Stoke Mandeville hospital in England, where Bikila took part in games for wheelchair sportsmen. He was there, too, at the beginning of the Olympic marathon in 1972, in his wheelchair by the Munich starting line. But in October 1973 his life was ended by a stroke. The equivalent of a State funeral suggested the standing he enjoyed among his countrymen, the emperor himself among the mourners.

We have become accustomed, in our catastrophic times, to seeing Ethiopia in a different light: as a land of endless conflict, endless famine, endless struggle for life. But as Gezahgne Abera triumphantly reminded us in Sydney at the turn of another century, Abebe Bikila had done more than win two Olympic gold medals. They told stories about the hero Abebe Bikila in the schools of Ethiopia, and Abera had been among the listeners. In a land where hunger has become tragically commonplace, the life-affirming feats of Abebe Bikila fuelled another appetite. It, too, has yet to be assuaged.

19. ADDIS ABABA – TRIUMPH OF THE AFRICANS

At the centre of a country known for its poverty and famine, a place aided by the West in times of drought, where the people fight a constant battle against the problems of diseases like AIDS and malaria, lies a heart that beats with the pride of a struggling nation. The rising summit of Mount Entotto may cast a shadow over the sprawl fighting to free itself from its glum slum history, but the place, founded little more than 200 years ago, where old colonial buildings signal old signs of hope and sun-bleached shacks and empty building lots display the rigours of modern life, is bursting with sunshine and energy. The city is Addis Ababa, a place where marathon legends are born.

The misty, pine-covered hills surrounding Addis lay claim to many of the sport's Olympic greats and are, as time goes by, still bearing future pretenders to a crown that almost deserves a permanent home in the capital of Ethiopia. The *mercato*, a colourful 25 square kilometres of open markets offering everything from local food to paintings of biblical scenes, displays the hustle and bustle that is typical of North African life; pungent odours wafting from stoves, shouts clamouring one against another to be heard, all the colours of the rainbow spread through a variety of goods balanced precariously on rickety stalls and uncertain foundations.

Immediately to the north, Ankober hides a past as a trading centre for African wealth destined for ports in the Red Sea, while Debre Libanos of Shewa hosts a thirteenth-century monastery with mineral waters claimed to heal and relieve. Further north, deep in the Ifat Desert, lies Debre Berhan, the Church of the Divine Light, a fifteenth-century church built when the area was the empire's capital. Further still and the Blue Nile gorge tracks the life-giving river towards the sea. All are facets of a growing nation and have helped create a motherland for names that grace the record books through the history of modern marathon running.

Now swollen to a population of more than two million people, Addis Ababa is the political capital, the economic core and the social nerve centre of Ethiopia. It is a big, sprawling, hospitable city that rambles across wooded hillsides and gullies cut through with fast-flowing streams. It is as cosmopolitan as any of the world's great metropolises with architecture as varied as the city itself: tall office buildings, elegant villas, functional bungalows, fashionable hotels, conference halls and theatres. All gleam in their marble and aluminium and vie for attention alongside traditional homes made of wattle and daub, surrounded by cattle, sheep, goats and chickens.

It was in a traditional home of that kind where, in 1932, in a town named Jato, about 130 kilometres from Addis Ababa, in the district of Nea Denba near Debre Birhan, that perhaps the world's greatest marathon runner, Abebe Bikila, came into the world. His humble beginnings, as part of a large and poor peasant family, saw him grow up as a shepherd while completing the traditional Qes schooling as an on-off student. He was forced to enlist in the army when he was seventeen as a convenient way to earn his daily bread. It was a turn of fate that led him to the Imperial Guard and, in turn, planted the marathon seed that would grow so strong.

Eleven years later, in Rome on 10 September 1960, almost at the very place where Italian dictator Benito Mussolini and his army has passed under the famous Arch of Constantine on their way to invade and conquer Addis Ababa some thirty years before, the noble African athlete won the Olympic marathon. On a humid evening one of the most striking moments in Olympic history was played out as Bikila astonished everyone by running on the cobbles of the city and up the Appian Way barefoot, his soles hardened by the Ethiopian soil in the fields of his homeland, to cross the line and take victory in only his second marathon. Asked why he ran barefoot, Bikila replied, 'I wanted the world to know that my country, Ethiopia, has always won with determination and heroism.' Olympic marathon gold was, for the first time, heading back to Ethiopia, and Bikila had won it in the way he had wanted.

One of Haile Salasssie's imperial bodyguards, Bikila, 28, had not been rated before the event, despite an impressive time he set a month earlier in his high-altitude training area in Addis Ababa. Instead, European champion and world-record-holder Sergey Popov, of the Soviet Union, Olympic champion and silver medallist Alain Mimoun, the Algerian-born Frenchman, and Yugoslavia's Franjo Mihalic, were all favourites for the race, which snaked around the city and outside the stadium to ensure the best views of Rome were displayed to the world. Instead, it would be the achievements of the man from Addis Ababa that stole the show when he cruised by the soldiers standing with flaming torches along the darkening course and crossed the line at the Coliseum, victorious at dusk, almost half a minute ahead of his closest challenger, Rhadi ben Abdesselem of Morocco.

Bikila's achievement, which saw him become the first black African to win Olympic gold, sent shockwaves through the sport and penetrated into the very heart of pure African nationalism. Here was an athlete from the poorest continent on the planet at the height of decolonisation, yet his run that day, with a time of 2 hours, 15 minutes and 16 seconds, comfortably broke the best efforts of all his rivals. It began a career that would eventually see him enter the athletics' hall of fame as a widely acknowledged claimant to be the finest marathon runner on earth. Furthermore, as both of the two duelling leaders hailed from North Africa, the Rome event marked a change in the marathon legend, a change that had been hinted at before Bikila was even born, through the performances of Algerian-born Frenchman Mohamed El Ouafi.

El Ouafi could have claimed the first African marathon victory 32 years previously had he not chosen to run for France. Born on 18 October 1898, on the fringes of the Sahara Desert in a place near Biskra, 300 kilometres southeast of Algiers, the Algerian, like Bikila, was a farmer before being struck by the bug of the marathon at the age of 23. He was hamstrung by the constraints of competing for an unfavourable African nation, however, and moved to France to pursue his dream ahead of the 1924 Paris Olympics. On 13 July that year, after consistent defeats by French champion Jean Manhes, El Ouafi won the French Olympic trial when his rival dropped out and he went on to finish seventh in the Olympic Marathon. He would have to wait four gruelling years to achieve his ultimate success.

Running despatches for the French Army in his Algerian homeland during 1926, he was forced to run long distances under tough conditions and consequently grew stronger before returning to France, in 1927, to stake his claim for a place at the next Olympic Games in Amsterdam. In a race alongside 67 others, he paced himself perfectly to take over the lead 3 kilometres from the finish before entering the stadium to a trumpet fanfare. Newspaper reports described him as 'the dark-skinned little man in the French Olympic colours' and the first African-born champion had been crowned.

In Melbourne, in 1956, the second African-born Algerian Olympic marathon winner was crowned when Alain Mimoun defeated a field that included the great Czech legend Emile Zatopek. But Africa's success in the marathon was never proclaimed until Bikila's achievement in 1960 and his subsequent success at the 1964 Games in Tokyo. There, this time wearing running shoes on his tough leather-like feet, he ran out victorious again to become the first athlete to retain the Olympic title in the marathon. Once again, he set a record time, bringing the mark down to 2 hours, 12 minutes and 11.2 seconds and setting a then-unprecedented record speed of 11.9 miles per hour.

Once again, he had used his African spirit to battle through adversity and achieve his astonishing success. Just months before his second Olympic Games, he was accused of playing a role in a conspiracy to overthrow the government. The claims were false, but the allegation forced him to spend several months in prison and miss out on essential pre-race training, as did an attack of severe appendicitis, which saw him undergo an operation just one month before the start of the marathon. But still he won the event comfortably and even had time to amuse the spectators with an array of different warm-down stretches as he patiently waited for the silver medallist to arrive in the infield.

Aiming for a hat trick of three successive Olympic triumphs at the next Games in Mexico City, in 1968, Bikila was forced to withdraw after seventeen kilometres. He had been so determined to fight for victory that he ran despite a hairline fracture in his right foot, which was complicated by stiffness and circulation problems. The pain became too much for him to continue and, in a sad end that saw him driven off in the back of an ambulance, a chapter of Olympic marathon history came to a close. Just months after that moment, an even worse fate followed as his career ended in a car accident in Sheno, just seventy kilometres from Addis Ababa, that left him paralysed from the waist down. His spirit would not fade, however, and he continued in wheelchair races until, at 41, he suffered a fatal brain haemorrhage. He was buried in the grounds of the St Joseph Church in the presence of a huge crowd and the then-emperor, Haile Selassie.

By the time of his death, Bikila had already passed on the African spirit of success having metaphorically handed over the team baton to his compatriot Mamo Wolde in the Mexico games. There, Ethiopia's new hero Wolde claimed a hat trick of Olympic marathon victories for the country. Hailing once again from the surrounds of Addis Ababa, in the village of DreDele about sixty kilometres from the city, Walde was born one year before Bikila, in 1931, and followed almost the same life path, having a traditional upbringing and joining the Imperial Guard. He followed his passion for running into the Olympics at shorter distances, but ran in the 1964 Olympic marathon and was beaten by Bikila.

The same, quite probably, would have been true in 1968 were it not for Bikila's injury. He had just won his first silver Olympic medal in the 10,000 metres and the day before the marathon race, team trainer Negussie Roba heaped pressure on his shoulders when he revealed that his team-mate was unlikely to finish the event and that, suddenly, he was Ethiopia's only hope for their third consecutive medal. 'At the twentieth kilometre, coaches Negussie and Major Niskanen got out of their car and told me, "You are Ethiopia's only chance, Ayzoh Berta,"' recalled Wolde. But helped along by cheering journalists travelling alongside the runners in cars clad in the national flag, he took the win and, like his predecessor, became an instant hero.

'Any Ethiopian child can tell you, too, that Bikila was running hurt,' recalled runner-turned-journalist Kenny Moore, who was competing in the event for the United States. 'After ten miles, he turned and beckoned to his team-mate, Mamo Wolde. Wolde wove through the pack to Bikila's side and Bikila said: "I'm not finishing this race, but, Lieutenant, you will win this race. Don't let me down." Wolde responded: "Sir, yes, Sir" and, thinking some runners were out of sight ahead, took off. None were, but until the tape touched his chest, he couldn't be sure. He won, to his great relief, by a masterful three minutes. I was in the stadium tunnel when Abebe Bikila emerged from an ambulance. He caught Wolde's eye, came to attention and saluted. Wolde, mission accomplished, crisply returned it.

'Wolde's victory meant his country hadn't produced a lone prodigy, but a succession. Wolde had made the marathon Ethiopia's own. Wolde went home, had his portrait enshrined among the Olympic rings atop his national stadium and eventually would inspire Olympic champions Miruts ("Yifter the Shifter") Yifter,

Derartu Tulu, Fatuma Roba, Gezahegne Abera and Haile Gebreselassie. The tale of Captain Bikila's order to the good soldier Wolde became a legend in Ethiopia.'

Four years later, at the age of 39, Wolde participated in the Munich Olympics and won the bronze medal in the marathon but, after a total of 62 international competitions, that was effectively the end of his athletics feats. He also served as a national coach afterwards, but little was heard of him in later years. African success continued and grew stronger when Ethiopia's Kenyan neighbours came to the fore, albeit never yet in an Olympic marathon. The continued long-term dominance of African runners has derived numerous theories, research projects and in-depth investigations into how and why they were and continue to be so successful.

In Bikila's day, the famous Swedish trainer Onni Niskanen helped the Ethiopian athletes to hone their apparent natural fitness advantages with innovative training methods involving saunas, basketball practice and long highway races. Training is, of course, crucial to climb the steps up to the level of an Olympic champion but, as with all naturally talented athletes, it is the initial base, the fundamental internal capacity, that provides the flair and aptitude to reach the top of their game. It is clear that something is present inside the DNA make-up of the African nation that does just that.

Perhaps the greatest advantage claimed by runners from the Great Rift Valley, a great mountain range that cuts across East Africa through Kenya and Ethiopia, is their high-altitude backgrounds, which gives them a natural strength from birth that their rivals can only attain through hard training outside their own countries. Addis Ababa, located in the Shewa province and nestled in the central mountain region on the western ridge of the Great Rift Valley, lies at 2,440 metres above sea level while the Kenyan marathon 'capital' of Eldoret, situated to the northwest of the country's capital Nairobi, lies at around the same height and forces athletes from the region to develop a greater lung capacity as they have to become accustomed to thinner air. But, with countries in the world's highest mountain range, the Himalayas, unable to portray similar achievements, the African successes must be down to more than a simple terrain advantage.

The long-term running culture seen in the inhabitants of the Rift Valley is often touted as a reason for their impressive success on the world marathon stage. But claims that Rift Valley runners develop strength on long distances because, as children, they are forced to run to and from school, sometimes as much as ten miles a day, are often rubbished by top Kenyan runners. Other suggestions that the cattle-herding background of tribes in the area might play a role because the faster a man can collect the cattle, the more wives and, consequently, the more children he can have, are also denied. Claims, too, that the circumcision ritual found throughout the area, in which adolescent boys must endure tremendous pain, help them cope with the grind offered by a 26.2-mile marathon run and instil in them the traits of courage, endurance, determination and restraint that the tribe values above all are equally unsupported.

Diet, another crucial contributing factor in the make-up of the marathon runner, is also touted as a reason for the East African success, with claims that the 'complex carbohydrates' and starchy food that Kenyan and Ethiopians eat is a strong source of their strength. Such diet, however, is common of many third-world countries and, if at all relevant, can merely play a part in their physical attributes. It is almost certain to be an important part of the make-up of the East African athlete, but it is not the be-all-and-end-all reason for their immense success in marathon running. No, work ethic, most athletes say, is the real reason for their success, with the training regimes in their countries notoriously difficult.

On top of that, the high interest in running, created by the great names such as Bikila and Wolde, creates an in-built natural competition and sees strongly fought battles for the highly sought-after places in competition squads. The ever-growing financial benefits, too, of competing on the global stage, leads many to believe success will offer a ticket out of poverty, a way to escape the rigours of everyday life in the strengthening, but still third-world lives they lead. Even the small winnings gained by second- or third-tier athletes represent a gigantic rise on the money that would be available through more mundane everyday jobs in the depths of Addis Ababa. But the region was turning out world-class runners long before such material incentives became available.

Others ponder that the reason lies in the gene pool, and a study into the topic by the Danish Sports Science Institute in 2000, which compared the distance-running prowess of several African youths against a Danish track star, Thomas Nolan, controversially concluded that Kenyans had a born advantage through 'birdlike legs'. 'Very many in sports physiology would like to believe that it is training, the environment, what you eat that plays the most important role,' Bengt Saltin, director of the Copenhagen Muscle Research Center and one of the world's premier sports medical researchers, told Jon Entine, the author of *Taboo: Why Black Atheletes Dominate Sports and Why We're Afraid to Talk About It*. 'But based on the data, it is "in your genes" whether or not you are talented, or whether you will become talented. The extent of the environment can always be discussed but it's less than 20, 25 per cent.'

This can also explain why East and West African runners, whose genetic populations are very different, have opposite talents in running. Between the two regions, there is more genetic variation than any other population, as short- and long-distance running require relatively specific body types. While West Africans tend to have the perfect biomechanical packaging for sprinting, combining small and efficient lungs, muscular 'mesomorphic' bodies and a high proportion of fast-twitch muscle fibres, those qualities make for poor distance runners. In comparison, many East and North Africans have slim, short 'ectomorphic' bodies with large-capacity lungs and 70 to 75 per cent of their muscle fibres being defined as slow-twitch, which is the ideal profile for endurance sports, but puts East Africans among the world's slowest sprinters.

Linguistic data links the Ethiopian areas to elsewhere in East Africa, including Kenya's Kalenjin tribe, which occupies an area approximately the size of Wales and accounts for 12 per cent of Kenya's population and can lay claim to three-quarters of the country's best runners. The climate in that area, like much of Ethiopia's marathon-runner training area, is ideal for sustained outdoor activity, with comfortable and warm days, cool nights and low humidity throughout much of the year. Unlike many other areas in the country, rural western Kenya is not a teeming slum but rather a land of green rolling hills, supplied with basic necessities where the troubles of sickness and infection are limited, life expectancy is high and prosperity is strong enough to fund the athletic opportunities.

While the theories remain just that, offering only sceptical suggestions rather than firm facts, science offers no claim to the more popular notion of harder training and tougher mental aptitude. The genetic reasoning, too, has little support, but it seems clear that thousands of years of evolution have left a distinct footprint on the world's athletic map, and put a talent for long-distance running on the shoulders of those in the Rift Valley. Astonishingly, the area coupling Kenya with Ethiopia can lay claim to more than 60 per cent of the best times ever run in distance races. And, while their great champions died off through ill health and old age, their future success stories continue to build.

The 1968 champion, Wolde, spent the last decade of his life in prison, charged, unfairly, he claimed, with the killing of a fifteen-year-old boy during the regime of Mengistu Haile Mariam, following the revolution. He died at the age of seventy, back in Addis Ababa, after a long illness, and was fittingly laid to rest alongside Bikila in St Joseph's Cemetery in Addis Ababa.

But while the great champions faded, Belayneh Dinsamo became the next in a long line of Ethiopians to enscribe their names in the history books of marathon running when he shot to fame in 1988 with a new marathon world record in Rotterdam, Holland. In April, on a windless spring day and on an out-and-back course that was a late substitute for the original planned course in Boston, he set a time of 2 hours, 6 minutes and 50 seconds. He was the first African to claim a world marathon record since his great predecessor Bikila and his time stood into the next decade, when it was finally beaten in 1998 by Brazilian Ronaldo da Costa in Berlin.

While the Ethiopians continued to claim records and successes in the major international championships, Kenyans also began to stamp their mark. In the inaugural IAAF International World Championships in Helsinki in 1983, Ethiopian Kebede Balacha was pipped to the gold medal by Australian Robert de Castella and, in the following championships in Rome in 1987, the door finally opened for the first Kenyan marathon victory of note when Douglas Wakiihuri claimed the gold. That heralded the rise of the Kenyans, who went on to enjoy tremendous success in the famous marathon events around the globe, both in the men's and women's categories. When Kenyan pair Martin Lel and Margaret Okayo won the famous New York City Marathon in 2003, they recorded the fifth Kenyan male victory since 1997 and the fifth Kenyan female victory since 1994. On top of that, Kenyan men had been victorious in all but one of the preceding twelve Boston Marathons and both Kenyan and Ethiopian women have seen strong success in the London Marathon.

Ethiopian athletics took another giant leap forwards in the 1996 Olympic Games in Atlanta, when Fatuma Roba, hailing from Addis Ababa, running in red shorts and an azure-blue top and with her black hair distinctively dyed orange on either side, surprised her rivals and her own team by outstripping her 29th-best ranking and becoming the first African woman to win a gold medal in the marathon. Just three years after her first 26-mile run, the then-22-year-old came into the event on the back of tumbling times for her personal best and strode away with the race, reaching the halfway mark with a 9-second lead and steadily drawing away to win by 2 minutes with another personal best time, before kneeling to kiss the track in celebration. Hers was the first Ethiopian marathon success at the Olympics since Wolde won a bronze medal in 1972 and it displayed the fact that the East African talent for marathon running could transcend the genders.

Roba looked to be one of those Ethiopian children who conformed to the rule that running ten kilometres to school and back each day was the foundation, but she claims the long-distance demands came too early to develop her marathon mind. It was the legend of Bikila that managed to do that. 'He opened the door, not only for all Ethiopians but for all Africans,' said Roba, born just a year before Bikila died in 1973. 'My Olympic win was not only a very special thing for me, but also for my country and all African women. I am not a hero like him, but a lot of people know me because I make the same history at the Olympics. Especially children. Now they want to be like me and hopefully that is the way our country can continues its success.'

After her surprise arrival, she had little success anywhere other than in the Boston Marathon, which she won for the first time in 1997 and went on to claim three consecutive times. But world championship success passed her by, first through injury in 1997 and then due to intense heat in Seville in 1999. The 2000 Olympic Games in Sydney also failed to yield a medal and eyes turned to the next Ethiopian runner in line to continue the Bikila success, Gezahgne Abera. In what seemed to be a culmination of the development of African running, the 22-year-old Ethiopian was to contest for the gold medal with a Kenyan runner, Eric Wainaina and, with a strong finish, claimed a second successive marathon gold for his country. To round off the East African rout, Tesfaye Tofa claimed the bronze medal in Sydney to drive the crowds in Addis Ababa wild.

In typical Ethiopian style, Abera, one of a family of eight, grew up on a farm in the village of Etya that nestles in the hills above Addis. He ran the long trip to school and back and, as is the trend in modern times, collected a coach at the age of sixteen then began putting the nation's renowned training regime to work. Six years later he was front-page news, accompanied by a squadron of MiG jets on his way back from Australia and returning to Addis Ababa in a cavalcade through streets packed with a million cheering spectators. His gold medal now hangs in his Christian church. 'Winning the Olympic marathon title in Sydney has changed my life so much in such a good way,' he told the London *Daily Telegraph* after his victory.

The people love me because they know I work hard and do a good job. I think they are proud of what I do. So I want to work harder to do better to show my people what is possible with hard work.

I actually really loved football when I was young and would often dream of having the life of a professional footballer. I did mainly football at school and also a range of athletic disciplines, but I didn't make the national junior team until I was seventeen. I entered a regional race after hearing about a 22-kilometres race on the radio, which sounded the right kind of distance for me, did well in the regional race and was invited into the national junior squad. I knew I could do well because I was the only one of my parents' eight children who ran so far to go to school. When I was in junior school, from six to eleven years old, I ran twelve kilometres every day. When I went to high school, it was 25 a day. I ran there in bare feet and it's funny when I look back because most of the students there were weekly boarders, even though some of them lived not too far from me. Now, all I want to concentrate on is running. I would like to win the Olympic and World Championship titles again. Being a champion is about getting to the top and staying there.

There is no designated 'city centre' where the crowds celebrate in Addis Ababa because, until very recently, there was no planning. Like its athletes, it simply grew in a natural, organic way, and its present appearance reflects this unforced and unstructured evolution. The spirit in the streets remains strong and the continuation of the Kenya–Ethiopia rivalry into the 2001 World Championships ensured interest remained high. Abera did not disappoint, out-sprinting Kenya's Simon Biwott in one of the closest and most thrilling finishes ever seen in a major marathon. The two runners entered the Commonwealth Stadium together, with Abera on the Kenyan's shoulder. He made his move with just 200 metres to go, pulling clear round the bend, but Biwott fought back and missed out on gold by just a second. Abera's win clocked up another record for Ethiopian running as he became the first man to hold both the world championship and Olympic titles at the same time.

Whether Addis Ababa will remain home to the records in the coming years will depend not only on their own athletes, but on their Kenyan neighbours'. Heading into the spring of 2004, Kenya had stolen the march, with 34-year-old Paul Tergat silencing the Ethiopian cheers by taking the record mark in the men's marathon down to 2 hours, 4 minutes and 55 seconds in Berlin in September 2003. Daniel Njenga, born in 1976, represents the next wave of Kenyan men's talent, while the emergence of Catherine Ndereba has ensured Kenya, not Ethiopia, is now at the forefront of marathon running. But the spirit flowing through the dusty streets in Addis Ababa, the natural talent of the children running to school and working in the fields around the capital, and the legend of runners like Bikila, Walde and now Abera will ensure the cheers in Addis will not be silenced for long.

20. HISTORY 10 – MEXICO AND MUNICH: BLACK POWER TO BLACK SEPTEMBER

In a long and ultimately tragic life, Mamo Wolde obeyed two higher powers. One was life-enhancing, all-embracing and the object of the great Olympian's undying faith. 'Everything,' said Wolde, simply, 'comes from God.' The other was life-threatening, malevolent and the scourge of his later years in a war-torn homeland. 'Those were revolutionary times,' he said. 'Orders were given from above, and you disobeyed them at your own peril.' Between those two extremes, Mamo Wolde found the strength and stamina to pursue Olympic gold from Melbourne to Munich. The high point of his career came literally and metaphorically in Mexico City in 1968.

The decision to award the Games of the XIXth Olympiad to the Mexican capital was, like so many before and after it, shrouded in controversy. At 2,300 metres high, the city's air would contain something like 30 per cent less oxygen than at sea level. It was not expected to be a problem in the explosive events. But what of the endurance runners? Would there be some real advantage for the men who ran and trained habitually in the African highlands? Conversely, were others, the non-Africans in particular, putting themselves at risk in that rarefied atmosphere? Bob Beamon gave us confirmation of the first suspicion, that Mexico might help the explosive athletes' cause: the American leaped into unknown territory when his long jump carried him 8.9 metres and literally past the measuring system for a world record that would stand for 22 years. In the endurance events, however, black power was supreme. From 1,500 metres to the marathon, Africans – one of them an African Arab – swept the Olympic boards: Kip Keino of Kenya in the metric mile, Mohamed Gammoudi of Tunisia in the 5,000 metres, Naftali Temu of Kenya in the 10,000 metres, his compatriot Amos Biwott in the 3,000-metre steeplechase – and Mamo Wolde of Ethiopia in the marathon.

The drastic effect altitude might have on runners of a different provenance was to be illustrated in the 10,000 metres, in which Mamo Wolde also took part. It was, moreover, the first track-and-field event to reach its conclusion in those Games. Australia's Ron

Clarke pushed himself beyond the limits of his own endurance in his lionhearted bid to reach the finish of that gruelling encounter. When the ashen-faced Clarke collapsed at the end of the race, some observers – the Australian team doctor among them – wept in the belief that Clarke had paid the ultimate price for his conspicuous gallantry. Resuscitated after ten minutes on oxygen, Clarke remains convinced that the damage he did himself that Mexico day contributed directly to his need, years later, for open-heart surgery. 'I was sucked into it,' he said, 'because it was the last lap. I wouldn't have done it, if there had been a lot further to go, because yes, I was feeling a bit queasy.' Clarke had tried to anticipate the problems he eventually encountered. 'I had been working at the Royal Melbourne Hospital's cardiac unit, running on the treadmill and having the full ECG afterwards, and reducing oxygen to simulate the percentage that would be available in Mexico City. And it wasn't the same I have to say! But the point is that there had been no sign of any leakage, or of a heart murmur, so yes – I believe what happened that day was the major contribution to the need for open-heart surgery.'

Biologists and others in sports medicine believe that something in the African make-up lends itself to extreme tests of endurance. Jon Entine has referred to African runners as 'a near-perfect biomechanical package for endurance: lean, ectomorphic physiques, huge natural lung capacity, high proportion of slow-twitch muscle fibres'; the genetic propensity to have less body fat is said to offer a critical edge at this level of running, in both senses of that expression. Little wonder, then, that Keino and Temu claimed silver and bronze behind Gammoudi at five kilometres, or that Wolde and Gammoudi did the same behind Temu over twice that distance, and Benjamin Kogo was second to his Kenyan compatriot in the steeplechase. Black power, indeed. But before Mamo Wolde could run into history in his own right, black power of another kind would have its day.

The 1960s live in the memory as one of the most turbulent decades of a tumultuous century. The Mexico City Olympics were fated to become the sports event at which the struggle of a people for its place in the sun first reached an unprepared and shocked worldwide audience. The first tremor came when the concert of black nations forced the International Olympic Committee to revoke its invitation to South Africa to send her athletes to the Olympic Games. The real wave broke, however, at the presentation ceremony for the men's 200 metres. Americans Tommie Smith and John Carlos were the gold and bronze medallists respectively: black men, both, and proud. The moment when they each raised a black-gloved fist – Smith his right, Carlos his left – atop the Olympic dais has become part of the collective memory of sport in the twentieth century. Whether or not he was moved by his fellow athletes' gesture, Mamo Wolde had other things on his mind as the moment of truth in the marathon came nearer. One of them was Abebe Bikila.

As we have seen, Bikila's bid for a third consecutive Olympic marathon success was thwarted by injury. The Rome and Tokyo champion suffered a fractured bone in his leg as well as ligament damage. Some accounts say that Bikila was almost literally unable to walk in the days preceding the Mexico marathon: a man broken in spirit as well as in body. Famous Ethiopian coach Negussie Roba said quite simply to Wolde, the great man's understudy, that Ethiopia now expected him to don the marathon mantle. It was lucky indeed, then, that Mamo Wolde was already well accustomed to serving Ethiopia in her time of need. His formative years ran in remarkable parallel to those of his predecessor as Olympic marathon champion. Born in 1932 and orphaned early in life, he joined the Imperial Bodyguard in 1951 and benefited in both educational and athletic terms. In 1953, however, Mamo Wolde was sent to Korea as part of the UN peacekeeping mission to that war-torn country, where he stayed for two years. In 1956 he gained Olympic selection for the first time, though last places in his heats of the 800 metres and 1,500 metres and an equally fruitless 4 × 400 relay run did little to suggest the greatness that lay ahead.

According to his own recollection, Mamo Wolde was the innocent victim of an unfortunate tug-of-war when the Rome Olympics came round. As civil war raged in the Congo, the Ethiopian authorities wanted him as part of another peacekeeping initiative. His country's Olympic Committee fought to have him sent with the team to Italy. In the end, predictably enough, he did neither, and indeed the Wolde version has been debunked by his contemporaries. In Japan, four years later, he came fourth in the 10,000 metres, behind American Billy Mills, Gammoudi and Clarke. While he started the marathon, he was unable to finish it. But Mexico was to be an altogether different story. Wolde took silver behind Temu in a brutally fast finish to the 25-lap race early in the Games, but when

72 runners from 44 nations assembled at the marathon start he must have felt the weight of a country's hopes on his shoulders. Mamo Wolde once said, 'Bikila made me want to run: he was my guiding light.' Now the hobbling Bikila would call on him more directly. Though the brave two-time champion took the start and kept pace with the front of the race for fifteen kilometres, he could not go on. His exhortation to his fellow countryman was, 'Mamo, make the ultimate sacrifice.' Wolde duly did, breaking the spirit of familiar adversary Temu at the thirty-kilometre mark, and went on to win by three minutes, beating Japanese runner Kenji Kimihara and New Zealander Michael Ryan. Kimihara was no mean runner in his own right, a winner of the Boston Marathon in 1966, while Scots-born Ryan had won bronze in the Commonwealth Games and taken the Fukuoka race that same year. Wolde's time of 2:20:26.4 was a full 10 minutes and 50 seconds outside the world's best, set by Clayton of Australia at Fukuoka in December of the previous year, and over 8 minutes slower than Bikila's Tokyo Olympic mark. No matter: Ethiopia was still on top of the marathon world with an unprecedented third successive Olympic title, a feat no other nation has ever matched. In the words of Kenny Moore, Mamo Wolde had seemed like 'a black and green wraith, vanishing ahead'. As Moore learned much later, the wraith was to vanish in far more sinister fashion as Mamo Wolde's tragic life unfolded.

Before that, however, there was more marathon business to attend to. From their highest altitude in Mexico City, the Olympic Games sank to the lowest ebb in their history when Black Power gave way to Black September in Munich in 1972. There is little need to revisit the horrifying facts, etched with such grim honesty by Kevin MacDonald's Oscar-winning documentary, *One Day in September*. We should simply remind ourselves that the Black September movement took its name from the month in 1970 when Jordan erupted into bloody civil war, government forces against Palestinian guerrillas who, once defeated, fled to such places as Lebanon and Syria. Hijackings and other politically motivated activities were not yet commonplace, though were on their way to becoming part and parcel of modern life. But 5 September 1972 was the day the Olympic Games lost any vestiges of innocence. As James Lawton has so memorably written, 'The truth is that the Olympic Games have never been able to do more than hold up a mirror to the world in which they operate, and there is neither time nor space to list all the examples.' Between four that morning and one the next, eleven Israeli athletes, five terrorists and one policeman would lose their lives. And yet the Games would go on, delayed by a mere 24 hours. With the marathon scheduled as the final major event, the obvious question was: were the athletes safe to run? None asked the question more directly of himself than the man who would eventually win that race.

Coincidence is a wonderful thing. Frank Shorter was born in Munich of American parents in 1947. By the time the Olympic Games brought him back to the Bavarian capital, Shorter was ready to break a 68-year drought in his country's Olympic marathon history. 'My good fortune,' he would later say, 'was that I happened to be pretty good at it at the right time.' It didn't just happen, of course. Not until his senior year at Yale, where he was a psychology major, did Shorter start taking his running seriously. But once his first degree was over, Shorter made a very sensible move: to Colorado. His coach, Bob Giegengack, had been in Mexico City and seen the effect that running at altitude could have. Shorter was convinced altitude training would develop more of the red blood cells that increase oxygen capacity, and thus be better equipped to excel when he came back down to sea level to race. He proved it by winning the Fukuoka Marathon in 1971, and by the time that tragic September came around, Olympic glory beckoned. Not since 1904 had the United States produced a marathon gold medallist at the Games: but was history about to deny Shorter the chance to bridge the gap back to St Louis and Thomas Hicks?

Shorter, in his room only some fifty metres away from the scene of the Munich crimes, heard gunfire and knew something appalling was in the air. By the time the full scale of the tragedy became known, running a marathon or any other race was close to the last thing on his enquiring mind. 'The first reaction,' he said afterwards, 'was that people died, and nothing is more valuable than human life. So we shouldn't be here, we should all go home. But people started to realise, after they got through the grief and the shock, when they emerged out the other side, that it had to go on because the terrorists wanted it to stop. We have to go on, because otherwise they win. There's no more powerful argument you can make to an athlete.' And so, in the Olympics where his country had perhaps performed worse than in any other year in the Games' history, Frank Shorter went to the line.

So did Mamo Wolde. But, like Abebe Bikila before him, the Ethiopian was to be plagued by problems with the most important part of the distance runner's anatomy: the feet. Years before, Bikila had reacted to ill-fitting shoes by casting them aside. Wolde must have wished he had done the same. 'I lost that competition,' he said, 'because I didn't select shoes for myself.' In fact his toes were painful from the start. Imagine that feeling, with 26 miles ahead . . . 'Had it not been for that problem,' he maintained, 'I'd have won the race. I had four more years' experience compared to Mexico, after all.' Shorter and Wolde apart, it was another high-class field: in it were the fastest two men in marathon history at the time, Clayton of Australia and England's Ron Hill, who had also been training high up in the Alps. But Shorter, surely the epitome of the thinking man's athlete, would beat them in his mind; then beat them on the road.

He surprised everyone with a tactical burst at the fifteen-kilometre mark. Too soon, his American colleagues feared. Not for Frank: 'We ran down a leafy fountain area and we were going to do a 180-degree turn. I was in the back of this huge group of people and I said, "You know, these people may slow down. I'm just going to let my momentum carry me." ' It carried him all the way to the Olympic gold medal. By the 20-kilometre mark Shorter had taken his lead to over 30 seconds, by 25 kilometres it was out to just under a minute, and by 30 it was 65 seconds and growing. 'In no way,' he claimed, 'was this, for me, a race against time. It was a race against other people. The minute I upped the pace, the race was over.' He may not have been racing the clock, but that did not prevent Shorter from setting a personal best of 2:12:20, nearly four minutes outside Clayton's world best from May 1969 but still over two minutes too good for silver medallist Karel Lismont of Belgium. Mamo Wolde ran his own fastest time to take the bronze despite those aching feet. At forty, he was the oldest medalist in Olympic marathon history.

Insignificant though it was in the face of what had happened just five days earlier, Shorter had another disappointment to face. As he entered the Olympic stadium, a young prankster in a garish running outfit somehow got on to the track. After a beautifully worked-out race, Shorter was denied the welcoming roar his mind had started to anticipate. This, he felt, was anti-American feeling taken too far. Kenny Moore, fourth that day and later a gifted columnist for *Sports Illustrated*, had once said Shorter was perfectly equipped for long distances because 'he runs like a ghost'. A ghost Shorter must have thought he was on that lonely lap, asking himself, 'Doesn't anyone see me?'

No one was to see the Mamo Wolde of that day, and especially of the golden day four years earlier in Mexico, again. Ethiopia descended into a nightmare of its own following the revolution of 1974 when the Dergue overthrew Haile Selassie. It brought Mengistu Haile Mariam to power and with him the time in the late 1970s that eventually became known as the Red Terror. Though Mamo Wolde would always protest his innocence, when the Ethiopian People's Revolutionary Democratic Front in turn seized power, he was imprisoned in 1993, accused of killing several people and one teenaged boy in particular. Wolde made that statement quoted earlier about higher powers, and insisted he had deliberately shot to miss the child, already dead. Finally brought to trial nine years later, he was given a six-year sentence and released because he had already spent so much time behind bars, in a part of his prison known, tragically, as 'Alem Bekagne' – 'The End of the World'. And so it was: his health had deteriorated dramatically, and within three months of his release Mamo Wolde was dead. On his release, Wolde had said, 'Thank God I am free at last. I bear no malice towards anyone.'

The journey from Black Power to Black September was complete, and in that eight-year spell perhaps more than in any other phase of history, the Olympic Games were forever altered. Wolde's personal tragedy takes its place alongside the collective sorrow of Munich, where Frank Shorter gave the world his personal, defiant response. As Kenny Moore so movingly wrote, 'It was the finest example of somebody turning all the dross and misery of life into golden performance.' Such is the cycle of violence to which the world, and its mirror known as the Olympic Games, are now prey, that Shorter was able to say three decades later, 'I think you can almost draw a line from Munich to 9/11.' The line only grows firmer when you remember that the Olympic Games in Munich ended one day late – on 9 September 1972.

21. NEW YORK, NEW YORK – THE ENDLESS RACE OF UNIVERSAL APPEAL

Listen carefully and you can hear Frank Sinatra crooning his anthem to their town as the runners limber up for the New York City Marathon. It is different to the rest. It is big and it is brash and it is fun and original. In the city that never sleeps, it is the race that never ends. True to American style, few marathons can match the New York City one for enthusiasm and spectacle. Bigger and bigger each year, the race, which winds its way through the famous Five Boroughs, draws hoards of people out into the streets and sends the buzzing city to a gridlocked standstill. The organised streets, usually home to bright-yellow taxis, bustling dark-suited businessmen and streams of shoppers, bulge with anticipant crowds aiming to infuse that American spirit into every one of the committed and, some may say, crazed entrants in one of the city's biggest events. As one local said, 'You're either in it or you are supporting it. You can't ignore it.' Not even Ol' Blue Eyes himself could have put it better.

Out of humble beginnings, the Big Apple's marathon has ripened. Initially, on its inauguration in 1970, the course streamed through the grassy, tree-filled urban oasis that is Central Park and took in four laps of the same route. The course was undulating, seemingly endless and immediately drew interest for its gruelling and challenging nature. One hundred and twenty-seven runners paid the $1 entry fee, fifty-five of them finished the course and only about a hundred spectators were there to see the finish. The New York Road Runners Club gave co-directors Fred Lebow and Vince Chiappetta just $1,000 for organisation and promotion, unused bowling trophies were recycled to be presented to the winners, and Lebow dug into his own pocket to buy some wristwatches as prizes. American Gary Muhrcke, in a time of 2 hours, 31 minutes and 38 seconds, put his name in the history books as the man who claimed the city's first title, while the race succeeded in claiming the city's hearts.

After New York's arrival in the world of marathon running, the city's inhabitants wasted little time in making sure it secured a rapid place in the folklore of the event. Now, the field has swollen to more than 30,000, organisers term it 'the daddy of big-city marathons' and, while more recent marathons, such as London, have overtaken the event in size, the very nature of the course and the history that the event is steeped in, many believe, are second to none. Total prize money is more than $250,000, with the male and female winners in the open division receiving $50,000 each (a fact that makes a stark comparison, for the women, with the prize money offered in some other cities). But it is the unique and typically American atmosphere that makes the event what it is and it is that which draws people into the event, be they runners, spectators or the 12,000 volunteers that help it happen.

At the turn of the millennium, the event drew more entry requests than ever. In a special year, what better than to run the most special marathon in the world? That is the thought that occurred to a young Italian, sitting with friends discussing life, the universe and everything as they, like the rest of the world, prepared to welcome in a new dawn. That Italian Formula One driver Jarno Trulli, suggested the idea of running a marathon in 2000 but, rather than stay close to home and compete in the Italian International Marathon, sponsored by Italy's most famous Formula One ambassadors Ferrari, he suggested that it should be done in New York.

'I was just on holiday with a few friends and we were chatting towards the end of 1999 and we decided to do the first marathon of the millennium in New York,' said Trulli, who was racing for the Jordan team at that time and is now challenging at the front of the Formula One field with Renault. 'New York is the most representative marathon, the most popular and the most supported. To me it is the biggest one. I have never had an interest in running a marathon, but we just decided it would be good to do. We thought, "Let's do something special for the millennium." It didn't matter if we finished, it is just that it is a nice place and to be able to say that you ran New York is something very special.

'Once in your life you have to run a marathon. I would not do it again, but I would recommend anyone to do a marathon once and I would definitely recommend that they do it in New York. It is such an absolutely fantastic atmosphere. It doesn't look like a marathon. It looks like a carnival. We arrived on the Thursday morning and went for a two- or three-mile run then had lots of tours around, visiting all sorts of places. But we didn't drive the course so I didn't know the route at all so it was difficult to understand how you should be feeling, when you should be tired, and when it was ever going to end!'

The race, originally completely run through Central Park, moved from its original location in 1976 to celebrate the US bicentennial. Organisers decided to draw on the success of the early events and take it to the streets through the now-famous five-borough course that takes in Staten Island, Brooklyn, Queens, the Bronx and Manhattan. The initial course plans were sketchy and there were strong concerns over the ease of clearing the city's sprawling streets. But New York's marathon came of age as a competitive event that year. Men's winner Bill Rodgers turned in the fastest marathon time in the world for 1976 and women's winner Miki Gorman set course and race records.

From the start on Staten Island runners cross the huge expanse of the Verrazano Narrows Bridge into Brooklyn where they run through several ethnic communities from Italian to Hispanic to Hasidic Jewish. At halfway, the route crosses into Queens and rises up on to the Queensboro – or 59th Street – Bridge. Once across, the runners head into Manhattan and emerge to a stadium-like crowd on First Avenue. Running north, under the shadows of the famous Empire State and Chrysler Buildings and past the endless enthusiastic crowds that are now in excess of two million, the runners briefly enter the Bronx before returning to Manhattan to enter Central Park for the gruelling last four-mile run to the Tavern on the Green and the finishing line. On marathon day, First Avenue and Central Park become a street party, with bands playing every half-mile. And it is that atmosphere that helps to make the New York marathon a very special day for everyone taking part.

'It was my first ever marathon, it was my first time on the route and, looking back, I now know that it helps to know the route,' joked Trulli, who managed to complete the event on 5 November 2000 in a respectable time of 4 hours, 4 minutes and 21 seconds. 'I remember when we were running I thought that once we went into Central Park we had virtually finished – but that is definitely not the case! That is where it starts to get really tough! There is so much up and down, it is so hilly and you get very tired very quickly. The one area that sticks in my memory is Central Park. No matter how much you train, how much you have been pacing yourself, or how much you are being willed on, that final run to the finish is tough and you need as much support as you can get.

'And that is the great thing. There are people everywhere. All year they prepare to welcome you. There are bands playing live music, people are urging you on, saying "go on, go go, you can do it, don't stop now". But the thing is, actually, you just cannot stop. It is physically impossible to stop. When I was running I saw some images that will stay in my mind forever and one of those I remember was a long straight full of people where you couldn't stop because people would jump over the fences and start patting you on the back and willing you on. If you decided to pause for a moment you would almost immediately have to start to run again because all the runners just carried you forwards and you had to run along with them. The crowds were not rough, there weren't any things being thrown, no ticker tape and no mess. They were all well composed, but they probably put as much effort into supporting as the runners do in running.

'The last two hundred metres . . . no, actually, the whole of the final bit around Central Park was amazing. When you arrived the crowd cheered you up and it was fantastic for the last few miles. Central Park is just full of people. The city just stops and everyone participates in the marathon, be it running, helping out or cheering. When you finish you finally realise how tough it was and you are really satisfied, even if it hurts. To be honest, I have never had a real interest in marathons. I watched the Olympic marathon, but have never watched the London Marathon because it is in the middle of a really busy period in the Formula One season. I only did the New York one as a special one-off. But I experienced a lot.'

Trulli is a decent athlete in the strenuous world of Formula One, has a passionate hobby as a chef and is, because of his job, a very healthy eater. He is honed to the peak of physical fitness through a stringent exercise regime, aided by a personal fitness instructor and regular visits to his Renault team's high-tech Human Performance Centre in Enstone, near his Oxfordshire home, in England. If he is not driving, he is training. If he is not training, he is in his favourite kitchen apron preparing healthy dishes and, if he is not eating the food he has prepared, he is sleeping, dreaming of the next challenge in his fitness-fanatical life. His decision to do the marathon was based on the fact that, while he knew it would not be a walk in the park, he thought it would be a relatively simple challenge to put his already fit body to a different test. That is where he was wrong.

'A marathon requires totally different training to that needed for Formula One,' Trulli explained. 'A marathon is a long way and it is not easy, especially for me because I needed a lot of time to do specific training for long distance. The marathon came one or two weeks after the last F1 race of the season and although I am fit, I am not fit to run that kind of distance. The difficulty of a marathon, and training for it, depends on what your target is, what time you want to achieve. It takes a lot of effort to train for it and there are lots of problems. When you run that far it is always going to hurt! It is not the best thing to do for a Formula One driver either. The maximum I had run before the marathon was three hours and I got problems after three hours and twenty minutes – it gets tough when you pass your maximum, I tell you!

'At the time I started training for the marathon I was quite fit, but I could then go and play football for twenty minutes and be absolutely knackered, absolutely dead, because it is a totally different thing. People who do a particular sport are trained for that particular sport. It doesn't mean you can change to another sport and be just as fit for that one, and that is strange to me, difficult to understand. I did it with seven or eight people, including my girlfriend and my engineer. We didn't run together though, everyone had done different levels of training. We had someone do it in three hours and ten minutes, one in three hours forty, me, and people who did it in six hours. The biggest challenge is not the time, it is getting to the finish. I did it with four jet lags! I had four consecutive jet lags in about one and a half months because I was in the USA then back to Europe then to Japan then Europe again then Malaysia, then Europe then out to New York. That made it tough! It was a challenge and I finished it in four hours and a couple of minutes. Those bloody couple of minutes! It is nice to be able to say I finished it in under four hours but I can't.'

Trulli, a man among the masses in bib number 2309, aimed, like many numbers before and after him, simply to finish the event, to collect his medal, and to proudly tell his friends and Formula One rivals that he had completed the great New York Marathon. He did so, albeit disappointed to finish outside three hours and even more aggravated by the fact his race engineer, Dino Toso, a fellow Italian, completed the run in 3 hours, 59 minutes and 12 seconds. But while he was one of the many fun runners and amateur competitors on whom the event thrives, there are many others at the sharp end of athletic competition for whom New York is now one of the chief prizes on the list. It was not long into its life that New York's event drew professional interest and, when it did so, it attracted marathon debutante Grete Waitz, whose name is now synonymous with the event and omnipresent in its history.

It was one year after the 1977 race – in which the number of entrants had grown to a then-world-record 4,821 and the number of finishers had increased from just over 300, in 1975, to 3,885 – that the Norwegian's name appeared on the record books. While American Bill Rogers was continuing his run of four consecutive victories, begun in 1976, Waitz, a blonde 25-year-old track runner with pigtails arrived in New York to begin stamping her mark on the event. Although she was world dominant in 1,500- and 3,000-metres running, she had never taken on the challenge of a marathon. Astonishingly, she won, breaking the world record by more than two minutes. The draining event left her insisting she would never attempt the distance again. But the lure of the marathon and, in particular, the lure of the New York spectacular, drew her back again, and again, and again. She went on to win the race eight more times in the next ten years.

Hers was a time when women athletes were not taken seriously, not given equal opportunities and not supported financially or personally. In her teenage years at home in Oslo, Norway, she was always focused on trying to get to the next race and constantly fought with her family to do so, because her brothers were seen as the athletes while she was simply a young girl who should not be concerned with physical exertion. Somehow, she made it into international competition, finally winning the respect and support of her parents, and went on to pioneer the movement of women into athletics. In 1972, she saw women allowed to compete at the 1,500-metres event in the Olympic Games in Munich and three years later became one of the first women to run 3,000 metres in competition as she continued to strive for more women's events to be instigated on the international calendar.

There were no female finishers in the inaugural New York Marathon in 1970 and, until the arrival of Waitz in 1978, fresh from teacher training school, where she studied as back-up in case her running came to nothing, all the female winners were American nationals. But her arrival heralded a new era, one in which women finally proved they could compete on such a distance. She became the first woman athlete to break 2 hours and 30 minutes in 1979, when Roberts won his final event, clocking a time just 16 minutes quicker. During a period of six years she improved the women's marathon world record on no fewer than four occasions – three times in her adopted 'home' of New York in 1978, 1979 and 1980, the latter with her best ever time in New York of 2 hours, 25 minutes and 41 seconds, at a time when the event was not recognised as a race at which women could or should excel.

Waitz went on to continue her stardom on the opposite side of America when, in the 1984 Olympics in Los Angeles, women were allowed to compete in the marathon for the first time in the history of the Games and she brought home the silver medal. It was fitting that, after leading the movement to develop marathon running for all by competing and succeeding in New York, she would achieve an Olympic medal for her efforts. Hard training in cold winter months had paid off and she is proud of the mould-breaking her success achieved. 'Looking back on my career and thinking that I almost retired in 1978 except for that infamous New York City Marathon, I am glad I got a shot at a second distance-running career,' she said. Now, after retiring in 1990, she is making sure women from all walks of life are given as much chance as possible to live their dreams in marathon running.

Those sorts of emotional achievements are typical to the spirit of marathon running and they continue throughout the world year on year. A wheelchair category was introduced to the New York Marathon for the first time in 2000 and the following year, less than two months after the 11 September terrorist attacks on the city's trademark twin towers, the marathon became a race of hope and renewal for participants, spectators, and all New Yorkers; and patriotism ran high as the race hosted the USA Marathon Championships. The 2002 race had a separate start for the women's field, highlighting the most competitive women's field in race history and, in 2003, in unseasonably warm temperatures and high humidity, a record 98 per cent of the 35,286 people who started the race crossed the line at Tavern on the Green, led by Waitz as the event's first ever grand marshal.

Organisers, helped by extra funding from ING, the first ever title sponsor of the event, set up designated cheering zones, complete with mini-megaphones, at miles 8, 12, 13.8, and 19, where excitable fans could offer the runners extra boisterous support as they followed the race on plasma-screens. The emphasis has grown into charity fundraising, with musician, fashion designer and entrepreneur Sean 'P. Diddy' Combs one of the many celebrities continuing the tradition by completing the marathon in 4 hours, 14 minutes and 54 seconds – beating Oprah Winfrey's personal best time of 4 hours and 29 minutes – and raising two million dollars for charities dedicated to improving the lives of New York City children. Combs's two million dollars was double what he initially sought to raise. 'I want to thank the people of New York City who came out in droves to support me in every borough,' says Combs. 'The New York City Marathon is an unbelievable experience – both physically and mentally and I'm so blessed to have finished it and shared the experience with so many wonderful people.'

Little more than three hours after Combs crossed the finish line, another impressive story of the 2003 marathon came to a conclusion when 92-year-old Sikh man Fauja Singh finished the gruelling event. Running in bright yellow T-shirts, saffron turbans and carrying the Akhanda, a Sikh religious knife, he hoped to help to educate the public about Sikhism, a religion founded in Punjab, India, in the 1500s. Singh endured taunts of 'Hey, Osama Bin Laden' and 'Look at Saddam' along the way but, thankfully for the spirit of New York and its historic marathon, such taunts were out-shouted by cheers and continuous clapping that kept the Londoner focused on the road ahead. 'When the people were cheering at me I was getting all of their energies,' he said after his sixth marathon, an event he took up only recently after the death of his wife.

Singh, a great grandfather with members of his extended family living in Italy, Canada, India and the US, ran his first London marathon in 2000, aged 89, having not run for 53 years. It took 6 hours, 54 minutes and 42 seconds. When he ran a near-identical 6 hours, 54 minutes 55 seconds in 2001, he found he had knocked almost an hour off the world record for the over-90s. 'You only die once,' he said. 'At this age, I may die any time at home and no one will notice. But, if I die while running, at least people will know me as a Sikh that ran the marathon. Running in a marathon is no more dangerous than walking on the street.'

22. HISTORY 11 – MONTREAL TO MOSCOW WITH A DISGRACED DOUBLE WINNER

'My running was very simple,' claimed the peerless Zatopek. 'It was out of myself.' If only the same could be said for the man who became the second double marathon gold medallist in Olympic history after Abebe Bikila. The controversy surrounding East German athlete Waldemar Cierpinski emerged in full only long after the Montreal Olympics were over but, like the Games' cost to Montrealers, it would never really go away. Cierpinski emerged from almost total obscurity, and a steeplechaser's background, to astound himself, his team-mates and especially Frank Shorter by winning Olympic gold at the first time of asking. The obvious question was: how did he do it?

The Cierpinski question was only one of a long list of controversies surrounding Montreal's elevation to the elite club of Olympic cities: bad weather, strikes, construction delays all had their part to play in leaving the Olympic facilities short of their full splendour by the time the Games began. More important than any of those, however, was the first major boycott of the Olympic Games, which meant that Cierpinski had none of the great black Africans to beat. It came about because the black African nations objected to the IOC's inviting New Zealand to the Games when that country's rugby union touring squad had graced South Africa, apartheid and all, with its presence. And sadly, it was only the prelude to an even more dramatic boycott four years later.

On the face of it, Cierpinski – dismissed by some of his East German team-mates as 'a living example of mediocrity' – should not have had the ghost of a chance. He had tried his hand, or rather his feet, at the marathon for the first time only two years before. Up against him were two medallists from Munich: gold-winner Shorter himself, now 29 and arguably at his peak, and Karel Lismont, one of the great Belgian runners of that golden age in his country's distance-running history. The dangerous Canadian Jerome Drayton was in there too, and to add intrigue the outstanding athlete from Munich and Montreal, double gold medallist at 5,000 and 10,000 metres, Lasse Viren, had decided to 'do a Zatopek' and have a tilt at this marathon thing himself.

As rain fell on the city of Montreal, it was American ace Bill Rodgers who led them through the first quarter of the 1976 Olympic marathon. Unlike Munich, where his early break had caught the entire field napping, Shorter this time opted for the more traditional waiting game. His mind, though, was still working just as hard as his body, helping him to implement a carefully planned sequence of surges designed to break the hearts of those around, and soon behind him. Even the great Viren could not keep up, falling back after around 25 kilometres to come home a creditable fifth. Nor could anyone else – until the East German interloper appeared at Shorter's side. Cierpinski would later claim that, as he was an unknown quantity who knew all about Shorter, the psychological advantage was what carried him clear of the surprised American. Shorter would take a different view.

First, though, there was a minor farce to be played out, just as there had been in Munich four years earlier when another, less serious interloper stole Shorter's thunder on the final lap inside the Olympic stadium. This time the confused individual was Cierpinski himself. He arrived just as the strains of his own national anthem were playing, not in anticipation of his feat but at the medal ceremony for East Germany's women's $4 \times 4,000$ relay squad. Inspired perhaps by the music, and stunned at seeing the figure '1' on the lap board, Cierpinski embarked upon an extra lap. It may be the only time in Olympic history that the silver medallist has been waiting at the tape to greet the winner of the gold, for Shorter in the interim had completed the course in his own right and was waiting to give the victor a sporting pat on the back. Perhaps that is when the rot set in, for the American was stunned to hear the winner address him in German. 'Sprechen Sie Deutsch?' Cierpinski asked. 'Do you speak German?' 'I thought to myself, "That's a hell of a thing for a guy from Portugal to ask me!"' Shorter said later. He had mistakenly persuaded himself that the unfamiliar individual running alongside and then away from him was, in fact, Carlos Lopes of Portugal. He was eight years ahead of himself and Lopes, who took gold in Los Angeles in 1984.

While Lismont distinguished himself with a second successive Olympic marathon medal, this time the bronze, the fourth-placed man that Montreal day was another American, Don Kardong. Kardong would later jokingly introduce Shorter as 'the only man twice to have an impostor finish the Olympic marathon ahead of him'. Sadly, Kardong was not referring to Shorter's case of mistaken identity, but something far more serious – something that was about to become commonplace in the Olympics and in sport generally. In retrospect, Shorter has always claimed to have had his doubts about Cierpinski from the very moment he knew the Olympic marathon double was being taken away from him. 'I suspected the minute he ran away from me,' the American wrote later. 'Just the way he did it, the ease with which he did it. It sounds like sour grapes when you say nobody could do it that easy. You know what kind of effort it would take for a normal person. Now I know . . . there was a reason for it. And it didn't have to do with anything I did incorrectly.' What that reason was became clear and apparently incontrovertible only 22 years later, thanks in no small measure to the persistence of Shorter himself in pursuing the truth about the man who denied him that Olympic double. For the present, though, Waldemar Cierpinski could bask in Olympic glory, an additional lustre lent to his achievement by a personal best and Olympic record of 2:09:55 – the first time the Olympic marathon winner had dipped below 2:10. In the absence of the great African runners, behind fifth-placed Viren came Drayton of the host nation, Leonid Moseyev of the Soviet Union and Italian Franco Fava. Viren had every right to be thrilled with a time of 2:13:10, three-and-a-quarter minutes off the winning pace. It would bring the Finn back for another crack at the marathon in Moscow four years later.

If Viren was in Moscow, 65 invited nations were not. If Olympic-watchers had thought Montreal four years earlier was a major political boycott, it had nothing on what happened in 1980. It was what happened in 1979 that triggered it. On Christmas Eve of that year, the Soviet Union invaded Afghanistan, provoking righteous anger around the world, nowhere more vociferous than in the White House. As President Carter fulminated against Soviet aggression and threatened to take the passport of any US athlete who dared travel to Moscow, Prime Minister Margaret Thatcher expressed her solidarity with the American stance – but stopped short of actually preventing British athletes from taking part. It was an interesting volte-face by a leading politician who had earlier condoned and justified the position of UK rugby union players bent on touring South Africa – the catalyst for the Olympic boycott four years earlier when their New Zealand counterparts did the same.

If there was a pre-Moscow marathon favourite, perhaps it was the Dutchman Gerard Nijboer. On 26 April of Olympic year, he had set not only a Dutch record in winning the Amsterdam Marathon in 2:09:01, but also the time that would stand as best in the world that year. Once again, though, the big names of marathon running were not really there – except the biggest one of all in Olympic terms, the reigning champion. Bidding to emulate Bikila with a second successive win, the East German lay doggo for much of the Moscow race. Lasse Viren was a frontrunner for much of the first half until Mother Nature intervened, forcing the Finn into less than glorious retirement when an attack of diarrhoea seized him. Mexican runner Rodolfo Gomez was quick to spot an opportunity, making a break on the leading group and trying to make it decisive with a marked increase in pace. Running a five-kilometre stretch in well under fifteen minutes, though, was too much to ask of himself even on this momentous day, and Gomez's challenge withered. He would eventually finish sixth. Into the breach stepped Nijboer, who must have been confident at that stage that Olympic gold would be his.

That confidence was shattered within less than one kilometre. The reigning Olympic champion strode past. As in his attack on Shorter, Cierpinski, now just a couple days short of turning thirty, seemed totally in control, able to shift to a higher gear at will even after forty gruelling kilometres, and even with the weight of Communist anticipation on his shoulders. He responded with a sprintlike finish that carried him through the final half-lap in a mere 33.4 seconds, the icing on the cake of a total time of 2:11:03 – a good 2 minutes shy of Nijboer's Amsterdam performance. Nijboer, whose Amsterdam mark stood as the Dutch national record until a man called Maase broke it in 2003, clocked 2:11:20 to take silver: he would go one place better two years later in the European Championships in Athens. The Dutchman was, in turn, fifteen seconds ahead of Soviet runner Satymkul Dzhumanazarov, who was a Kirgizian. Early pacemaker Vladimir Kotov, also from the Soviet Union, came fourth ahead of team-mate Leonid Moseyev – two places higher than his Montreal finish.

Cierpinski's apparently distinguished career was not yet over. In 1983 he would take bronze at the Helsinki World Championships behind Robert de Castella and Ethiopian Kebede Balacha. Nowadays, in the freer markets of the new Germany, the former East German sports master has begun to do rather well for himself in the sports goods business, a burgeoning enterprise centred on the city of Halle. Ironically, he has followed a similar path to the man he beat in 1976, for Frank Shorter has also done well out of Frank Shorter Sports and, like Cierpinski, has been a frequent expert analyst on marathon telecasts. Shorter, though, is also a trained lawyer with a degree completed at the University of Florida two years after his own Olympic success. The sheer doggedness of the marathoner, together with an incisive legal brain, have kept him running after Cierpinski in metaphorical terms for more than two decades. Not only that, but Shorter has also been the founding father and first chairman of the US Anti-Doping Agency. The combination of all these qualities and roles seemed certain to bear fruit as Shorter sought to establish that it was he, not Cierpinski, who should have been the second double Olympic marathon winner after Bikila. The impostor who beat him in Montreal was a man on drugs or, as one American commentator pithily put it, 'juiced to the gills'. So Bikila 'the barefoot' was joined by Cierpinski 'the cheat'.

It was not until 1998 that Shorter received confirmation of what he claimed always to have believed. As the walls of the Communist world came tumbling down, so did those of its most secretive institutions. One of these was the East German secret police, the Stasi. Documents formerly classified became available in the late 1990s and Shorter received a package of them. It contained details of what the world had long known but been unable or unwilling to say out loud: that a government-backed programme of sports drug-taking had been the real key to East German excellence throughout the 1970s and 1980s. How else, for example, would an East German women's swimming team that had finished nowhere in Munich in 1972 come away from Montreal just four years later with no fewer than eleven of the thirteen gold medals on offer in the pool? Athletes on the East German programme were set out by specially allocated numbers. Shorter was able to establish that number 62 would become more infamous than the vests that Waldemar Cierpinski wore en route to marathon gold: for that was the number at which Cierpinski figured on the Stasi list. A memorandum quoting that list and Cierpinski's place upon it was dated February 1976, six months earlier than the Games at which Cierpinski denied Shorter his second gold.

At the height of his career Waldemar Cierpinski had made this claim: 'Running as long as possible – I've made that into a sport. I have no other secrets. Without running I wouldn't be able to live.' Frank Shorter knew he did have other secrets, and Frank Shorter was just as determined to keep running. As he said of his job at the USADA, it called on the mindset that had served him so well in his own athletic career: 'What you want to be to cheaters is the person running on their shoulder, and you're still there and you're smiling at him. You're not going away.' Those words were eerily similar to the way Cierpinski had summed up his strategy in staying physically close to Shorter. This time the American would refuse to be shaken off. The IOC eventually imposed a three-year statute of limitation on drug-related disqualifications, though what Shorter must have felt on seeing disgraced skaters and cross-country skiers instantly ousted from medal-winning positions at the Salt Lake City Winter Olympics is anybody's guess. Such are the ironies of life that Cierpinski is still fêted in his native country, and still as much an ambassador for marathon running there as Shorter was to be in the United States, a trainer and mentor to budding triathletes including his own son Falk. Cierpinski Senior ran the Sydney Olympic course long before the Games went Down Under and finished 32nd in a field of 1,600 in the thoroughly respectable time of 2:45:22. Recent wholesome gestures include his involvement in rebuilding schools in the war-ravaged Vietnamese village of Ai Tu, a joint venture with Vietnamese kung fu grand master Chu Tau Cuong, and his involvement in the 'Middle German Marathon' from Halle to Leipzig designed to boost the latter city's bid to host the Games of 2012. In 1980, a hysterical East German commentator urged his watching audience to name their newborn sons Waldemar. How many of those young men will have opted for their middle names in recent years?

23. LONDON – RUNNING, AND SINGING IN THE RAIN

It rains in London. People run to escape it. They splash through puddles and arrive home with damp clothes. Foreign visitors often cry for blue skies and sunshine. The grey skies can depress even the most optimistic natures. Central London, the middle of the city that embraces Piccadilly, Oxford Street, Regent Street, Marble Arch and Park Lane, is often no more than a solid mass of metal, cars fuming in queues and belching exhaust smoke. London, after all, is the city made famous by its smog, bad weather and unappetising food. It is a wonder any tourists visit at all; if it was not for the history, the museums, the theatres and the Royal Opera House, maybe they would not. So, it is the last place anyone would expect to find people wanting to run in a marathon. Yet, against all expectations, it is a marathon city. More than that, it is a city that hosts one of the best marathons on earth.

The London Marathon was born on 29 March 1981. The brainchild of Chris Brasher, a former Olympic 3,000-metre steeplechase champion, it was realised as the inaugural event was held when 7,747 people ran through the English capital (more than 22,000 had applied to compete, only for the numbers to be restricted by police) and 6,255 made it to the finishing line at Constitution Hill. It was the start of something special, the birth of one of the top events for long-distance runners and weekend joggers in the world and it was held in a vast and colourful city of humour, heart and endless distractions.

Brasher, who had run along with Chris Chataway as a pacemaker on the famous day in 1954 at Iffley Road, Oxford, when Roger Bannister broke the four-minute barrier for the mile for the first time, was a man of courage, ideas, vision and action. Two years earlier, he had run the New York City Marathon and been captivated by the true essence of it. With a £50,000 contract from Gillette, a manufacturer of razors and shaving products, Brasher was able to bring to bear what had been no more than an idea.

Brasher, a multitalented individual who worked in television and journalism and who was awarded an MBE later in life, enjoyed a successful career as an elite athlete. In 1956, two years after his famous pacemaking role in Oxford, he claimed his steeplechase gold in the Melbourne Games having, as he put it, given up smoking, mountain climbing and girls to achieve his ambition! After running in New York, Brasher wrote in the *Observer* newspaper,

> To believe this story, you must believe the human race to be one joyous family, working together, laughing together, achieving the impossible. Last Sunday, in one of the most trouble-stricken cities in the world, 11,532 men and women from 40 countries in the world, assisted by over a million black, white and yellow people, laughed, cheered and suffered during the greatest folk festival the world has seen.

Within two years, he ensured London could host such a carnival.

The inaugural marathon was organised with a total budget of £100,000, half of which came from the Gillette deal, from which 2,000 foil blankets, 75 portable lavatories, 400 gallons of coffee and 50,000 plastic cups were supplied. The boom of a 25-pound cannon that started the marathon in Greenwich Park, 200 acres of parkland making up London's oldest Royal Park in the southeast of the capital, sent the field, which ranged from a 15-year-old girl to septuagenarians, on their way at 0900 BST (British Summer Time). The competitors wound their way along the banks of the River Thames, the route containing more turns than its New York sister and 30 yards more road than the official marathon distance, with 1,000 volunteers, 500 constables and 300 St John Ambulance personnel helping along the route before the finish at Constitution Hill. More significantly, television coverage from the BBC helped give the marathon wide exposure across Britain and its popularity has grown ever since.

In the 24 years that have followed, London's roads have been witness to triumph and tragedy, brilliance and bravery. Inge Simonsen, of Norway, and American Dick Beardsley were both crowned the first victors of the men's race after a dead-heat finish, with Briton Joyce Smith claiming the first of back-to-back wins in the female race. The sportsmanship, camaraderie and comradeship Brasher had been part of in New York ensured the outcome of the inaugural marathon will stand out in history. Beardsley, 24, and Simonsen, 25, crossed through the tape hand in hand after 2 hours,

11 minutes and 48 seconds. About seven hours after the cannon had started the race, Marie Dominque de Groot, from Paris, and British runner David Gaiman, came home at the rear of the field, replicating Beardsley and Simonsen's finish by holding hands as they crossed the line.

Other names like Steve Jones followed in their footsteps. Jones won in 1985 and his time stood as the course record until Portugal's Antonio Pinto recorded a new best across the capital in 1997, five years after he had won for the first time. In between, of course, other greats have taken the honours. Ingrid Kristiansen, of Norway, won the female race four times in five years between 1984 and 1988, her compatriot Grete Waitz won in 1986 to add to the success she had enjoyed in 1983. Germany's Katrin Dorre completed a hat trick of victories in 1994 before Mexico's Dionico Ceron achieved the same feat of three back-to-back wins in the men's race in 1996. Ceron also won in 2000. Paula Radcliffe, the embodiment of so much that is quintessentially English in her running and her nature, gave the London public a home win to savour in 2002 and 2003, Liz McColgan having also won the race on home soil, or asphalt, in 1996. Radcliffe also broke a tradition of the event when she was allowed to start at the same time as the elite men, the first time a woman had been permitted to do so.

It is now an historic event that more than 500,000 athletes have started, though not all of them have finished for a wide variety of reasons. The London Marathon has seen seventeen different male winners and fourteen female winners to the end of 2003. Of those half-million starters, the casual runner and the individuals running for charity have played as much a part as the leading athletes at the forefront of the field. Now, it is a global marketing dream. More than 500,000 people clog up London's transport system on one Sunday every April to line the streets of the route, while television viewing figures are at an all-time high with the marathon, still covered by the BBC, broadcast in more than 100 countries worldwide. In 2003, a total of 46,500 competitors started from a record 80,500 applicants as the streets were filled to capacity. On the other 51 Sundays in the year, the route of the marathon is home to no more than a few strolling dog-walkers, or families driving out to lunch; or, perhaps, on a rare sunny afternoon, a couple enjoying the glorious English weather on their way to a walk in the park.

*   *   *

'The greatest marathon ever completed.' That was the assessment of Michael Watson's 6-day trek to cover the 26.2 miles the London Marathon could throw at him. His was an achievement few would contemplate, it was nothing short of heroic, and it was a lesson and example to others. In ambling the distance across England's capital in April 2003, he completed a superhuman effort and with it recorded the slowest time ever in the event. None of it was for him. It was all for others.

The accolade bestowed upon the former boxer's feat came from neurosurgeon Peter Hamlyn, the man who saved Watson's life with six brain operations, who set up the Brain and Spine Foundation, for which the marathon quest raised cash in 1992, and who persuaded his former patient to take part. Hamlyn, who accompanied Watson on the entire route from Greenwich to The Mall, knew only too well the bravery that had been shown in order to raise funds for the benefit of others.

On a terrible day in 1991, Watson, then aged 26, had suffered brain injuries in the final round of a world super-middleweight boxing fight with Chris Eubank at White Hart Lane, the north London home of English football club Tottenham Hotspur. He was in a coma for forty days and even experts of Hamlyn's medical calibre did not expect him to talk, let alone walk again. He was warned speech and movement were over. As Watson recalled, he was branded a 'cabbage' who would never live a normal life for his remaining years. But he decided to prove them wrong.

He did not regain the full use of his left side as a result of the paralysis that prevented him from walking until his true grit got him out of his wheelchair. He also suffers from dizzy spells and a stiffening back. Before contemplating the marathon, Watson struggled to walk across a room. But that was all put to one side as, in January 2003, he began three months of training that would ultimately see him complete his goal and earn a place in people's hearts throughout the length of Britain. Watson, competitor number 60,199 and captain of Team Telegraph, the group charged with raising money for the Brain and Spine Foundation, completed four miles a day, two in the morning and two in the afternoon, along with closest friend and carer Lennard Ballack, Hamlyn and Patrick Dayton, the trainer of then-world heavyweight boxing champion Lennox Lewis, who took three weeks off to help with the marathon.

In between his double stints, Watson rested, slept and ate on a double-decker bus.

In addressing Team Telegraph in December 2002, Watson was an inspiration. Few were left with dry eyes after his captain's speech. 'I have come a long, long way. I will set a milestone in this race for the marathon,' he said. 'As far as I am concerned, the race has already been accomplished. I will raise a substantial amount of money. I have a lot to repay the Brain and Spine Foundation for because of what they have done throughout my life. But I do love a challenge. I have a strong memory of preparing for fights. Except the victory in this fight will be crossing the line, and the belt will be the money which will go to helping people. I hope that every step I take in the marathon helps someone in hospital, or helps towards facilities to improve their lives. I'm looking forward to this marathon and I'm going to make the most of it. I don't feel the pressure, and I won't crack.' Hamlyn, a man who had seen some grisly sights in a boxing ring, added, 'If he achieves it, it will be one of the greatest achievements the marathon has ever seen.'

There was great irony in the two major stories that came from that 2003 London Marathon and it was exemplified most dramatically before the race began when Watson, conserving his energy for what lay ahead, sat in the elite athletes' tent at Greenwich Park, chatting to Paula Radcliffe. Little more than two hours later, the British female athlete had finished her own marathon in a world-record time while Watson was hoping to complete the first of his 26 miles. As Radcliffe lapped up the plaudits, Watson, who started after all the other competitors had left the start line, for safety reasons, was in the infancy of his own 'marathon' effort, some would say Herculean, and had covered the first mile and reached Woolwich. It had taken him, and the group of followers, 22 minutes, but he arrived at the one-mile marker to a chorus of 'You'll Never Walk Alone'. Road cleaners sent to remove the markings for the route from London's roads passed him, as did a late starter, but his pace was not a concern. More important to him, and to the members of his team, was to ensure that the buckets carried by the Team Telegraph members were circulated and filled with cash. Tearful well-wishers emptied their pockets, purses and wallets to honour the effort Watson was making. 'It means more than having a world-champion-ship belt around my waist. The honour of being a champion of the people is much greater,' he remarked at the time.

The measure of the man came at the two-mile mark when he went against the advice of his training team, who had told him to keep his momentum going at all times, when he felt he had to stop to console a Japanese female wheelchair competitor who sat at the side of the road. 'Although the plan was to keep my momentum going, I felt I had to stop to shake her hand. The wheelchair athletes are truly inspiring,' he said. Equally inspiring for Watson was the presence of Alex Robinson and Jenny Gritt for part of his marathon. Robinson, a fourteen-year-old boy, walked two miles for the first time since being knocked down by a car eleven months earlier and suffering injuries. Jenny is the mother of Hayley Gritt, one of the founding members of the Brain and Spine Foundation who had died before Christmas 2002. Hamlyn had performed numerous operations to keep Hayley alive from the age of eight, before she eventually died at eighteen. 'Her mother told me the family will always celebrate those extra ten years. That's what my London Marathon is all about. This marathon is about helping people's lives,' Watson said.

It is an inspirational story. A homeless man, with only a cardboard box for shelter, gave the seventy pence he had raised while sitting begging under the bridge at the Embankment, and an ice-cream vendor on the route happily handed over his entire takings for the day. By the end, Watson had raised in excess of £200,000 for the foundation. Chris Eubank, the opponent who had inadvertently inflicted such horrendous injuries on Watson, was there to walk the final 1.2 miles from Blackheath Common to The Mall with Watson on the final Saturday, six days after the odyssey had begun. Watson's former boxing promoters Frank Maloney and Frank Warren walked with him during the six-day challenge, as did boxer Audley Harrison, footballers Ashley Cole, Chris Powell, John Fortune, Jason Euell and Kevin Lisbie, former sports minister Kate Hoey, London Marathon organiser David Bedford, Robert Darko, another boxer to suffer brain injuries, David Prescott, the brother of Michael, who had been in a bed next to Watson's, in St Bartholomew's Hospital. Lennox Lewis, the world heavyweight boxing champion, sent a good luck message as did the greatest boxer of all, Watson's hero and idol, Muhammad Ali.

Rightly, the finish line was re-erected once again in The Mall on Saturday so that Watson could finish his marathon just as all of the other competitors had. The Chief Inspector of the Metropolitan Police, who was in charge of the finish section on Sunday, was there to see his task through to the finish, as were hordes of adoring supporters captivated by the spirit, fight and determination Watson had shown. They all wanted to pay their own tributes and respects to such a brave man. Watson stopped at the finishing tape to savour his moment before walking through the tape and into the arms of his mother, Joan, who proudly hung the medal around his neck. The cheering from the supporters said it all. He had achieved his goal. A clock used to time his marathon showed 6 days, 2 hours, 27 minutes and 17 seconds. It meant he had completed the course at an average speed of one mile per hour. It also registered as the slowest time ever set, one year after Lloyd Scott had taken more than five days to walk the distance in a heavy diving suit.

'One Michael Watson . . . There's only one Michael Watson,' was one of the cries from the crowd gathered to witness the culmination of a real feat. It was followed by 'We love you, Michael, we do.' Many of those gathered were in tears. Eubank, who had stood back on the approach to the finish line to let his former rival in the boxing ring complete the final steps of his epic journey alone, led the post-event tributes: 'Twelve years ago, a lot of people looked into his head and said that he would not live. This is the ultimate proof that Michael Watson is alive and vibrant. It's an incredible day.' Watson revelled in the fact that he had achieved his goal and reached the finish. The fight in the man was unbelievable. 'It has been an amazing, epic journey for me,' he said. 'The longer it has gone on, the stronger I have felt. In truth I didn't want it to end. That's how much I enjoyed it. There are so many memories that will stay in my mind; memories that will stay with me for a lifetime. Memories of people, and of the power that the human spirit possesses, people who gave their all to me. I remember the man who rose from his cardboard box under the bridge on the Embankment to give me seventy pence and the deaf and mute man who came to meet me. These are the people I hope I can inspire. They said I was going to be a cabbage. What a horrible way to describe a person. And look how wrong they were. They said I would not walk. They said I would not talk. But look at what I have achieved. And I won't stop at the marathon. I will take on new challenges. The more I take on, the better I will feel, the stronger I will become.'

Hamlyn has witnessed so many brain-injury victims succumb to their ailments, but Watson has amazed and inspired him. He knows the fact that Watson made the start line is a miracle in itself and acknowledges the feat that has been achieved. Hamlyn said in his final diary in the *Daily Telegraph*,

> He rose from the edge of death to strive across twelve often desolate years just to reach Sunday's start line. He has been an inspiration to me throughout, as he was to all those who have met him. He is a noble man who, unbowed by a burden, which even now would extinguish most of us, has walked not for himself but for others less fortunate. Michael's marathon is 12 years, 6 operations, 3 hospitals, 26 miles and 365 yards long. The psychical feat is truly unimaginable. Remember his words: 'I'm doing this for others less fortunate than myself.'

Watson's walk earned him an MBE in the Queen's New Year's Honours List, which he then received in February 2004. It saw him given the Helen Rollason Award for a special achievement and bravery at the BBC Sports Personality of the Year awards and given an accolade for outstanding courage by the Variety Club. British Prime Minister Tony Blair and his wife Cherie invited Watson to tea at Number 10 Downing Street. The success of his marathon forced him to contemplate a second walk for charity, but Watson decided to seek alternative challenges. He knew his special marathon had added a great chapter to the history of the London Marathon and given inspiration to millions.

It can be held on a dull April day, with rain, or a pleasant spring morning with sunlight brightening the streets. The cool temperate British climate ensures that the London Marathon is not one of the most demanding, from a physical perspective, but more of a scenic trip across England's capital. Passing Big Ben, Buckingham Palace, Tower Bridge, Birdcage Walk and the Cutty Sark, as the route winds alongside the River Thames to the finish area at The Mall, it provides a great spectacle. For the elite, the conditions are favourable for quick times, as Paula Radcliffe proved in achieving a new world-record time in 2003, but for the fun-runners, those dressed as a big bird, elephant, clown or even Elvis Presley, it is simply that – a weekend of fun, aimed at raising funds for charities. Unfortunately, however, it has also been the source of stories of tragedy, having been the scene of seven cardiac deaths since the maiden marathon in 1981.

Twelve months before Watson completed his feat, Lloyd Scott, the man who would become known as 'the diving suit man', took 'fancy dress' to a new extreme when he walked the distance in his authentic 120-pound deep-sea diving suit in aid of leukaemia charities. Scott, a former fireman who had contracted the disease in saving the lives of two young boys, ran a marathon shortly before, and then after, undergoing a bone marrow transplant to save his life. His saga in the diving suit, which weighed as much as an average teenage female, took a total of 5 days, 8 hours, 29 minutes and 46 seconds to complete and was classified as the slowest time until Watson finished his own remarkable trek. Scott's diving suit is a story that has taken in the New York and Edinburgh Marathons, the latter running to a seventh day, illness detracting from his pace, and, of course, a march across the floor of Loch Ness.

Others have tales to tell. Jenny Wood Allen continues to hold the world-record time for women over seventy, set in London. Having taken up marathon running at the age of 71, she finally hung up her training shoes in 2002 at the age of 91 after completing the distance for the last time. One year earlier, she was forced to abandon her marathon after being knocked over as another competitor passed her. Her male equivalent Fauja Singh, a Sikh living in London, entered the marathon for the first time at the age of 89, and took less than 7 hours. Behind him trailed 407 entries, many in their thirties. When recording an almost identical time, one year later, he earned a place in the record books after knocking almost an hour off the world record time for the over-nineties. It is evidence that the London Marathon is for everyone: record-breaker Radcliffe, record-breaker Wood Allen, record-breaker Singh and the brave Michael Watson. Age is no barrier. All you need is that marathon spirit.

24. HISTORY 12 – LOS ANGELES TO SEOUL: INTO UNCHARTED WATERS

The Portuguese have long been famous for covering long distances. Where would the world have been without such men as Vasco da Gama and Ferdinand Magellan, after all? When the Games of the XXIIIrd Olympiad went to Los Angeles, however, those great men of the fifteenth and sixteenth centuries were long since consigned to the pages of our history books. Ground-breaking Portuguese had been rather thin on the ground they were supposed to be breaking, not least of all in the realm of sport. Remove Eusebio and Benfica from the list of options, and who could name even a handful of outstanding Portuguese athletes? Far from covering long distances, that great maritime nation's athletes had scarcely figured at all on the Olympic radar. But by 1988, when the Games swung from the rampant commercialism of LA back to the grimmer realities of an ideologically divided nation in South Korea, two Portuguese runners would have made their own remarkable contributions. When they donned their Olympic tracksuits they were representing a nation of some ten million souls. One of them, by virtue of being female, had behind her the far greater force of womanhood in its entirety: LA introduced several previously unstaged Olympic sports for women, among them the toughest race of all. It fell, not to the woman from Portugal, but to a diminutive runner from Maine, on the north-eastern seaboard of the United States, to be the first woman to etch her name in the history of the Olympic marathon.

Los Angeles was the third city, after Paris and London, to enjoy the privilege of staging its second Olympic Games. Between 1932 and 1984, however, the world had changed in ways even the most optimistic American of half a century earlier might not have dared imagine. Whether in response to the controversial mounting of the Olympics in Moscow four years before, or not, the Americans seemed determined to impose upon the Games the razzmatazz, the hype and the money-making energy that only they can summon up. The energy of LA Mayor Tom Bradley and president of the city's Organising Committee Peter Ueberroth took the Olympics arguably from the last vestiges of their amateur origins into the harsh light of a rampantly commercial modern society – one that contrived to turn a $250 million profit on the first Games to turn advertising on tickets and anywhere else into a minor art form. As now seemed common-place, someone had to try and spoil the party. Was it genuine concern over security, or merely tit-for-tat after the 1980 boycott? Whatever the real reason, the Soviet Union declined its invitation, as did the Communist bloc, with the exception of Romania. Neverthe-less, 140 nations attended and, of the 6,797 participating athletes, 1,567 were women.

The allegedly gentler sex had not been short of outstanding Olympic representatives in track and field before Los Angeles 1984. The list includes such names as Fanny Blankers-Koen in 1948, the wonderful trio from Australia's golden age of sprinting Marjorie Jackson, Betty Cuthbert and Shirley Strickland in 1952 and 1956, and Soviet middle-distance star Tatyana Kazankina in 1976 and 1980. But the way the Stars and Stripes dominated the women's track and field events in 1984 – Evelyn Ashford in the 100 metres, Valerie Brisco-Hooks in the 200 and 400, Benita Fitzgerald-Brown in the 100-metre hurdles, to say nothing of the winning quartets in the 4×100 and 4×400 – seemed to herald a new coming of age for American womanhood under the aegis of the five rings. But the marathon? Surely that was a different kettle of fish altogether? Anyone who thought so reckoned without the proudly independent State of Maine, where fish is part of the staple diet. And Maine had few prouder inhabitants than the tiny American who was about to become a giant on the world running stage. Her name was Joan Benoit.

Like so many marathoners before her, Benoit was lucky in her own way to make it to LA. Less than three weeks before the USA's Olympic trials, she had undergone arthroscopy – then in its relative infancy – on a seized knee, the surgeon simply snipping an inch-long, severely tightened length of collagen fibres to release the joint back to free movement. The knee had let her down in March of that year. Joan Benoit was no stranger to serious injury: she had begun running as part of her rehabilitation after breaking a leg doing what she loved first, if not best – downhill skiing – and had undergone Achilles tendon operations on both heels. But her absence from the Games would have been a major disappointment, for at that stage the girl from Bowdoin College had two strong Boston Marathon wins under her belt from 1979 and 1983, the latter in a then-world-best time of 2:22:43. In August of 1984 there was perhaps one major threat to Benoit's chances of emulating her fellow Americans and winning LA gold. Her name was Grete Waitz, who came in with fairly serious credentials: she was the reigning world champion, she was undefeated after seven marathons and she had always had the wood on Joan Benoit. With her would be her Norwegian compatriot Ingrid Kristiansen, returning to the world stage gradually after the birth of a son in 1983. There was also a young Portuguese runner, who it seemed had turned to the marathon only after finishing back in the pack in the 3000 metres in the European Championships in Athens two years before. She was called Rosa Mota, and she was destined to be the first woman from her country to win an Olympic medal. Next she would convert that medal from bronze to gold. But not yet . . .

The 1984 Olympic marathon for women began, curiously, in the midday heat. It ended just a quarter of an hour later. That was when Joan Benoit decided to throw caution to the winds and make her first break. It was the first – and last, for no one else dared go with her, Waitz and Kristiansen included. 'I didn't use my head then,' Kristiansen would later tell an interviewer. 'If I had followed Joanie, maybe three or four other girls would have come too. It might have been a different race.' Conditioned, at that stage, to defer to the great Waitz, who was three years older and had customarily finished ahead of her whenever they had run against each other, Kristiansen left her own move too late and finished one place out of the medals. In the end, Benoit won by a minute and 26 seconds in the relatively slow time of 2:24:52, beating Waitz into second pace and Mota into third, a further 39 seconds adrift. But with Benoit seizing the initiative so soon, the drama lay elsewhere in the 1984 women's Olympic marathon.

You might say that LA marathon was a severe example of tunnel vision as it afflicted two women. The first was the winner, for Joan Benoit knew that as she ran through the tunnel into the Memorial Coliseum she was running into history as the person she had once been, and into a new existence as an Olympic winner. 'I really didn't want to change my life,' she later mused of those few seconds when she flirted with the idea of turning tail and fleeing from the notoriety it would bring. But with women's emancipation, their new freedoms to express themselves alongside male athletes, came the occasionally burdensome consequences of fame. Joan Benoit ran through that tunnel and into her new life. 'I was determined not to cry,' she said of her appearance on the top step of the podium, citing the men as her example. 'But I sure blinked a lot.'

Another runner in that LA women's marathon looked for a moment as if she might be on the brink of changing her life in the most appalling way. Gabriella Anderson-Schiess, a ski instructor in Idaho's Sun Valley, took advantage of dual nationality to compete for Switzerland. She entered the Coliseum some twenty minutes after Benoit. In severe physical distress – one leg stiff, one arm hanging limp by her side – she must have felt she was tottering into a tunnel from which she might never have emerged. The athlete took an agonising 5 minutes and 44 seconds to cover her final lap, occasionally clutching her head as if in horror at what was happening to her. 'The last two kilometres are mostly black,' she says simply. 'My mind wasn't working too good.' Alert medical staff noticed, however, that she was still sweating profusely, a good physical sign, and opted not to intervene. Gaby may have staggered to the line, but those who watched her do it were staggered to hear that two hours later she was well on the way to recovery and apparently unharmed by her ordeal.

Joan Benoit, by then Joan Benoit Samuelson, missed the next two Olympics for a variety of reasons: foot, back and hip injuries, and more importantly the birth of her first child in 1987 and another less than four years later. She decided to attempt a comeback to the Olympic arena in 1996 but was placed thirteenth in the USA trial won by Jenny Spangler. She had said she wanted her children to see that 'you don't have to win to have fun at something', the sort of statement outsiders might associate with House Committees on Un-American Activities. She had set a US record of 2:21:21 in winning the 1985 Chicago Marathon, where there was the thrilling top three of Benoit–Kristiansen–Mota, and held it for far more years than she ever anticipated. As late as 2003, in Boston, Joan Benoit Samuelson ran 5 minutes and 20 seconds a mile pace in winning over a much shorter distance in the 40–49 age group of the US Track and Field Masters. While she ran into history as the winner of the marathon gold at the Games of the XXIIIrd Olympiad, it was the number nine that seemed to have just as much bearing on her case. It was Title IX of the United States' Education Amendments Act of 1972, effective in 1975, that formally prohibited discrimination on grounds of gender in federally funded programmes including athletics. Within nine years the number of women in American college sports had increased nine-fold, and one of them was the first Olympic champion at the marathon.

If Rosa Mota put Portugal on the map of women's athletics with her bronze-medal-winning performance in LA, Carlos Lopes put the country at its very centre. The Portuguese 'novice' did it in the most comprehensive fashion: not only did he establish a new Olympic record of 2:09:21, he also became the oldest gold medallist in Olympic marathon history. This, too, was a star-studded field, with reigning world champion Robert de Castella of Australia the probable pre-race favourite. It also contained Japan's enigmatic Toshihiko Seko, protégé of the legendary coach Yoshiro Nakamura, American crowd favourite Alberto Salazar, Kiwi Rod Dixon and a man coming in off a rather good year of his own, England's Charlie Spedding. Remember what Ron Clarke said about going under 2:09 and making it a somewhat specialised event? That 1984 Los Angeles field boasted no fewer than seven individuals who had broken that magic barrier, the world-best time at that stage belonging to 'Deek' with his 2:08:18 from Fukuoka in December 1981. Lopes, for his part, had claimed silver behind Viren back in Montreal in the 10,000 metres, and had since been head to head with de Castella over the marathon, pushing the great Australian all the way to lose by a mere two seconds. And then there was an Irish interloper by the name of John Treacy who, not content with finishing ninth in the LA 10,000 metres, decided to follow the Zatopek and Viren example by having a crack at the marathon too.

As things turned out, the catalyst in that 1984 Olympic marathon was the irrepressible Spedding, from the northeast of England – the breeding-ground for gritty runners like Brendan Foster, Steve Cram and Mike McLeod. Charlie was then 32 and had been running for exactly half his life. He had had time to mature as an athlete and as a man – but he had also had time to set his heart on an Olympic dream. Coming into the Olympics, Spedding was perhaps in the best form of his athletic life: he had already had outstanding wins in marathons in Houston and London earlier in that Olympic year. In an interview many years later, Spedding recalled the moment he sensed something was on. 'No one went crazy at the start,' he said, 'which was good because it was pretty hot. I got to twenty kilometres and was waiting for de Castella to make his move, but when I looked round he wasn't even there and I thought it was time to get rid of some of the others so I started shaking it up.' As 'Deek' has told us, perhaps he overtrained for that Olympic day. He also made a move that seemed innocuous, but later proved fatal to his chances. Drinks stations, by that stage, were a common sight along Olympic marathon routes. With around seven kilometres left to run, Robert ambled over to a water-stop for a drink. 'When I looked up after finishing that drink,' he said matter-of-factly, 'the leading pack of eight or nine runners had opened up a fifty-metre gap on me. There wasn't much I seemed to be able to do about it. I tried to pick up my pace and pull them in but they just seemed to be getting further and further away.' Two lost toenails were merely the physical accompaniment to the pain of seeing his Olympic dream evaporate.

Given the highs on which men like de Castella and Spedding must have approached their rendezvous on the Pacific coast, Carlos Lopes must have felt the sporting gods were against him. A fortnight before the Games got underway the Portuguese athlete was hit by a car while on a training run, rolling across the bonnet and smashing its windscreen with his elbow. Happily for him, the injuries were trifling and his running was not greatly affected. Still, as omens go . . .

Omen or not, Carlos Lopes was in the thick of it from the outset, though as the halfway mark approached it was the great Tanzanian runner Juma Ikangaa who led the way. After de Castella's watery demise, however, the leading pack dwindled and Spedding made his move. 'In the Olympics,' he cheerfully stated, 'you have one shot and give it everything.' But as Treacy and Lopes gave chase, the Portuguese runner began to exert the pressure that would bring him gold. A withering burst in which he covered five kilometres at an average of less than three minutes a kilometre was too much for other flesh and blood to bear. As Lopes ran away with the gold, Treacy produced his own lung-bursting last lap of 67 seconds to take silver by 2 seconds from the gallant Spedding. In a rare burst of Olympian modesty, Charlie analysed his achievement: 'My wildest dream had come true and I'd performed to the very best of my ability. What more could I want? I couldn't have done more – the other two were better than me.' While Treacy went on to become a senior sports administrator in his native Ireland, Spedding was not yet finished with the Olympic Games. Lopes, for his part, had left a mark that is yet to be erased: his winning time is still the Olympic marathon record.

Anyone who thought the move from the Memorial Coliseum in 1984 to Seoul in 1988 might put the brakes on the commercial momentum of the Olympic movement might have been stunned to hear that the Korean spectacular raised the Games' profit to $288 million. Once again politics raised its unlovely head: the North Koreans at first laid claim to a share of the events, then stayed away altogether, keeping a gaggle of hardline states with them. But 159 participating nations were there, and a quarter of the 8,000-plus athletes were women. Pursuit of the gold medal in the second women's marathon at the Olympics ran in tandem with the pursuit of another milestone: the first sub-2:20 run over the distance by a female athlete. The mid-1980s were, by any measure, a golden era of women's marathon running. Joan Benoit Samuelson from the States, the great Norsewomen Kristiansen and Waitz, Mota: all of these great runners reached the peak of their careers – and were joined by a new emergent force in the waiflike Lisa Martin, later Lisa Ondiecki. Born Lisa O'Dey, the Adelaide runner went to the University of Oregon as a 400-metre hurdler but from 1983 onward she embarked upon a road-running career that was to lead all the way to the podium at Seoul. And then there was East German prodigy Katrin Dörre, who seemed set to win every marathon she entered as she embarked upon her own blistering challenge to the record books.

All of them seemed bent on making the marathon their exclusive territory. In April 1985 in London, Kristiansen established a women's world-best time of 2:21:06 that would last for two days short of thirteen years. Olympic silver medallist Waitz claimed the world title, and took sole ownership of the New York City Marathon with a staggering nine victories to 1988. By the time she came to Seoul, Martin was Commonwealth Games champion at the distance: like compatriot de Castella she would win that title twice, and 1988 would also see the Australian set her career-long personal best when she won Osaka in 2:23:51. And then there was Rosa Mota . . .

If Joan Benoit was diminutive at five-foot-three, then Mota was positively tiny – she stood two inches smaller than her great

American rival. Like Benoit, she had had to fight adversity to establish herself as a marathon runner, for in 1979, aged 21, she was afflicted by career-threatening asthma. It had been induced by exercise, but the medical man who helped her recover, Jose Pedrosa, would go on to become her partner and the guiding light behind possibly the greatest marathon-winning career yet seen. By 1982 she was well and fit enough to win the first of two European Championships at the distance, in Athens; the following year she took superb victories in Rotterdam and Chicago, and that same year, 1983, she finished fourth in the inaugural World Championships in Helsinki, behind gold medallist Waitz. Her run to the bronze medal in Los Angeles in 1984 was merely the prelude to an astonishing spell of sustained competitiveness that would carry Rosa Mota to the very top of her profession. En route to Korea in 1988, the Portuguese runner won Chicago in 1984, came second there to Benoit Samuelson the following year but set her all-time personal best of 2:23:29, won Tokyo the following year, and claimed the 1987 world title in Rome by a stunning margin of more than seven minutes. From 1987 to 1991 Rosa Mota would be the undisputed world-ranked number one women's marathoner, and she took with her to Seoul the additional baggage of overwhelming favouritism for Olympic gold.

With three-quarters of the race run, there were four candidates for the three medals: Mota, Martin, Dörre, and Soviet runner Tatyana Polovinskaya. When the last-named started to wilt around the 35-kilometre mark, the only question to be answered was: who would finish on which step of the podium? Mota had tried in vain to persuade one of the others to share the frontrunning burden with her. Getting 'no' for an answer, she listened to the advice coming from Pedrosa, who had pedalled out to see how she was faring, and use one of the few inclines coming up to stamp her authority on the race. She struck for home, and a nearly spent Martin could never close the gap to less than the 13-second winning margin, with Dörre a further 28 seconds behind. Like Benoit years before, Waitz had endured arthroscopic surgery, just six weeks before the Games, and was never a contender. Martin would later rank that Seoul silver as second only to her subsequent superb run in the 1992 New York Marathon where she set a course record in the process, but her greatest days – fired by the intense rivalry with Scotland's Liz McColgan – lay ahead, not on Olympic tracks but in the other great city-based races. She would be back to try again in Barcelona. For now, though, she had become only the second Portuguese athlete to claim Olympic gold – and she joined brother-marathoner Carlos Lopes in doing it. The Magellans and da Gamas of this world who went in search of wealth far beyond the shores of Portugal would have been proud.

If anyone had unfinished business in the Olympic marathon it was the Italians. In 1988 a runner claimed by both Vicenza and Milan would cast aside eighty years of Olympic history and, in many watchers' eyes, set the record straight. Ten decades after the gallant Dorando Pietri's disqualification in London, Gelindo Bordin became the first Italian winner of Olympic gold in the marathon. Many of his compatriots would claim that the 29-year-old Bordin's achievement that October day in Korea was the greatest in the history of Italian athletics. Amazingly enough, Bordin, too, was on the list of marathon medallists who ought not to have been there in the first place. Had he not been presumed dead after being hit by a car while training seven years earlier? In between that accident and his Seoul apotheosis, Bordin distinguished himself with victory in the European Championships of 1986. The significant fact about Seoul, though, was that Bordin managed to reverse the order of the top three from the 1987 World Championships in which he had claimed bronze behind Douglas Wakiihuri and Djibouti's Ahmed Saleh.

Wakiihuri is perhaps one of the most intriguing marathoners of recent times. A Kikuyu tribesman raised in the shadow of Mount Kenya, he travelled to New Zealand before he was twenty to meet the legendary Nakamura, coach of the equally legendary Seko, and uprooted himself to take up life in Japan. In 1987 he upstaged Bordin on his home streets in Rome to take the world title. With 1987 World Cup winner Saleh, he formed a formidable threat to Bordin's hopes of bridging that eighty-year gap. So, too, did men like the returning Spedding, double Seoul course winner Takeyuki Nakayama, Seko himself and the still-menacing de Castella, whose compatriot Steve Moneghetti – beaten to the World Championship bronze by Bordi – was also in the field. Nor could any of them discount the Tanzanian who seemed destined always to be the big city bridesmaid, never the groom, Juma Ikangaa.

It was Ikangaa who dominated proceedings for more than the first half of that Seoul encounter. When Bordin himself decided it was time to make a push, it was short-lived: Nakayama went too, Saleh joined him and what Bordin later called 'the war' was on. The Australians tailed off, de Castella in particular paying the price for a preparation disrupted by injury, Nakayama could not sustain the pace, and Bordin had again resigned himself to bronze. But in the closest Olympic marathon in almost as many years as it had been since Pietri's heroics, the Italian took heart from the way first Wakiihuri, then Saleh started turning round. Clearly they were in distress and concerned about the man from Europe closing the gap. The Italian warrior drove past the Kenyan, then took him with him past Saleh with just over a kilometre remaining. In the end Bordin headed Wakiihuri home by fifteen seconds, Saleh just twelve seconds behind the Kenyan. The gallantly recovering Nakayama was only six seconds out of the medals, ahead of Moneghetti and Spedding, with early pacesetter Ikangaa seventh ahead of 'Deek'. As another famous Italian-based individual later made a habit of doing, Bordin crossed the line and immediately kneeled to kiss the foreign soil on which he had just triumphed. 'Life,' he later admitted, 'became very hard at first, because all the people in Italy wanted to meet me. So they organised parties . . .'

As a postscript to Seoul, it is interesting to remember that the start of those Olympic Games had already bridged a gap to previous marathon achievement. It was in Berlin in 1936 that Sohn Kee-Chung did – and didn't – win the Olympic marathon for Korea. His country occupied by Japanese forces, he had been compelled to run under the Japanese flag and endure the Japanese national anthem as he accepted his medal. Now, more than half a century later, a still-fit Sohn carried the Olympic torch into the stadium for the opening ceremony. At last the man who wanted to let the world know he was a Korean could do so, and how he seized the moment. Just four years later, another Korean would span the decades by winning Olympic gold. By then, alas, Sohn Kee-Chung was dead. President Kim said in 1990 that 'Sohn . . . left a footprint that awakened the spirit of the Korean people.' That spirit would carry Young-Cho Hwang to a form of immortality of his own in Barcelona.

25. BEDFORD – THE WOMAN WHO RUNS FOR GLORY

It could be one of many rural county towns in central England, a place that blends into its surroundings. It is an unexceptional collection of roads, streets, shops and homes, but in its heart, among noisy, chewing, laughing gangs of all ages that busy the pavements, there is another statue of another man of action. Swans, their long necks stretching vertically towards the overhanging trees and away to the riverbanks, glide across the surface of a tranquil waterway, the River Ouse. From a bridge, not far from the clubhouse of a rowing club and a square and imposing building, the Swan Hotel, a high street leads away towards a bustling town centre, spilling teenagers from several well-known schools with sporting pedigrees, a decent library and a famous red-brick prison. It was in this gaol, one of the high-walled features of the town, that writer and preacher John Bunyan was locked away for twelve years in the mid-seventeenth century. He was a man of great principle, determined and meticulous, who had earlier fought in the Parliamentary Army, against King Charles I, during the English Civil War. Afterwards, he spoke with his own voice, wrote many books, the most famous of which was *The Pilgrim's Progress*, and several fine hymns. For all of that, the town to which he was attached has remembered him with a statue from which he can keep an eye on affairs as they unfold more than three centuries later.

Bedford, benign in nature, modest in size, but bristling with good ambitions, sits on the river on flat land in the north of its own county, fifty miles north of London. The town was once known as a centre for market gardening and farming, for cars, general engineering and brickworks, as well as the preaching and thinking of Bunyan. It has grown much since his days, of course, but changed little in character and, in the closing years of the twentieth century, it produced an athlete who characterised most of its virtues and more. She was Paula Radcliffe, marathon woman and world-record-breaker who in 2004 was expected to travel to the Athens Olympic Games and challenge for glory in the ancient footsteps of Pheidippides and Spiridon Louis on the run south from Marathon itself and inland to the capital of Greece. Like the swans on the Ouse, she had her own familiar style; from afar it seemed she ran so smoothly, making serene and rapid progress, but closer examination always revealed that, like the swans' webbed feet below the waterline, she was exerting every muscle, her head and neck bobbing with effort. To some, it was reminiscent of Zatopek. This may have been the same gutsy determination and unforgiving sense of purpose that took Bunyan to prison for his outspoken beliefs and criticism of the Quakers, or Zatopek to semi-exile after the Prague spring in 1988. In her running, her intelligence, her modesty and poise, Radcliffe reflected well on Bedford, the town that adopted her athleticism and fostered her progress, and maintained a marathon tradition of highly principled runners.

This distinctive, awkward style in her running, that saw her head loll from side to side, her face contort in a grimace, has become her motif since she began to sweep all opposition aside following her debut over the classic marathon distance in 2002. Twice, she broke the world record as she won races, gained popularity and attracted lucrative commercial contracts, reflecting the commitments and sacrifices required in top-class modern sport and the rewards on offer for those prepared to endure them. Yet Radcliffe, who achieves such extraordinary things with her long legs, her slim frame and her iron resolve, is in many ways just an ordinary village girl blessed with a special talent and the mind to know how to use it – although she was placed fiftieth – with an annual income of more than 2.2 million pounds sterling. She appeared in one of the 'highest-paid women' lists published by a British Sunday newspaper in December 2003. In the modern jungle of sporting success, full of media temptations, commercial sideshows and celebrity traps, she has emerged as a perfect professional, the signal example to her peers, a girl that Bedford and Bedfordshire is proud to claim as an ambassador who fights for her principles. An asthmatic, too, she has overcome her own ailment and, on the way, denounced all drug cheats in sport.

Growing up in her native home town of Northwich, in Cheshire, Radcliffe tasted long-distance running for the first time when she was nine and began to join her father Peter, a brewery executive and athletics fanatic, on his training runs. She enjoyed it, but it was not until the Radcliffe family moved south to Bedfordshire, to live in the modest, quiet and rural village of Oakley, that the talent of the tall, asthmatic, long-limbed and blonde-haired girl became apparent. When it did, the husband-and-wife coaching duo of Alec and Rosemary Swanton were on hand at the Bedford and County Athletics Club to guide her through her formative athletic years. Under the Swantons, she overcame her asthma, and then anaemia, and embarked on the well-trodden trail of school, club and county athletics meetings.

'I have exercise-induced asthma, which was first recognised when I started training seriously at the age of fourteen,' recalled Radcliffe. 'I still sometimes get a tight chest, become short of breath and feel dizzy. I am also sensitive to other common triggers such as house dust mites, air pollution, tobacco smoke and some pollen.' By guarding Radcliffe against these threats, the Swantons prevented asthma stalling her progress; but Radcliffe then found that resisting asthma was one thing and establishing herself among the bright-eyed youngsters in the junior ranks was quite another.

In many ways, though talented, Radcliffe was far from a being child prodigy and this was demonstrated, most famously, in 1986 when a young Radcliffe, barely in her teens, finished 299th in the English women's cross-country championships at Western Park in Leicestershire. Radcliffe did not let the setback deter her and, six years later, she rose to prominence by winning the world junior cross-country championships in the snow at Boston. 'Sport was my real passion at school,' she explained. 'I enjoyed languages and maths, but athletics was what I excelled at. But it wasn't until my second year at University, when I competed in the World Champion-ships and finished seventh, that I decided to pursue a career in athletics.' Her modesty hid a talented all-rounder who, in 1992, achieved all her goals and, in effect, transformed her life. She left Sharnbrook Upper School with four A levels (in Mathematics, French, German and General Studies), each passed at grade A. No one could have done better than that.

'If anyone had told me at the start of the year when I was suffering from anaemia that I would win the cross-country, get such good A level results and be fourth in the world, I would have laughed in their face,' she said. After winning the junior cross-country cham-pionships in the United States that year, she had gone to Seoul in South Korea, sliced four seconds off her personal best time in the 3,000 metres and taken fourth place in the junior world athletics championships. Aged eighteen, she said, 'Junior championship are for learning and enjoying. I certainly enjoyed it and I learnt from that race. I made mistakes that I won't make again in the seniors.' Her target, in Seoul, was to break 9 minutes and, in fact, she ran in less than 8.52.

Her move to sport-focused Loughborough University, to read European Studies, did not, however, break Radcliffe from her Bedford roots. Radcliffe would return home during the holidays to train with the Swantons and continue her rapid development as a runner of pedigree and potential (her father was vice-president of the Bedford and County club and her mother managed the cross-country team, so she was never short of encouragement). But after meeting her future husband, trainer and manager, Gary Lough, at the Leicestershire university, she began to take her first steps towards world recognition as the fastest woman to run the marathon. As Radcliffe's career progressed, during and after university, she refused to allow herself to be forced into a particular distance specialisation, instead running in 1,500-, 3,000-, 5,000- and 10,000-metre races in domestic, European, Commonwealth, world and Olympic competitions, while continuing to compete in a variety of cross-country championships. She gradually built her reputation on the world stage as a serious talent, but was still a challenger and a contender rather than an all-conquering champion. Kenyan rivals frequently denied Radcliffe victory, with matters coming to a head in the final of the 10,000 metres at the World Athletics Championships, in Edmonton, Canada, in 2001.

In a bid to outsmart the Kenyans and give herself a hope of victory, Radcliffe set a blistering pace, leading the race from the early stages, pursued by a pack of Kenyans. The race continued with Radcliffe in front, Kenyans behind and the rest of the field nowhere until the final lap. One by one, the Kenyans came past an exhausted Radcliffe, leaving her in fourth place. The defeat was a hammer blow to Radcliffe, but one that galvanised her resolve to gain success in the future. It was a blow, too, that would help Radcliffe decide to step up to the ultimate distance race for a runner of her class – the marathon. Many believed Radcliffe better suited to the 26.2-mile event and so it proved when she set a remarkable time of 2 hours, 18 minutes and 56 seconds in London, in her first competitive marathon, in 2002. The time, the fastest by a marathon debutant, sent shockwaves through the sport, but Radcliffe knew there was more to come. Her next marathon outing in Chicago saw her set a new record of 2:17:18, 2 minutes faster than world champion Catherine Ndereba, who finished in second place.

Then, in 2003, Radcliffe returned to London to set another new world-record time of 2:15:25. This time was all the more remarkable because the organisers had agreed to allow Radcliffe to start alongside the leading male runners, a move that was designed to ensure a good enough pace would be set for a world record attempt. Money, fame and adulation followed in quick succession for the seemingly ungainly girl from Bedford, with expectations mounting that she would be a virtual certainty to win the Olympic marathon gold medal in Athens in 2004.

Yet how, and why, did this girl with four A grades in her A levels, and a decent, if not outstanding, record as a junior, find herself propelled to the pinnacle of one of the world's most gruelling and highly regarded events? Natural talent was obviously a useful, if not essential, attribute for any world-beater and Radcliffe had a fair pedigree. Her great Aunt Charlotte won a silver medal as part of Great Britain's freestyle relay swimming team in the 1920 Games and her father Peter and mother Pat were both keen and talented runners, who would go on to help establish Bedford and County AC as a proving ground for many of Britain's young athletic talents. But genetics alone cannot explain Radcliffe's rise and rise according to the man who has coached her since she was eleven, Alec Swanton. 'She trains so hard and gives so much,' says Swanton. 'She is so dedicated and she will shut herself away at her home in the mountains and just train. She's run some great times and done great things. But she remains hungry and she would pack it all in if she didn't enjoy her running. She's got a great team working around her, and when all that clicks together, you are suddenly in a position to make the right times.'

Swanton's belief that a combination of determination and simple, old-fashioned professionalism is the source of Radcliffe's success is backed up by her clinical, almost fanatical, approach to training, and her approach to the team she allows to help her to reach her targets. When it comes to concentrating on her fitness, Radcliffe allows only a select few to help her. Swanton and husband Lough are accepted into the Radcliffe inner sanctum, as is physical therapist Gerard

Hartmann. Naturally outgoing and friendly, Radcliffe is able to shut herself off from the outside world accompanied by these select few and concentrate entirely on realising her potential as an athlete. Those allowed to share Radcliffe's pursuit of perfection are each a mixture of friend, confidant, motivator and professional.

Radcliffe's praise for Swanton indicates that reliability, honesty and dependability are key characteristics of those she will allow to influence her training regime. 'He [Swanton] knows me well and has not let me down yet,' says Radcliffe of her mentor. 'It's not an accident that I've improved every year. It was planned that way. He could have trained me hard, when I was fifteen or sixteen, and I might not have made it through. I might have been a great junior, but not made it through to senior level.'

It is evident that Radcliffe is fiercely professional in her approach to achieving success and determined enough to put outside consider-ations on hold as she pursues her aims. In addition, Radcliffe remains true to her roots and loyal to those who have helped her achieve all she has already. She is a down-to-earth person and still a Bedford club runner at heart, when her mind is not bent with ironlike strength towards athletic success, which currently means winning the Olympic marathon and attempting to beat her own marathon world record.

While her character seems suited to the challenges she has chosen, it is clear a decision made by Radcliffe through her heart alone has helped her to dominate the marathon as much as any of her carefully made choices of coach, diet or tactics. By marrying Gary Lough, Radcliffe was joining her most vehement critic and her most staunch protector. As well as coaching Radcliffe, Lough protects Radcliffe from the outside world. He pushes her to her limits on days when her resolve flags and pushes her to even greater effort when she is at her best. He will berate her for her failures and try to build on her successes. At the end of the 10,000-metres final at the 2001 World Athletics Championships in Edmonton, where Radcliffe had finished a cruel fourth, Lough was on hand to criticise her unorthodox tactics. His harsh words prompted a high-profile argument televised around the world, but one Lough believes has ultimately made Radcliffe stronger. 'When something rips the heart out of you, you have a choice,' reflects Lough. 'Either you let it get you down or you get up and get on with it. Paula wanted to get on with it.'

Radcliffe is the epitome of the modern athlete: a professional in every sense, determined to strive for success and not to accept failure, factors that make her well suited to the mental and physical demands of the marathon. While she may be the best there is in terms of times and achievements, it is interesting to note that many of her characteristics are shared by other runners who have dominated marathon history, notably the modest pride she takes in setting an example to her Bedford club and her many friends and admirers. Like Zatopek, Spiridon Louis and the rest, Radcliffe uses her running to give rather than take. This was evident as long ago as 1992 when, on leaving school, she told her local newspaper the *Bedfordshire Times*, 'There's no way I'm going to leave Bedford.' This was great news for Bedford and County Athletics Club, her coaches Alec and Rosemary Stanton and her fellow athletes and friends, like Claire Peet, Vicki Russell, Juliette Parkin, Eleanor Caborn, Liz Talbot, Anna Mills, Michelle Matthews and Sarah Desborough, who all looked up to Radcliffe as an example.

Her sense of loyalty has given her strength, too, when it has been reciprocated. In the early 1990s, having overcome asthma, she struggled with injuries. In 1994, she suffered a stress fracture under the arch of a foot and missed several major events. At one time, she was told she may never run again and to prepare for the worst. Instead, ignoring this specialist's advice, she went to another ten physiotherapists in Britain and finally found the advice she wanted when she visited a sports medicine expert in Munich, Germany. Dr Hans-Mueller Wolfhardt had previously helped Boris Becker, Linford Christie and several members of the German football team.

Radcliffe learned that her foot should not have been put in plaster, as it had been, and that the key to her treatment was salmon calcium extract. She vowed never to accept British medical advice unreservedly again. For a woman whose strengths include loyalty to flag and home, it was a difficult decision, but the right one. It was a clear example, too, of her pragmatism and professionalism. After winning the BBC Sports Personality of the Year award in December 2002, in which the British public gave her 600,000 votes, putting her well ahead of her nearest rival, footballer David Beckham, she gave an insight into what it is that has made her, the girl from Bedford, into an international star. 'Bascially, I always want to get the best I can out of myself,' she said. 'If I choose to do something, I want to be able to say I did my best. Hopefully, that is good enough to achieve what I aim to achieve and what I am dreaming of achieving. I want to be able to walk away at the end of my career and know that I have achieved all I was capable of doing.' If she achieves that, the good folk of Bedford may need to build another statue, not though in memory of a man who wrote hymns and books, but the daughter of a brewery executive and a headmistress, whose scruples are as well respected as her running.

26. HISTORY 13 – SPAIN TO SYDNEY: RUNNING FREE

It is often said that long-distance runners, at some stage, 'hit the wall'. Between 1988 and the Barcelona Olympics of 1992, one of the most famous walls in history came tumbling down. The removal of that odious artificial division in the great German city of Berlin was the prelude to an even greater fall, as the whole edifice of communism – or at least the corrupted version of it practised in the late twentieth century – was itself reduced to historical rubble. There was, it seemed, a new world order taking shape as the Olympic movement began turning its mind to the New World again at the end of the century. Another wall, invisible but no less hateful, collapsed as apartheid was swept away and South Africa was free to return to the Olympic fraternity for the first time in 32 years. For the first time in twenty years the Olympics were not disfigured by a boycott: every National Olympic Committee in the world was represented, all 169 of them. Nowhere was the new unity more visibly or more poignantly expressed than in the aftermath of the women's 10,000 metres in Spain, when winner Derartu Tulu of Ethiopia – the first black African woman to win Olympic gold – and silver medallist, white South African Elana Meyer, set off hand in hand on their lap of honour.

In the three Olympics from Barcelona to Sydney, five nations would share the marathon gold medals. The only one to claim two would be, so fittingly, the one with the greatest distance-running pedigree of them all. First, though, a slight young man was to savour one of the sweeter moments in Olympic history. Like Bordin, building bridges back to Pietri so many years before, Young-Cho Hwang had unfinished business to attend to when the field assembled for the Barcelona marathon. Seoul had drawn inspiration from the sight of Sohn Kee-Chung, still so young in heart, asserting his Korean nationality for all the world to see. Now Young-Cho Hwang of Korea was about to claim Olympic gold in his own nation's name rather than in that of an unwanted invader. This was, in some ways, a hiatus in marathon running: some of the great names of the 1980s and 1990s were in the twilight of their careers, Robert de

Castella among them. By the time he headed for Barcelona, 'Deek' was already in a senior position at the Australian Institute of Sport in Canberra and the pressures of time no longer meant simply a stopwatch to run against. 'I was working full time,' he concedes nowadays, 'and trying to cram my normal training routine into a long, demanding work schedule.' The voice tails off as he concludes, 'Maybe I could have run a bit better . . .' In short, the great Australian was not to be a major factor. The time was ripe for some lesser lights to occupy centre stage.

Hwang had simply not had time to be anything else: he was still short of his 21st birthday when he claimed Olympic gold. The previous year he had won the 10,000 metres in the Asian Games, then distinguished himself with a first-time victory in the Seoul marathon with a time of 2:12:35. His personal best followed in February of Olympic year, a 2:08:47. Armed with four marathons, Hwang set off for Spain and the biggest event of his young life on 9 August. His eventual victory was to be made all the more satisfying because of the man he beat into second place. Not that he had anything against Koichi Morishita, but the symbolic significance of the silver medallist's nationality – the country that had denied justice to Sohn all those years ago – could not be overlooked.

As things turned out, the demanding Barcelona course, with its long climb up to the finish through Montjuich, left those two to fight it out between them once the pack had broken up beyond the thirty-kilometre mark. Overcome by his victory, and perhaps its unseen importance to his people, Hwang collapsed to the track and kissed the ground on winning. Sadly for him, subsequent serious injury to his ankle kept him from building on that pivotal moment of his life: unprepared, he came only 29th in his country's pre-Atlanta trials and promptly retired from marathon running at the ripe old age of 26. Not so much a lesser light, more of a shooting star . . . Hwang also had something in common with the man who claimed bronze in Barcelona in 2:14 dead, German Stephan Freigang. The two had competed in the 1991 World Student Games staged at Sheffield, Hwang winning the marathon and Freigang the 10,000 metres, before graduating to the larger international stage. A champion over shorter distances from his teenage years, Freigang reached the pinnacle of his own career that Barcelona day, though he had claimed victory at Fukuoka two years earlier and would go on to win his country's championship in 1994. Freigang registered a DNF in Atlanta four years later but continued winning city marathons in places like Hanover, Leipzig and Lisbon into the early years of the next century.

By coincidence a Japanese runner would also win silver in the women's marathon at the Barcelona Olympics. Yuko Arimori was the athlete referred to as 'the Michael Jordan of Japan', so famous did her Spanish silver and other marathon exploits make her in her own country. Born in 1966, she would become the first athlete to be granted professional status by the Japanese Amateur Athletics Federation. Coached by Yoishi Koide, Arimori came to Barcelona buoyed by fourth place at the previous World Championships, building on a Japanese record-breaking performance in taking sixth place at Osaka in 1990.

As with the men, some of the great women marathoners had fallen victim to the ravages of time, injury or personal pressures of another kind. Rosa Mota had suffered injuries after Seoul and perhaps tried to force her way back to top-flight competition too soon; she was also fighting off-track battles with her own national federation, which may or not have inspired or equipped her for her subsequent move into the political arena. Lisa Martin-Ondieki was also in Barcelona but, still on the comeback trail after motherhood in 1990, she could not finish on the punishing course and in the unfamiliar humidity. Ondieki, whose change of name came with her second marriage to the Kenyan runner, had not responded well to the Kenyan training methods, where she felt the absence of emotional support from the coaching staff. 'No concept of resting up and peaking for races,' she told Australian interviewer Brian Lenton, 'absolutely no consideration of injury prevention. It's essentially survival of the fittest. If you don't die, you'll run great. Of course I did some great performances from this training . . . but I also DNF'd in Barcelona because I think there was no consideration for heat and humidity.'

Someone else who should not have been at home in hot, humid conditions was New Zealand's Louise Moller, but she it was who would follow the front two home to give the Barcelona marathon podium an unusual flavour. Moller was then 37. A PE teacher who had decided to go to the States to further her running ambitions, she saw her marathon career take off in London two years later and went on to claim three Osaka wins through the 1980s. By the time she approached the start in Spain, Moller was still recovering from a personal blow: four days before running the Barcelona race she had learned of the loss of ex-husband Ron Daws, himself a United States Olympic marathoner in 1968, to a heart attack. 'The best I could do to remember Ron,' she said afterwards, 'was to run as he taught me.' There were three problems. One was the final uphill stretch at Montjuich – Formula One cars had struggled round there with all their power in the Spanish Grand Prix many years before, so why should humans be any different? Another was Arimori. The last was the other member of the frontrunning duo, a lady by the name of Valentina Yegorova.

Yegorova was interesting in a number of ways, not least of all because her selection had caused controversy. In the first place, it was no longer for the 'Soviet Union', consigned with the Berlin Wall to the pages of the history books, but for a 'Unified Team' of former Soviet republics. In the second, it came at the expense of Olga Markova. Markova was, to all intents and purposes, the best marathoner around in that new-look part of the atlas. On the build-up to Olympic year she had won Boston in a personal best time of 2:23:43, a whopping five minutes better than anything Yegorova had achieved. But Markova's decision to miss the Los Angeles qualifying event cost her dear. Yegorova had credentials of her own, including silver – a mere three seconds behind Mota – in the 1990 European Championships, and bronze in the 1991 World Cup. In the end, Barcelona turned into an arm wrestle between the two best stayers in the field, and Yegorova outdid the Japanese to claim gold by a mere eight seconds. Significantly, the winning time was a slow 2:32:41.

Moller, whose patience in the earlier stages paid dividends, was beaten both by them and by the Catalan capital's topography: 'There was no catching anybody once you got to that hill,' she would later say. Winning Olympic bronze was Moller's greatest day; Yegorova and her Japanese rival would be back for more.

'More' was certainly the theme of the 1996 Olympic Games. Atlanta, capital of Coke, had more, it seemed, of everything, from security to sweltering heat. It had more athletes than any previous Olympics: a staggering 10,318 of them. It had its own brush with the darker side of history when a bomb killed one person and injured many more, and overall the southern city's effort at staging the world's greatest sporting spectacle met with something less than wholehearted enthusiasm. Not that it was any fault of the athletes', of course. In fact the winner of the men's marathon at these Atlanta Games would write one of the most extraordinary chapters in the history of this extraordinary event. His name was Josiah Thugwane, and it is no disrespect to any other runner in the field to say that the 1996 Olympic marathon was all about him.

In 1995 Nelson Mandela had rejoiced with his nation's rugby players as they won the World Cup on home soil. In 1996, on foreign fields, a little man would draw inspiration from Mandela's long walk to freedom as he embarked upon his own long run into history. 'Nelson Mandela inspired me to achieve in sport,' said Thugwane, whose ambitions as a footballer had been thwarted by his anatomy – just 158 centimetres and 45 kilos of it. Turning to a half-marathon instead, Thugwane soon realised running was the life for him. South African champion in 1993 at full marathon distance, in 1995 he won the Honolulu Marathon; the following year he took first place in South Africa's Olympic trials and greatness beckoned. Semi-literate at best when he went to Barcelona, Thugwane was still deferential when it came to his chances at Olympic level. 'The country has chosen me,' was all he would say. 'This is what is best for the country. So I will try my best today.'

Circumstances also conspired in his favour, at least once he reached American soil. Before doing so he endured the ordeal of a hijacking in the car with which he had celebrated Olympic selection. Shot at as he jumped from the moving car, Thugwane injured his back and also felt a bullet graze his chin – the resulting scar a trophy which he had already earned before Atlanta. 'I thought my chances of going to America were zero,' he confessed, but with typical determination he made it. After altitude training at Albuquerque, in New Mexico, under the watchful eye of coach and mentor Jacques Malan, Thugwane arrived in Atlanta to find the race was scheduled to start at 7.05 a.m. 'For me,' he later said, 'it was not difficult to run in the morning because in South Africa all of the races start early. Another thing about the Olympic marathon is that there aren't that many people in the field. Only the best are here to represent their country.' On the day, the best of all was Joseph Thugwane, heading home Korean Lee Bong-Ju and Kenya's Eric Wainaina (who would later beat him at Nagano). Thugwane was the first black South African to join the ranks of Olympic gold medallists.

In every respect it was a life-changing experience. 'I thought that after winning the Olympics I would go home and everything would be normal again,' said Thugwane. 'But I was surprised . . .' Not the least of those surprises was the unpleasant realisation of jealousy and resentment even from his own people. Threats, physical attacks and abuse combined to drive him from his home and into the more protected housing conclave of the mining company where he had once worked in the lowliest of capacities. With Olympic gold came all the trappings: relative riches, material possessions and, above all, new-found status. More than anything, however, Josiah Thugwane wished to assert one basic right: he sought the education which alone would make him truly free. Once again his inspiration was the peerless Mandela, who had come to meet him on his return from Atlanta. 'It is because of him,' said the deeply respectful Thugwane, 'that I started school for the first time in my life.' Already in Atlanta, fellow South African Gert Thys, who could not match the little man's performance in that marathon, had said, 'I really respect that man.' That man, Josiah Thugwane from the province of Mpumalanga – 'the place where the sun comes up' – had earned respect by running into the sunlight and into history as few Olympic medallists had ever done.

In the Atlanta women's marathon, Valentina Yegorova finished ahead of Yuko Arimori, just as they had done in Barcelona. The only problem was that another runner finished in front of them both. This, too, was a great Olympic story out of Africa. It may be appropriate to pause for a moment to wonder how miscreants in Addis Ababa train for their activities and in particular their aftermath, for the lady who won gold in the Atlanta marathon was a police officer and one unlikely to be outrun. At the age of 25, Fatuma Roba had never seen the Olympic Games on television. Her admiration for the peerless Bikila owed nothing to the images of his victories in Rome and Tokyo three decades earlier. From the same Ethiopian village as the great middle-distance runner Derartu Tulu, the first black African woman to win Olympic gold back in Barcelona, Roba was now in her third year of marathon running. Used to cooler climes, she, too, should have been uncomfortable in the swelter of Atlanta, but thankfully the skies were overcast when she kept her own date with marathon history.

Roba came to Atlanta off a three-race winning streak. Pre-race favourite was probably Uta Pippig, herself a three-time Boston winner later to become embroiled in a doping controversy that would lead to her switching nationality to become a United States citizen, though too late to qualify for the next Games in Australia. Yegorova brought her own unquestionable pedigree, enhanced since Barcelona by victories in Tokyo in 1993 and 1994. It was the German girl who went out hard in Atlanta to lead by almost half a minute at the quarter-distance mark. By halfway, though, when they reached the quaintly named Oglethorpe University, the black runner from Ethiopia had cast her considerable shadow over the field. She would later come out with perhaps the most succinct statement ever made of how to win a marathon: 'I picked up the speed and they would not follow.' They could not: Roba's relentless drive for the tape carried her home a staggering two minutes clear, the widest margin in the short history of women's Olympic marathoning, in a total time of 2:26:05 – nowhere near world-best performance levels, but far too good for anyone in that Atlanta field. It was Roba's first significant success in major international competition; it was also, by the margin of three minutes, a personal best performance.

For Arimori, the gallant silver medallist in Spain, there was a final moment of heartbreak in Atlanta. Her mindset before the race was that she would again be running for a silver medal. 'A gold medal was beyond my imagination,' she would later say, suggesting that coach Koide had never really conditioned her to pursue the highest honour. Silver might have been hers again in Atlanta had not her arithmetic let her down. She was still well in the running when she and Yegorova trailed into the stadium in Roba's wake – but the Japanese athlete believed she had to complete not one lap but two to finish the race. Yegorova, inspired by the presence of her husband and son, seized the moment and sped home with half a minute in hand. 'I am so unhappy,' admitted Arimori afterwards. 'It was my mistake, as I thought there was another lap to run inside the stadium and so I timed my run badly. I can't believe there wasn't another lap . . .' Time would add perspective to her disappointment: 'The medals are encouraging to look at,' Arimori said later, 'but also things of the past.' A new career in athletics administration beckoned when she was elected to the IAAF Council in 2003.

Roba, meanwhile, felt she had brought her country, already so famous for its distance-running dominance, to the threshold of a new era. 'This is not only a special thing for me,' she said, 'but also for my country and all African women. The Ethiopian women are coming up in the marathon. This was the breakthrough.' Not quite: where Arimori had twice suffered gallant failure, in relative terms, a Japanese compatriot would have her own say in the destination of the Olympic marathon gold medal at the turn of the millennium. Between Atlanta and Sydney, the face of women's marathon running changed utterly.

On 19 April 1998, Tegla Loroupe of Kenya won the Rotterdam Marathon in 2 hours, 20 minutes and 47 seconds. The chase for that magic 2:20 mark was well and truly on as the Kenyan sliced 19 seconds off the previous world best held by Ingrid Kristiansen since 1985. Loroupe was one half of a 'Terrible Twosome' who emerged from Kenya in the mid-1990s and seemed set to dominate women's distance-running for years to come. If Addis Ababa thieves feared the footsteps of Fatuma Roba, Kenyan correspondents loved those of Loroupe and compatriot Joyce Chepchumba: they both worked in the Kenya Post Office delivering mail, presumably express. Born in 1970, Chepchumba was three years older. Forsaking her native land to go and train with the elite squad of Volker Wagner at Detmold in Germany in 1993, she was reunited with Loroupe there as the two of them set out to conquer the world from their new European base. Loroupe's siblings would have made up a decent marathon field – she was one of 22 children from her father's 4 marriages in that polygamous Kenyan society. A tiny four foot eleven and less than 40 kilos, she won the New York Marathon in 1994 at the first time of asking and again in 1995. The full extent of the threat she posed to the marathon world order emerged, though, that April day in Rotterdam. It was merely underlined when Loroupe bettered her own world-best time in winning Berlin in September 1999. Chepchumba, meanwhile, had not been idle. Fourth on debut in New York in 1995, she had gone on to claim back-to-back Chicago wins in 1998–99 and added Tokyo with a course record time in 2000.

But women's marathoning was not all about Africans. Out of Eastern Europe in 1996 had come Lidia Simon of Romania to claim sixth place in Atlanta. By 1999 she had improved to double bronze-medal winning level in the World Championships. From Craiova in the south of her home country, she did the African thing as a child and ran to school. She came to prominence in 1995 with a top-ten finish in the Gothenberg World Championship marathon, and a switch to altitude training in Boulder, Colorado in 1997 had undoubtedly paid dividends. She was a tough customer, too: she ran through illness to bronze in the World Championships at Athens in 1997, and two years later she had to bounce back from appendicitis. Simon also racked up three Osaka titles en route to Sydney to lay serious claims to the Olympic title. Defending champion Roba would be there too. But none of them would catch the daughter of the wind.

'When Naoko Takahashi takes on the marathon it will shock the world,' said highly regarded Japanese coach Yoshio Koide. It did: at 28, Takahashi would take the final step her compatriot Arimori could not and win Olympic gold. Her Sydney performance in itself would be only the prelude to greater things. It was Takahashi who, after an undistinguished student running career, sought out Koide and convinced of her own potential. It began to be realised in the mid-1990s, and on marathon debut at Osaka in 1997 Takahashi was placed seventh. A Japanese record followed in 1998, 2:25:48, and after that a superb 2:21:47 to win in Bangkok at the Asian Games in the same year. Her final year of Olympic preparation was marred by injury, though a good win at Nagoya set her back on track.

The Sydney marathon started at nine in the morning in the harbour city's northern suburbs. First to show the way was Belgium's Marleen Renders, who led the field across Sydney's iconic Harbour Bridge. They went through the first 10 kilometres in 34:08. Unlike Arimori, Takahashi had been made to feel by coach Koide that she had it in her to win gold. They had discussed a possible move before the halfway mark if the Japanese runner felt in the groove. She did. At seventeen kilometres Takahashi started to test the rest, and the ones who went with her initially were both familiar to her: they were her team-mates Ari Ichihashi and Eri Yamaguchi. And then Simon arrived on the scene to remind them that the Old Continent still had its role to play here in the New World of marathon running. Takahashi, however, had an ace up her sleeve. The Sydney course became hilly towards its final stages, beginning around the 27-kilometre mark and continuing up and down for some time afterwards. Takahashi had trained specifically by running the marathon course segment from kilometre 32 to kilometre 37 daily in her build-up to the race. When she made another move at 35 kilometres the others had no answer. Past the 40-kilometre mark she had a lead of 28 seconds: within the remaining distance the lionhearted Simon would pile on the pace and cut that to just 8 seconds at the line as Takahashi claimed gold in a Games record of 2:23:14.

'Sometimes,' said Simon, 'you realise during the race that you should try harder and harder and this is why I ran faster in the last part of the race.' The tragic memory of Tsuburaya, and the bitter disappointment of Arimori were set aside as Takahashi claimed Japan's first athletic gold since 1936 – when a Korean ran under the banner of the Rising Sun. Joyce Chepchumba came home third to uphold Kenyan honour, but Roba's promise of a breakthrough by the Ethiopian women was unfulfilled. In a Games where Ethiopians of both sexes dominated the middle-distance events, Roba could manage only ninth this time, while Kenya's and the world's best, Loroupe, was thirteenth on the day.

'I enjoyed myself,' said Takahashi in a masterpiece of understatement. 'I had a lot of hopes and dreams – I always envisaged this day.' Fêted like no predecessor in her native land, she even had a comic strip built around her in which she was given that title, 'Daughter of the Wind'. Her own reaction, though, was one of mild let-down. 'Once it's over, I feel as though I've lost my objective,' she concluded. 'My goal is achieved and I'm a little saddened. So from tomorrow I have to set another goal.' As an interesting postscript to those wonderful Sydney Games, Takahashi did set herself another goal – to eclipse the word best by going under 2:20 – and she did achieve it by running 2:19:46 to win Berlin on 30 September the following year. One week later Catherine Ndereba clocked a staggering 2:18:47 to remind the world that Kenya would not lightly let go of her running heritage.

If the Daughter of the Wind triumphed in Sydney, that wind did its best to upset the marathon men. Vying with sister marathon venue Chicago for the title of 'the windy city', Sydney produced 25 to 30 mile-per-hour gusts that made life even more difficult for the field in the final event of what Juan Antonio Samaranch would describe, without demur, as the best Olympic Games ever. It seemed wonderfully appropriate that the last Olympic marathon gold medal of the century should go to the greatest nation in the event's history. Not only that but, at 22, Gezahgne Abera became the youngest winner of the marathon gold, coming home in 2:10:11, well outside Carlos Lopes's Olympic record of 2:09:21 but a comfortable 20 seconds clear of Atlanta bronze medallist Eric Wainaina of Kenya and Abera's compatriot Tesfaye Tola. 'Comfortable', in that Abera's previous reputation rested on a six-second margin of victory at Fukuoka in 1999 and a hair's-breadth loss to Kenyan Elijah Lagat in Boston when both men were given the same time. Uncomfortable in the extreme, though, because of other circumstances. 'Terrible, terrible winds,' said Abera after Olympic triumph in only his sixth marathon. 'Sometimes from the front, sometimes from the side. Sometimes it slowed us to a walk.'

Sometimes, too, the eventual champion was not even walking: at the 16-kilometre mark he had a fall that jarred his knee, lost him 25 metres and forced him to sprint back into the fray. He did have help, though, chiefly from two sources. One was Botswana's Tiyapo Maso, who went out heroically or foolishly and led the first half of the race by as much as 70 seconds before enduring the heartbreak of seeing almost the entire field sweep past to leave him 77th overall. The other was Abera's team-mate Tola, who took up the brunt of the frontrunning work and sheltered him for much of the time in the crucial later stages of the race before saying, 'I am tired now. You catch him and win.'

The 'him' in question was the gallant Wainaina, who tested Abera with a series of well-thought-out accelerations before eventually giving best to the young Ethiopian. Wainaina, his Atlanta effort notwithstanding, was lucky to be there in the first place. Kenya's well-documented political difficulties within its athletics administration had led to the three athletes originally selected – Lagat among them – being dropped again for allegedly not training hard enough. Wainaina for his part had trained hard in Japan. 'Next time,' he vowed, 'I will try to win the gold,' a promise he looked likelier to keep after eclipsing his personal best by a minute and a half en route to victory in Tokyo early the following year. England's John Brown was a gallant fourth, just six seconds adrift of Tola, after running through a painful stitch with ten kilometres left and despite only six weeks' full-scale training following a hip injury. Reigning champion Thugwane could manage only twentieth, almost seven minutes behind the winner. For now, though, the Olympic marathon spotlight was back on Ethiopia, and never had it shone so brightly. Not only did Abera's performance crown a wonderful track effort by Ethiopia in which Haile Gebreselassie, Millon Wolde and Derartu

Tulu all won gold, it also bridged the decades to make Ethiopia the only four-time Olympic marathon-winning nation. 'I couldn't believe it, actually,' he said modestly. 'It's been thirty years [since Wolde's win]. It is an upset for all of Ethiopia.' Upset? Perhaps that was a mistranslation on Abera's behalf by the team doctor. To the rest of the world, his run into history was one of the most uplifting moments of the last Olympic Games of the twentieth century.

27. LAST LAP

From the solitary pain, real or invented, of Pheidippides, to the shared agony of today's mass marathon fields is a long journey indeed. When the modern Olympics began, seventeen men fore-gathered at Marathon to make their symbolic advance on Athens; in the year 2000, 100 athletes – only the best of each country – flooded over Sydney Harbour Bridge and there was another 54-strong field of women for their separate event. And now, led by an upright English girl in search of gold, they will return to Athens, completing the circle the visionary de Coubertin began to draw so many years ago.

The symbolic distance travelled is far greater than the mileage racked up by runners in the thirty Olympic marathons to date, to say nothing of the street lengths covered in all those big-city events. More clearly, perhaps, than any other race, marathon running has built bridges from the oldest countries to the new; brought frail-looking men and women from the Dark Continent to challenge and finally sweep away the myth of white supremacy; welcomed athletes breaking through the man-made walls of political doctrine into the embrace of the Olympic family.

From Spiridon the Greek to Abera the Ethiopian, the story of the marathon is an almost seamless chronicle of human endeavour, often in the most trying circumstances, and more often than not with overtones of tragedy, personal or collective. In the long run, as it were, we remember not the cut and thrust of political in-fighting, nor the calamitous misuse of the Games by people with perverted views on how to change the world: we remember the individuals who made marathon running the summit of human striving.

Nurmi the Flying Finn; Bikila the barefoot blazer of trails; Lopes, the pioneering Portuguese who still holds the Olympic record set twenty years ago; Thugwane, the tiny warrior following in the giant footsteps of Mandela; Abera, the new face of the marathon's greatest nation; and alongside them brave Benoit, majestic Mota, triumphant Takahashi.

One name, though, still stands above them all, just as the man who bore it still stands above the lake on that hillside in Lausanne. The man whose exploits are the fulcrum of a century and more of marathon still stands guard at the gates of glory: Emil Zatopek is forever running into history.

INDEX